e 2.1
illion
ell as
o the

te, or
v, and
efore
ighly-
ated.

Human activity has damaged 15% of the world's land. **Deforestation** leads to land erosion by wind and rain. Poor irrigation and overgrazing lead to soil deterioration.

Each year 16.8 million hectares of the world's forests are destroyed. Currently 1.3 billion people are using up wood for fuel more quickly than it can be replaced.

Atmospheric pollution caused by industrial activity affects 10% to 20% of all trees in 13 European countries. Lakes are also being affected by pollution, especially by **acid rain**.

More than 10% of the world's rivers are polluted. Sewer drainage is responsible for a large part, but **industrial pollution** also contributes to making water unfit for consumption. In developed countries, chemical fertilizers are increasingly contaminating the ground water.

Air pollution exposes more than one billion city-dwellers to excessive quantities of dust and soot. Each year, thousands die as a result. In certain towns, for example Athens, authorities are sometimes forced to ban the use of cars for several days at a time.

Chronicle
of the year 1992

Chronicle
of the year 1992

Publisher: Jacques Legrand

Editor	**Andrew Hunt**
Picture Editor	Xavier Rousseau (Sipa Press), Catherine Seignouret
Writers	Christophe Balouet, Christopher Dobson, David Gould, Perry Leopard, Angela Read, Paige Rosenberg
Editorial Administration	Yves Kielan
Proofreader	Bob Mouncer
Production	Catherine Balouet, Emmanuelle Berenger
EDP	Martine Colliot
Artworks	Catherine Jambois, Patagonie

How to use this book

Chronicle of the Year 1992 reports the events of the year as though they had just happened.

The weekly chronology summaries do not aim to cover all the most important events since these are reported in greater detail in the reports adjoining the summaries. The summaries include less important events and those leading up to the main events reported elsewhere or their consequences. These chains of developments can be tracked through a system of cross-references which complements the index by pointing to the next link in the chain.

Arrows indicating the next link appear at the end of reports or summaries. They point only forward in time, but can lead to either an entry in the weekly summaries or one of the fuller reports. They work like this:

- If a cross-referenced event occurs in the same month only the day of that month will appear after the arrow – for example: (→15).
- If the next linked event occurs in another month, then the month will also appear – for example: (→March 15).

Where an arrow appears by itself after a weekly summary entry it means that the event and its consequences are reported in greater detail in the adjoining pages. Only one cross-reference appears per entry or report so the index should be used to find earlier entries on an event or individual.

© Jacques Legrand s.a., International Publishing, for World English Rights, 1993

© Chronicle Communications Ltd., Farnborough, United Kingdom

© Harenberg Kommunikation, Dortmund, for the Chronicle system

ISBN: 1-872031-75-7

Typesetting: Imprimerie Louis-Jean, Gap
Coulour processing: Beauclair
Printing and Binding: Brepols, Turnhout (Belgium)

Printed in Belgium

Distributors (except North America & Australasia):
Random Century Group Ltd.,
Random Century House,
20 Vauxhall Bridge Road,
London SW1V 2SA

USA: JL International Publishing Inc.
244 West Mill Street
Liberty – Missouri
64068 USA
Tel. (1) 816 792 19 81
Fax: (1) 816 792 19 32

Australia: Penguin Books Australia Ltd.,
487 Maroondah Highway
P.O. Box 257
Ringwood,
3134 Victoria

New Zealand: Penguin Books (N.Z.) Ltd.,
182-190 Wairau Road,
Auckland 10

Canada: Raincoast Books Distribution Ltd.,
112 East 3rd Avenue
Vancouver, V5T 1C8
British Columbia

Chronicle
of the year 1992

Su	Mo	Tu	We	Th	Fr	Sa
			1	2	3	4
5	6	7	8	9	10	11
12	13	14	15	16	17	18
19	20	21	22	23	24	25
26	27	28	29	30	31	

Buenos Aires, 1
A new currency, the peso, replaces the austral. One peso equals one dollar.

Sicily, 1
The army builds a barrier in an attempt to halt lava which has been flowing from Mount Etna for one week.

Lisbon, 1
Portugal assumes the six-month presidency of the European Community.

Berlin, 1
Citizens of the former East Germany are authorized to read their own files in the secret police archives.

Belgrade, 2
The 15th Serbo-Croat cease-fire is announced after an agreement by the two sides on the presence of U.N. military observers (→ 6).

Algiers, 2
Hundreds of thousands demonstrate against the dangers of Islamic fundamentalism (→ 11).

London, 2
Official figures showed that the richest 1% of the population own 18% of the marketable wealth, while the poorest 50% own 6%.

Tel Aviv, 3
Israel decides to expel 12 Palestinians from the Occupied Territories following a Jewish settler's murder (→ 6).

Miami, 3
After seizing a helicopter from Cubana Airlines, 34 Cubans flee to Florida.

Tbilisi, 3
Rebels open fire during a rally for Georgian president Zviad Gamsakhurdia, killing at least two and wounding 25 (→ 7).

Chad, 3
Government forces launch a counter-attack on rebels as France sends jets and paratroops.

London, 4
The first "Muslim parliament" is inaugurated with the question of Muslim schools as its priority.

DEATH

1. Mike Frankovich, American film producer (*1911).

Moscow's painful freeing of prices

Moscow, Thursday 2
Shoppers in and outside Moscow had a sharp taste today of the country's new market economy when state controls were lifted on

Russian steaks go sky-rocketing.

the prices of food and many other items. Television showed post-World War II footage with the message: "We've been there before." Still, consumers queueing in swirling snow were shocked once inside the grimy stores. Bread leapt from 60 kopeks to two rubles a loaf, carrots from 60 kopeks to three rubles a kilo, milk four times, butter and cooking oil five times. Gasoline, train and air fares and taxi rides soared.

President Yeltsin calls the hikes "a painful, necessary measure". Planners hope prices will settle and that production will be stimulated. Many shelves were bare today because of pre-New Year panic buying at the old subsidized prices.

Moscow scene outside Western store.

U.N.'s top post goes to veteran Egyptian

New York, Wednesday 1
Formidable challenges await the sixth secretary-general of the United Nations, Butros Butros Ghali, who took office today. The 69-year-old Egyptian diplomat takes over from Javier Perez de Cuellar at a critical moment in the organization's history. With the fading of the Cold War, the U.N. now has an opportunity to shape a new international system to replace the configuration of superpower confrontation. Apart from an expanded peacekeeping role, Butros Ghali wants to restructure the U.N.'s cumbersome bureaucracy, a plan supported by the United States.

A new world troubleshooter arrives.

El Salvador peace after bitter war

New York, Wednesday 1
For the Salvadoran people, the peace accord signed early today at the U.N.'s New York headquarters comes as a welcome New Year's present. Salvadoran government and guerrilla representatives signed a pact to end their 12-year civil war, which has cost 75,000 lives. The two sides agreed to a ceasefire beginning February 1 and culminating in the demobilization of the guerrilla forces by October 31. The U.N.-sponsored accord marks the end of one of Central America's bloodiest conflicts.

Jan 1. Mother Theresa, who underwent heart surgery on December 29, recovers slowly from pneumonia in a California hospital prior to release.

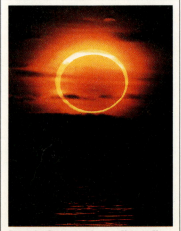
Jan 4. Spectacular eclipse dims the light in southern California.

U.K. employers fear 1992 economic fall

London, Wednesday 1
Prime Minister John Major conceded in a radio interview yesterday that the government had underestimated the length and the depth of the recession but was cautiously optimistic that a recovery was underway. However, even this cautious assessment is disputed by leading industrialists.

The CBI warns that the flood of job losses will continue. Sir Denys Henderson, chairman of ICI, forecasts "a very flat period ahead" with "very slow growth" in 1992. Sir John Quinton, chairman of Barclays Bank, says that last year had seen the worst collapse in business confidence since the 1930s and prospects for 1992 "were little better".

U.S. moves to aid Russia, 5 others

Washington, D.C., Friday 3
The Bush administration today established diplomatic relations with Russia and urged full membership in the World Bank and International Monetary Fund for six former Soviet republics. Full membership in the two Washington-based institutions for Russia, Belarus, Armenia, Kyrgyzstan, Kazakhstan and Ukraine will give them access to billions of dollars in development loans. U.S. backing virtually guarantees that the six republics will be admitted to the two institutions, to which 156 nations already belong.

Austerity for Cuba as fuel stocks fall

Havana, Thursday 2
President Fidel Castro had warned Cubans to expect a "trial by fire" in 1992. Already hard hit by the loss of Soviet aid, Cubans have now been told of drastic cuts in bus services as well as theater and television hours. Fuel is so short that on some Havana bus routes horses, donkeys or oxen will be used to pull the vehicles. Soviet oil imports dropped from 13 million tons in 1989 to just eight million last year, and further cutbacks are expected.

World's most eligible bachelor to marry

Warren Beatty and Annette Bening make their love story official.

Los Angeles, Sunday 5
Warren Beatty probably broke more than a few hearts when he announced that he is to wed his girlfriend, Annette Bening, his co-star in Barry Levinson's *Bugsy*. The 54-year-old Virginia-born actor and his 33-year-old fiancée are expecting their first child in the next few days. It seems that Beatty, who has starred in such hits as Arthur Penn's *Bonnie and Clyde*, *Reds* and *Dick Tracy*, has finally decided to settle down to family life.

Longest jobs queue shows slump's reality

London, Friday 3
The harsh reality of the recession is being seen all round the country in the ever-lengthening queues of men and women seeking help and jobs at social security offices. Last month's figure of 2,551,700 unemployed is expected to rise by another 100,000 this month in a bleak start to the new year.

There is worse to come. National Power expects to shed 6,000 of the 17,000 workers it inherited from the Central Electricity Generating Board. The Confederation of British Industry warns that 73,000 manufacturing workers will lose their jobs in the first quarter of the year. Behind these stark figures lie poverty and broken dreams.

Like their British counterparts, unemployed Americans have little to hope for.

Deaths rise among working journalists

Brussels, Wednesday 1
Last year was an even worse one for journalists than 1989, which had set a record for the number of reporters killed worldwide. A total of 84 media personnel died while covering the world's trouble spots and natural disasters in 1991, against 58 in 1989, according to a report published today by the Brussels-based International Federation of Journalists. Of these, 23 were killed in Latin America, including nine in Colombia and seven in Peru. The Yugoslav conflict accounted for the deaths of at least 22 journalists. The report stresses that few of these died accidentally. Fifteen reporters were killed last June 3 when Japan's Mount Unzen volcano erupted.

Somalia victims are put at 20,000

Somalia, Friday 3
As Somalia sinks further into chaos and civil war, the country's capital, Mogadishu, has become a free-fire zone. According to the latest estimates by U.N. agencies, at least 20,000 people have been killed or injured in the city since last November 17. That was when violent clashes broke out between rival factions. One is led by Somalia's acting president, Ali Madhi Mohamed, while the other is headed by rebel general Farah Aidid, whose well-armed forces hold the southern sectors of Mogadishu (→ Nov 16).

Jan 4. Gerald Ratner's jewelry empire loses its old glitter.

January

1992

Su	Mo	Tu	We	Th	Fr	Sa
			1	2	3	4
5	6	7	8	9	10	11
12	13	14	15	16	17	18
19	20	21	22	23	24	25
26	27	28	29	30	31	

Washington, D.C., 6
NASA announces that the Magellan spacecraft, on a Venus-mapping mission, has stopped sending signals.

New York, 6
U.N. Secretary General Butros Butros Ghali says 50 U.N. military observers will be sent to Yugoslavia.

New York, 6
U.N. Security Council condemns Israel for expelling Palestinians from the Occupied Territories.

Colombia, 6
The Medellin drug clan announces the resumption of the war against their rival, the Cali cartel.

Johannesburg, 6
Grenade attack on the offices of the firm that organized the tour of American singer, Paul Simon (→ 11).

U.S., 7
Arab delegations agree to resume Mid-East peace talks following the United Nations condemnation of Israel (→ 28).

Manila, 7
Imelda Marcos, widow of the late Philippine dictator, announces her candidacy in the presidential elections.

Beijing, 7
Three Canadian MPs are expelled for placing a wreath in Tiananmen Square.

Athens, 8
Palestinian Mohamed Rashid is sentenced to 18 years in jail for the 1982 bombing of a Pan Am jet (1 dead, 15 injured).

Switzerland, 9
Zurich woman claims that the "Ice Man" found last year in the Austrian Alps, thought to be 5,300 years old, is her father.

Tripoli, 9
Libya claims U.S. Sixth Fleet aircraft operating from the carrier *America* have violated its airspace.

France, 9
Airbus results show a decline in orders from 404 aircraft in 1990 to 101 in 1991.

Washington, D.C., 10
U.S. unemployment level reaches 7.1%, the highest since 1987 (→ March 3).

Bush collapses at dinner, but recovers

The watching world holds its collective breath as the president falls over.

Tokyo, Wednesday 8
The misfortune that struck President George Bush at 8:19 p.m. this evening will probably be remembered as the most public case of an intestinal flu attack ever. As the world's television cameras rolled during a formal state dinner in Tokyo, the 67-year-old president turned white as a sheet, flopped backward in his chair, vomited on Japanese Prime Minister Kiichi Miyazawa, and finally hit the floor as Secret Service agents scrambled to assist him.

The incident lasted less than a minute. As Bush was helped to his feet to applause from the dinner guests, he joked: "I just wanted to get a little attention." After the president left the Miyazawa residence, his wife Barbara remained behind and calmly participated in an exchange of toasts with the Japanese premier.

Bush's spectacular collapse cast a pall over his crucial visit to Tokyo, where he has faced an uphill struggle in his attempts to promote free trade and American exports. The president, flanked by the leaders of America's three main automakers - Harold Poling of Ford, Robert Stempel of General Motors and Lee Iacocca of Chrysler - have met stiff resistance from Japanese officials reluctant to open up their markets to American trade. Japan offered to buy an extra $10 billion in U.S. automobile parts by 1995. This fell well short of what the White House had hoped for in its efforts to narrow the $50 billion U.S. trade deficit with Japan.

EC observers killed in Yugoslavia crash

Helicopter falls north of Zagreb.

Zagreb, Tuesday 7
The European Community's efforts to defuse the crisis in Yugoslavia suffered a setback today at 2:09 p.m. That was when a MIG-21 jet of the pro-Serbian Yugoslav army shot down a helicopter, killing five EC military observers, four Italian soldiers and one French officer. The helicopter was downed about 30 miles north of here. The five were the first casualties among the EC monitors since they began operating in Yugoslavia after the Serb-Croat war began last July. In a bid to soften international condemnation of the attack, the Yugoslav Defense Ministry said it has suspended the air force commander, General Zvonko Jurjevic.

Georgian president flees his bunker

Tbilisi, Tuesday 7
Zviad Gamsakhurdia, the former leader of Georgia, fled his parliamentary bunker after a 12-day siege by his one-time supporters. They had accused him of having become a dictator. Gamsakhurdia had been jailed under the Communists as a dissident. He proclaimed Georgia's independence in April 1991, and was elected president with 85% of the vote. Then his ministers began to resign and a rival military council was established. Fighting broke out in Tbilisi. Gamsakhurdia has fled to Armenia vowing to return. His opponents say the new constitution will prevent any one person accumulating too much power (→ March 7).

Gamsakhurdia's popularity melts.

The Royals, particularly these two, work harder, says report.

Algeria's president forced to resign

Algiers, Saturday 11
Fearing a takeover by the Muslim fundamentalists of the Islamic Salvation Front, senior Algerian army officers today forced President Chadli Benjedid to resign. Tanks and armored vehicles have been deployed in Algiers. Benjedid had planned to continue ruling under a system of "cohabitation" with the Islamic fundamentalists, who were certain to win an absolute parliamentary majority in next week's second round of voting. The poll is now sure to be cancelled (→ 12).

Serbs create their own Bosnian state

Sarajevo, Thursday 9
Bosnian Serbs today declared their own republic in protest against Muslim and Croat attempts to seek European Community recognition of Bosnian statehood. "Bosnia is no longer united because Yugoslavia is no longer united", said Radovan Karadzic, leader of the 1.4 million Serbs who form a third of Bosnia's population. This development has brought fears that the civil war raging in Yugoslavia will spread to the centre of the disintegrating federation. There are reports of heavily-armed rival factions making ready for action (→ 15).

Branson accuses BA of unfair methods

London, Friday 10
Richard Branson has taken his claim that British Airways have been waging a dirty tricks campaign against Virgin Atlantic Airways to the European Commission. In an unpublicized meeting with officials from the EC's Unfair Competition Committee his lawyers claimed that BA had abused its dominant position in conducting a smear campaign and employing unfair practises in sales and marketing. This move in the extraordinary dispute between BA and its thrusting independent challenger could lead to the EC taking action under its unfair competition rules.

Low attendance mars first Paul Simon concert in South Africa

The American singer and his band in full swing before meeting ANC leader Nelson Mandela in Johannesburg.

America's new automobiles go on show

General Motor's futuristic Ultralite is a star at the North American stand.

Detroit, Wednesday 8
With America's car-makers about to unveil their new models in an attempt to revive an industry in which sales have slumped by 10% in the last year, attention is focusing on Chrysler's Viper, a "muscle car" powered by an eight-liter V-10 based on a truck engine with the block specially cast in aluminium by Lamborghini.

It represents a return to 1960s motoring with a top speed of 165 mph. It can reach 60 mph in four seconds from a standing start, has only two seats and is certainly not designed for a shopping trip with the family. It also eats up a gallon of fuel every 15 miles at cruising speed.

Environmentalists are appalled by its advent, but Chrysler, down 20% on last year, is confident the sunset-red Viper with 400 horse power under its long bonnet will attract the macho customer. At $55,000 this all-American dream machine is a snip.

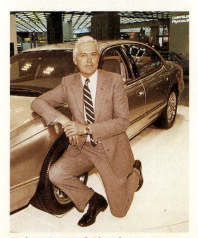

Robert Lutz, of Chrysler, optimistic.

Johannesburg, Saturday 11
Paul Simon's highly-publicized South African tour has got off to a shaky start. Only about 45,000 people, nearly all of them white, turned up to watch the American singer, leaving much of Johannesburg's 70,000-seat Ellis Park stadium empty. There was a heavy police presence around Ellis Park, as several radical black groups had threatened to disrupt the concert. Simon is the first international star to perform in South Africa since the cultural boycott against apartheid was lifted. Black opponents of the tour say the boycott should remain in force until there is a black government in South Africa. The low attendance at today's concert is being attributed to the high cost of tickets. These were priced at up to $30 each in a country where most black workers earn less that $300 per month.

Jan 9. Allison Halford, Britain's most senior policewoman, is suspended for misconduct.

January

1992

Su	Mo	Tu	We	Th	Fr	Sa
			1	2	3	4
5	6	7	8	9	10	11
12	13	14	15	16	17	18
19	20	21	22	23	24	25
26	27	28	29	30	31	

Algiers, 12
Algeria's parliamentary elections are cancelled to block victory by the Islamic Salvation Front (→ 16).

Sofia, 12
Zhelyu Zhelev leads in the first free presidential election in Bulgaria since the fall of the Communist regime.

Russia, 12
Ten thousand Communist supporters protest in Manezh Square against rising prices and demand the resignation of the government.

Strasbourg, 14
Egon Klepsch, a German Christian Democrat, is elected as the new president of the European Parliament.

U.S., 14
Dow Corning stops production of silicon breast implants following allegations that they are unsafe for women and could cause a health risk.

Moscow, 14
Twelve former Soviet officials, including the ex-chief of the KGB, are charged with conspiracy to seize power in the 1991 coup attempt.

U.S., 16
Doctors say legionnaire's disease can be caught via tap water as well as through air conditioning systems.

Algiers, 16
Mohammed Boudiaf, after 27 years of exile in Morocco, returns to head crisis-torn Algeria (→ June 29).

Ulster, 18
The British government, faced with a new outbreak of terrorism, decides to send more troops to the province (→ 20).

Berlin, 18
Chancellor Helmut Kohl takes part in 50th anniversary ceremonies against the Nazi Wannsee conference where the anti-semitic "final solution" was formulated.

Scotland, 18
In the Five Nations Rugby Union Championship, England beats Scotland 25-7.

DEATH
17. Charlie Ventura, American saxophonist (*Dec. 2, 1916).

Magic Johnson in president's AIDS panel

Basketball star, who admitted his condition, seeks to help other victims.

Woman on trial for serial killer case

Florida, Monday 13
Aileen Wuornos, alleged by police to be America's first-ever female serial killer, went on trial for the murder of seven men.

The case is being heard in De Land, some 30 miles from Orlando. Wuornos, a 35-year-old prostitute, was arrested at the Last Chance Saloon, in Daytona Beach. She is accused of having shot to death seven men she picked up between December 1989 and December of the following year.

America discovers its femme fatale.

Washington, D.C., Tuesday 14
Basketball star Earvin "Magic" Johnson today met with President George Bush, his first meeting as a member of the National Commission on AIDS.

Johnson was appointed to the panel after he shocked sports fans the world over by announcing last November that he had tested positive for the AIDS virus. After today's meeting, the 32-year-old former Los Angeles Lakers star said he had called on Bush to allocate more funds and to get more involved in the fight against the killer disease. Johnson is campaigning for greater awareness of the danger of AIDS among heterosexuals.

A need for Western jobs for scientists

London, Monday 13
Fears that unemployed Soviet nuclear scientists might sell their secrets to Libya and other "rogue" countries led MPs yesterday to urge that they should be offered posts at British and American universities. David Howell, chairman of the Commons Select Committee on Foreign Affairs, warned against a "vast increase in proliferation. We have had suggestions that nuclear warheads have gone for a walk and maybe are in irresponsible hands. This is the most urgent matter facing the world at the moment."

EC move means end of old Yugoslavia

Brussels, Wednesday 15
The European Commission today signaled the end of Yugoslavia as one nation by recognizing the independence of Croatia and Slovenia. This decision is seen as a victory for German policy but although all 12 EC members eventually succumbed to intense pressure from Bonn some, especially Britain and France, had grave reservations about its wisdom.

While Croatia and Slovenia celebrate their independence, reaction from Belgrade has been angry. Vladislav Jovanovic, Serbia's foreign minister, accused the EC of encouraging the break-up of the country and said it risked "reaping a whirlwind".

Independence feted by the Croats.

Jan. 14. Duke and Duchess of York before their breakup.

IBM announces its first-ever annual loss

New York State, Friday 17
In what must be one of the darkest days in Big Blue's 77-year history, the computer giant today posted its first annual loss.

International Business Machines Corp., which had reported a profit of $6 billion in 1990, suffered a loss of $564 million last year. The company, which is based near Armonk, said its revenues fell 6.1% in 1991, to $64.8 billion from a 1990 record of $69 billion. This was the first time in 45 years that the world's largest computer manufacturer's growth has fallen. However, IBM Chairman John Akers did not appear too disappointed with the company's year-end report. Last month he announced plans to slim down and restructure the corporation founded by Thomas Watson on February 14, 1924. These involve large-scale decentralization and further cuts in the workforce. IBM is expected to shoulder the $3 billion cost of incentives to induce some 20,000 employees to quit or retire. The company's management hopes the streamlining plan will cut operating expenses by 2%. Commenting on today's report, IBM executives attributed the poor 1991 results to the decline of the world's economy, increased competition and the problems associated with introducing new product lines. IBM's earnings have been hit by corporate computer buyers' move away from multimillion-dollar mainframe systems. Smaller microprocessor-based systems are slowly but surely replacing the huge mainframes.

Crisis-hit computer giant continues to cut back its worldwide workforce.

War anniversary finds Saddam still there

Baghdad, Friday 17
At 2:30 a.m. in Baghdad today, carefully rehearsed groups began chanting slogans in praise of Saddam Hussein, artists put the first strokes of paint onto giant murals, and Iraqi musicians played the opening bars of new works dedicated to their leader and to the war which began at this moment exactly a year ago.

Speaking to a group of tribal leaders, Saddam told them: "There is nothing to regret. I have never doubted, even for a moment, that we emerged triumphant from the war." With their country divided and in ruins, roads still impassable and bridges down, food scarce, inflation soaring and an international embargo preventing trade, Iraqis still turned out in their thousands to celebrate what Saddam had called "the mother of all battles". Foreigners present said the security police were everywhere, and the "spontaneous" demonstrations all seemed to have been carefully rehearsed. In Washington, the White House called on Iraqis to topple Saddam. It added America stood ready to work with a new regime in Baghdad, a new leadership that would accept U.N. resolutions and live in peace with its neighbors.

The reply from Baghdad crowds came in chants of "Death to Iraq's enemies", and "No to George Bush, yes to Saddam Hussein". Iraqi government officials confidently forecast Saddam Hussein would outlast President Bush.

Iraqi leader says he has no regrets.

East Europe is now drug gangs' target

Geneva, Monday 13
The U.N. has published a report on drug abuse in the world in 1991. Traffic is growing worldwide, and traffickers are intensifying and expanding their operations into countries where their presence had not been as strong, notably in the countries of the former U.S.S.R. and East Europe. Cocaine and heroin still have only a limited presence in East Europe, but the abuse of cannabis and psychedelic drugs is rapidly increasing there.

Jan 14. Mikhail Gorbachev starts afresh. He takes over as head of the new international study institute in Moscow.

Worst IRA terrorist bombing since 1988

Ulster, Friday 17
The IRA has made its worst attack in Northern Ireland since 1988: seven Protestant construction workers were killed instantly, and seven others injured, when a bomb destroyed a van transporting them from a worksite at a British Army barracks near the village of Omagh. It is not known if the workers were the intended target or not, but the IRA considers those who work for the British police and army as "collaborators". Prime Minister John Major declared the perpetrators would be punished (→ 18).

Jan 18. Artist John Keane puts Mickey Mouse in Gulf War painting.

January

1992

Su	Mo	Tu	We	Th	Fr	Sa
			1	2	3	4
5	6	7	8	9	10	11
12	13	14	15	16	17	18
19	20	21	22	23	24	25
26	27	28	29	30	31	

France, 20
An Air-Inter Airbus crashes into a mountain in eastern France killing 86 of the 96 people aboard.

Moscow, 20
Russia and Finland sign a new treaty which revises their post-World War II relations which were based on war reparations and neutrality.

Havana, 20
Eduardo Betancourt, opponent of Fidel Castro, is executed despite international appeals for clemency.

Ulster, 20
British Prime Minister John Major visits Belfast and vows to continue and win the anti-terrorist fight (→ Aug 27).

New York, 21
The trial opens of John Gotti, alleged organized crime leader and boss of the Gambino family, accused of ordering the killing of a rival (→ April 2).

Christchurch, 22
In cricket, England beats New Zealand by an innings and four runs in the First Test (→ Feb. 3).

Washington, D.C., 22
Fifty-four nations and international bodies attend the global conference to coordinate aid for the Commonwealth of Independent States.

Algiers, 22
The authorities arrest Abdelkader Hachani, fundamentalist leader, and seven members of the I.S.F. leadership.

Germany, 22
U.S. military materiel is seized as it is loaded onto a cargo plane bound for Libya.

London, 22
England is to reimburse the Baltic states for the 15.5 tons of gold sold in 1967. The sum involved is $162 million.

Moscow, 24
The Russian parliament approves an austerity budget for the first quarter. Cuts in military expenditure are expected.

U.S., 24
Dangerous and unusual forms of tuberculosis are detected in 13 states. Outbreaks mostly involve people with HIV.

Supreme Court places controversial abortion issue on docket

"The natural choice is life" lobby seeks to influence President Bush.

Washington, D.C., Tuesday 21
In a move that is sure to propel the abortion issue to prominence in an election year, the Supreme Court agreed today to rule on Pennsylvania's abortion law this term. The law that the court will review before it recesses in July imposes a 24-hour waiting period on women seeking to obtain abortions, states that married women must inform their husbands they plan to have an abortion and requires physicians to inform patients about alternatives to abortion. Anti-abortion groups hope the review of the Pennsylvania law will lead the court to overrule the landmark 1973 Roe v. Wade decision, while abortion rights advocates hope the court will reaffirm that ruling (→ June 29).

Auto thefts lead to U.K. crime increase

London, Wednesday 22
The number of stolen cars offered for sale to dealers in Britain has risen by a staggering 300% over last year. HPI, the vehicle information bureau, reports that dealers found 6,900 "dodgy" cars in the fourth quarter of the year against 2,200 in the same period of 1990. The rise reflects the dramatic growth in car crime with more than a million break-ins and thefts reported to the police during the year. Insurance companies paid out more than £400 million in claims.

Jan 21. London girl is the sex star of French film "L'Amant".

Magnificent Seven sets off in Discovery

Florida, Wednesday 22
The U.S. space shuttle Discovery blasted off from Cape Canaveral today carrying seven astronauts, among them a Canadian woman and a German man, on a scientific research mission which will last a week. The crew will conduct 55 experiments in physics, biology and medicine in the European-built Spacelab laboratory carried inside the shuttle's cargo bay. The flight marks the sixth anniversary of the disaster which destroyed the Challenger and its crew at lift-off. It was Discovery which took the U.S. back into orbit three years later.

NASA's latest mission in outer space.

Hand over Pan Am bombers, U.N. says

New York, Tuesday 21
The U.N. Security Council demanded today that Libya comply fully with U.S. and British requests for the surrender of two Libyans linked to the bombing of Pan Am Flight 103 over Lockerbie, Scotland, on December 21, 1988. The midair explosion killed all 259 people on board the New York-bound jetliner and 11 people on the ground. The tough U.N. resolution, adopted by a 15-to-0 vote, came after Libya refused to hand over the two men, saying they could stand trial in Libya (→ March 1).

Oxford is overrun by tourist hordes

Oxford, Monday 20
This "city of dreaming spires" is being drowned in a sea of tourists according to a survey commissioned by the local tourist board. While tourism supports more than 3,000 jobs in the city the side-effects are less welcome. The colleges are beset by parties which invade the hallowed quads and wander into halls during meals. Anthony Smith, the president of Magdalen, said Oxford was falling victim to an unthinking tourist culture. "People are invited to consume institutions rather than understand them."

Rash of murders is at epidemic stage

Washington, D.C., January
Violent crime in the U.S. reached epidemic proportions in 1991, according to a report by the Senate Judiciary Committee. A total of 24,020 people were murdered last year, an increase of 580 on 1990. California had a record 3,710 killings, ahead of Texas, where 2,660 people were murdered. The number of killings dropped by 2% in New York State, where 2,550 died, according to Senator Joseph Biden, the committee's chairman.

London court order winds up BCCI bank

London, Tuesday 14
The collapsed Bank of Credit and Commerce International was finally put into liquidation today by a High Court ruling on an unopposed petition by the Bank of England on the grounds that the bank "is plainly and hopelessly insolvent". Keith Vaz, MP, who has been fighting for compensation for the staff and creditors said the campaign would continue: "BCCI was given its last rites today but it has not yet been buried."

Buchanan champion of disgruntled Right

Fellow Republican launches campaign against Bush in New Hampshire.

Washington, Monday 20
Pat Buchanan, the heavyweight conservative journalist who has set his sights on the White House, has emerged as the champion of the disgruntled right wing of the Republican Party. Polls taken in the run-up to the New Hampshire primary show he has cut President Bush's lead by 10 points and is only 16 points behind.

His strong showing demonstrates his ability to reflect the feelings of troubled Americans. He accuses the president of spending too much time on foreign affairs and not enough on the problems of ordinary people at home: the poor state of the economy, costly health care and inadequate schools. His slogan is "America First".

Buchanan, a pugnacious Irish-American who is scathing about Jews, blacks and gays, is unlikely to defeat Bush but he could severely damage President Bush and the mood in the White House is said to be close to panic (→ Feb 18).

Premier is ensnared in telephone taps

Dublin, Wednesday 22
Prime Minister Charles Haughey of Ireland today strongly denied allegations that he knew about the wiretapping of two journalists' telephones. Haughey, who is fighting for his political life, called the charge "monstrous and unfounded". He said it was part of a plot within the ruling Fianna Fail party to topple him.

The allegations were made a few days ago by a former justice minister, Sean Doherty (→ 30).

Fares war rages in North Atlantic skies

London, Wednesday 22
Airlines on the transatlantic routes are waging a cutthroat war to win customers. The U.S. companies, United and American Airlines, have "frequent flier" programs: regular passengers amass points based on the miles they fly in order to qualify for free tickets. British Airways is offering hotel bookings, airport car parking and holiday breaks while Virgin gives points to "buy" health club memberships and lessons in hot-air ballooning.

Paris Spring-Summer 1992 haute couture fashion shows

Lacroix: Christian loves to provoke and always mixes genres. This year's show was luxurious with pink tartan taffetas and miles of tulle.

Ungaro: His 25th-anniversary show was worthy of the court of the Sun King. From the leg of mutton sleeves to the re-embroidered spencers, everything was dazzling.

Scherrer: This show was the story of a romantic and exotic voyage recounted in two tableaux: earth tones and feathered embroidery followed by opalescent chiffon.

Chanel: Kurt Lagerfeld gave us long and slender silhouettes in bright and gay pink, white and blue as well as more sober navy blue and black.

Su	Mo	Tu	We	Th	Fr	Sa
			1	2	3	4
5	6	7	8	9	10	11
12	13	14	15	16	17	18
19	20	21	22	23	24	25
26	27	28	29	30	31	

Australia, 26
Jim Courier (U.S.) defeats Stefan Edberg (Sweden) in the final of the Australian Open tennis championship.

Nagorno-Karabakh, 26
Heavy fighting again erupts between Azerbaijan and Armenia over this Armenian-dominated enclave.

Brussels, 28
France agrees to sign the NATO nuclear non-proliferation treaty (→ Aug 3).

Moscow, 28
The Mid-East peace talks resume despite a boycott by the Palestinian delegation.

Prague, 28
President Vaclav Havel's request for broader powers to solve Czechoslovakia's constitutional crisis is rejected by the federal parliament.

Buenos Aires, 28
Argentina suspends delivery of nuclear material to Iran.

Paris, 29
George Habash, Palestinian terrorist leader, is secretly hospitalized, causing a scandal and a purge at France's Foreign Ministry (→ Feb. 1).

Moscow, 30
Tass, the former Soviet government's news agency, changes its name to Itar.

New York, 30
Pan Am sues its new owner, Delta, for $2.5 billion over inadequate compensation.

Moscow, 30
Boris Yeltsin sets off on an international tour taking in London, the U.N. Security Council in New York, Washington, D.C. and Paris.

Dublin, 30
Veteran Irish politician, Charles Haughey, resigns as prime minister after being accused of telephone tapping.

U.S., 31
Boxer Mike Tyson, goes on trial for rape (→ Feb 5).

New York, 31
The pound is quoted at $1.78.

DEATH
28. Willie Dixon, American jazz musician (*April 15, 1915).

Bush disappoints with his Union message

President Bush, flanked by Vice-President Quayle, addresses Congress.

British child care is 'worst in Europe'

London, Wednesday 29
Only one in 300 children under five attend day nurseries sponsored by employers according to the annual report of the pressure group, Working for Childcare. Tax concessions introduced two years ago to help more mothers return to work after having babies have led to the number of nurseries being quadrupled to 425 but this still leaves Britain at the bottom of the European child-care league. Many companies are just too small to have nurseries.

Washington, D.C., Tuesday 28
Faced with sinking poll ratings, an embattled George Bush tonight went on a political war footing in his crucial election-year State of the Union speech. In a bid to give the economy a much-needed boost, he proposed tax cuts totaling about $25 billion and a $50-billion military expenditure reduction over five years. The proposed military cuts include ending production of the B-2 Stealth bomber.

The president's proposals were immediately scorned by Democrats, many of whom said it was "too little, too late". Others were disappointed that Bush did not plan to bolster social programs.

Jan 27. Recession threat to America's most famous department store.

German navy stops Syria-bound tanks

Bonn, Thursday 30
An embarrassed Defense Ministry official announced here today that two German warships have intercepted a German-registered cargo vessel carrying an illegal arms shipment to Syria.

The freighter, *Godewind*, was stopped last night as it cruised off the coast of Sicily in the Mediterranean. Aboard, German navy officers found 16 Soviet-made and Czechoslovak-owned T-72 main battle tanks. The *Godewind*, now being escorted back to Germany, left the Polish port of Szczecin two weeks ago. The 16 T-72s are part of a consignment of 300 Soviet-built tanks purchased by Syria.

Jan 27. Madonna goes shopping.

Heterosexual AIDS cases rise by 50%

London, Wednesday 29
Cases of AIDS acquired through heterosexual intercourse increased by almost 50% between 1990 and 1991 according to figures issued by the Department of Health today. This means that although the total number of heterosexual cases is still smaller than other groups the rate of increase of heterosexual AIDS in men and women is faster than in any other group. There were 121 cases in 1990 and 180 in 1991. Many of the heterosexual cases were infected in countries where AIDS is rife or by contact with someone from such a country.

Gennifer hits back, says Clinton is liar

New York, Monday 27
A furious Gennifer Flowers today called a news conference and publicly branded Governor Bill Clinton of Arkansas a liar.

The angry response came a day after Clinton, one of five major Democratic candidates for president, denied on television having had a 12-year affair with Flowers, a former TV news reporter in Arkansas. The 45-year-old governor, however, acknowledged "wrong-doing" in his marriage to his wife Hillary. Flowers, who claimed Clinton was "absolutely lying", also said the Democratic presidential contender had helped her get a state job in Arkansas (→ Feb 12).

Lady friend problem for candidate.

Yeltsin and Major agree weapons control

The Russian leader enters by the main door of Number 10 this time.

London, Thursday 30
Boris Yeltsin and John Major stood outside No 10 Downing Street today, shook hands and declared that there were "no ideological barriers" between Britain and Russia. The handshake and the smiles reflected the solid achievements of the talks between the two leaders.

They signed a 15-point declaration committing their nations to the peaceful settlement of disputes, the control of weapons of mass destruction and the non-proliferation of nuclear weapons. Yeltsin also told reporters that Russian nuclear weapons would no longer be aimed at British cities.

Other points in the agreement bind both sides to cooperate on defense matters, including the restructuring of the former Soviet armed forces to suit Russia's new circumstances, and to cooperate in handling surplus Soviet nuclear weapons and safeguarding nuclear materials.

They also agreed to set up a hotline between their offices to smooth the new relationship and to set up consulates in Edinburgh and St Petersburg. Referring to Major's support during the August coup attempt, Yeltsin said: "I can't hide the emotion I felt when he phoned me during some of the most difficult hours in Russia since the Second World War" (→ Feb 1).

Cuts coming in U.S. bases in W. Europe

Washington, D.C., Thursday 30
The Pentagon's post-Cold War policy of cutting overseas military costs worldwide took a step further today with the announcement of the closure of 83 military installations in Europe. Defense Department officials said the plan involved bringing home 17,000 troops. Apart from a site at Comiso, Italy, one at Thurso, Britain, and one at Maastricht, the Netherlands, all the installations are in Germany.

U.S. troop levels in Europe have decreased from 314,000 in September 1990 to 227,000. The Pentagon plans to cut troop strength to 208,000 by next September.

Chapter 11 cover is sought now by TWA

Mt Kisco, New York, Friday 31
TWA today became the most recent in a long line of U.S. airlines to declare bankruptcy and seek court protection from creditors. The once-great carrier, owned by Carl Icahn since 1986, filed in Delaware under Chapter 11 of the bankruptcy code. TWA stressed that schedules would not be affected and that tickets would be honored. Icahn believes TWA will recover from its debt of almost $2 billion and climb back to greatness in six months.

Redskins win the Super Bowl with victory over the Buffalo Bills

The Washington Redskins fly very high to grab the ball and trophy.

Minneapolis, Sunday 26
The Washington Redskins beat the Buffalo Bills by 37-24 here today to win the Super Bowl, one of the greatest prizes in the American sporting calendar. Although the Bills scored two late touchdowns to make the score-line respectable the Redskins won the game comfortably and the Bills are disconsolate after consecutive Super Bowl defeats. There was nothing disconsolate about the Redskins. Coach Joe Gibbs said: "I feel very humbled that the Lord has blessed me with great owners and a great organization." Washingtonians, glued to their TV sets, chanted the seconds to victory then went mad with joy.

Jan 30. Raincoat returns to haunt high society criminals.

February

1992

Twickenham, 1
In the Five Nations Rugby Union Championship, England XV beats Ireland 38-9.

Turkey, 1
The death toll, following avalanches in the south-east of the country, rises to over 100.

Spain, 1
Tens of thousands demonstrate in Bilbao, the Basque capital, against acts of terrorism by ETA Basque separatists (→ 6).

London, 2
Labour leader Neil Kinnock denies allegations of a "Kremlin connection" in the 1980's.

Auckland, 3
In cricket, England beats New Zealand by 168 runs in the Second Test.

Buenos Aires, 3
Argentina President Carlos Menem orders the release of secret police files on Nazi war criminals who fled to the country after World War II.

U.S., 3
The space probe Ulysses, launched in Oct. 1990 from the space shuttle Discovery, enters Jupiter's magnetic field.

Tunis, 3
The marriage is revealed of PLO leader Yasir Arafat, 63, and his economic advisor, Suha Tawil, 28.

C.I.S., 4
Despite memories of the Nazi regime, 25,000 Jews from the former Soviet Union apply to emigrate to Germany.

Indiana, 5
Three die in a blaze at an Indianapolis hotel housing the jury of the Mike Tyson rape trial. No jury members were injured (→ March 26).

Paris, 6
Boris Yeltsin, during an official visit to France, obtains $700 million in aid (→ April 1).

Mexico, 6
The Guatemalan government and rebels open their first peace negotiations under the auspices of the Mexican government.

New Jersey, 7
Minolta, of Japan, is fined $96 million, for infringement of Honeywell's self-focusing camera patents.

Palestinian leader causes scandal in Paris

Government is shaken by the fallout of the secret, but authorized, visit.

Paris, Saturday 1
"They're all crazy!" exclaimed French President François Mitterrand in reaction to the decision by French officials to let George Habash, leader of the Popular Front for the Liberation of Palestine, enter France. The decision caused an uproar in the country, with protests from members of the ruling Socialist Party as well as the opposition. Four government advisors, have under official pressure, offered their resignations over the affair. Habash was placed in police detention on Friday, but was allowed to leave France today after spending two days in the Henri-Dunant Red Cross Hospital in Paris.

Cossiga calls for new elections in Italy

Rome, Sunday 2
Italy's president, Francesco Cossiga, dissolved parliament today, five months early, and set April 5 as the date for a general election.

Prime Minister Giulio Andreotti's coalition will stay in power until a new government, almost certainly another coalition, can be formed after the election. The vote will take place against a background of severe economic problems, the murderous activity of the Mafia, and secret service scandals. A growing number of Italians are demanding a cleanup of the corrupt bureaucracy and a revision of Italy's political institutions.

Yeltsin returns to U.S. as head of state

Camp David, Saturday 1
Marine One, the presidential helicopter, flew Boris Yeltsin to Camp David. Then President Bush gave his Russian host a 61st birthday present: hand-made cowboy boots decorated with a map of Russia and the American and Russian flags. Smiling broadly, Yeltsin said: "The best present is meeting President Bush at Camp David." Yeltsin appeared delighted to be on the world stage at last. It was the first time he had come to the U.S. as a head of state. The two leaders discussed the proposal Yeltsin made yesterday at the U.N., where he called for merging the U.S. Star Wars system with Russian technology to create a global anti-missile shield (→ 6).

Cowboy boots will echo in the corridors of the Kremlin after Bush's gift.

Ancient city found in desert sands

Los Angeles, Monday 3
A group of American scientists and archeologists today announced the discovery of a 4,000-year-old lost city in Empty Quarter of the Arabian desert, on the border of what is now Oman and Yemen.

The American experts, who were helped by British explorer Sir Ranulph Fiennes, believe the find could be the fabled city Ubar, mentioned in the Koran and once a major center of the trade in frankincense. The U.S. team used old maps and satellite images. These helped them trace ancient caravan routes leading to and from the buried city.

Deaths, arrests as Caracas coup fails

Tank road blocks in capital's streets.

Caracas, Tuesday 4
The attempt by rebel units of the Venezuelan Army to overthrow the government of President Carlos Perez was finally crushed today when F-16 fighter-bombers strafed an armored brigade holding out at its base at Valencia in the hills south-west of the capital.

The rebels began to surrender when one of their captured leaders appealed to them to avoid further bloodshed. Most of the leaders are now under arrest. The rebellion, timed to mark the third anniversary of Perez' presidency, was sparked by discontent at his stringent austerity program designed to lift the country out of the economic misery brought by massive foreign debts.

Maastricht accord on EC cooperation

Maastricht, Friday 7
Music played today as 24 politicians gathered in a circular room on an island in the middle of the river Maas. The worthies of Europe – including, for Britain, Foreign Secretary Douglas Hurd – took out black fountain pens, and put their signatures to two hefty tomes.

They were signing first the Treaty on European Union and then the Maastricht Final Act. Together, these treaties commit the 12 members of the European Community to move closer to each other. Europeans will share common citizenship, economic and defense policies. But today's treaties only lay down broad outlines for European union. The details could be very difficult to thrash out. In Britain, doubts are already being expressed as to the wisdom of surrendering sovereignty to Brussels (May 12).

Madrid bomb havoc

Madrid, Thursday 6
A bomb exploded at 8:30 a.m. in the city center, the fifth terrorist attack in Spain this year. Responsibility has been attributed to ETA, the Basque separatist organization. The bomb, planted in a car, went off as the car passed a military van, killing four soldiers and a civilian and injuring six other civilians. With the Olympics in Barcelona and the Universal Exposition in Seville, further attacks are feared.

Spectacular start for Winter Games

The dazzling ice choreography staged by France in the stadium is admired by millions around the world.

Albertville, Saturday 8
The Winter Olympics opened this evening with a dazzling two-hour show that featured circus clowns, jet fighter planes, trapezists, Alpine hunters and walking snowballs. The extravaganza was witnessed by 30,000 spectators who paid 150 francs for a ticket.

The millions who watched the show on television, of course, were spared the expense of buying tickets to the opening and to the other events. But then the U.S. network CBS laid out $243 million for television rights, the European Broadcasting Union paid $24 million, while Japan had to cough up a mere $9 million. Sponsors are also footing a sizeable share of the Olympic bill. Companies such as Kodak, Coca-Cola and Bausch & Lomb are paying a minimum of $25 million each to use the Olympic rings in their advertising and packaging. The French government has also heavily invested in the region, with a new highway and an extension of the high-speed TGV railway.

The world has changed since the last Olympics, and this is reflected at Albertville. The Soviet team is no more: athletes from the Baltic states will compete under their national flags, and the countries of the Commonwealth of Independent States will be represented by a Unified Team. There is a Yugoslav team, but without Croatia and Slovenia, which are now independent countries and are represented by their own teams. German athletes will be united on one Olympic team for the first time since 1968.

More athletes – 2,196 – from more countries – 64 – are participating in this year's Winter Games than ever before (→ 23).

Posing for this historic photograph is one of the last survivors of the Gulag camps. He was released from camp Perm 135 near the Arctic.

Feb 6. Queen Elizabeth II, who celebrates 40 years on the throne this year, is seen in an off-duty moment with her beloved racehorses.

February

1992

Su	Mo	Tu	We	Th	Fr	Sa
						1
2	3	4	5	6	7	8
9	10	11	12	13	14	15
16	17	18	19	20	21	22
23	24	25	26	27	28	29

Senegal, 9
A plane, chartered by Club Med, crashes near the Atlantic coast killing 30 Club Med vacationers.

Moscow, 9
Rival demonstrations, for and against Boris Yeltsin, are staged in the capital where the leader continues to enjoy support.

Wellington, 10
England and New Zealand draw in the Third Test in cricket.

Moscow, 10
Mikhail Gorbachev warns that Russia's economic crisis could be followed by what he called "a general emergency... something quite different from democratization".

Russia, 11
Japanese officials repeat that aid to Russia depends on concessions on the former Japanese Kuril Islands, occupied by the Russians since 1945.

Ulan Bator, 12
Mongolia's new constitution introduces a multi-party system and human rights guarantees.

Lima, 12
Three police guards are killed by a car bomb that explodes outside of the U.S. ambassador's home.

U.S., 13
Colgate-Palmolive Co. agrees to pay $670 million in stock and cash to buy Mennen.

New York, 14
Disputes and incidents occur during the U.N. debate on alleged Indonesian massacres in East Timor, annexed by Indonesia in 1976.

Vatican City, 14
The Vatican denies allegations that following World War II it helped former Nazi war criminals escape from Europe.

Israel, 15
A Palestinian commando group breaks into a military camp and kills three soldiers.

DEATH

15. William Schuman, American composer (*Aug. 4, 1910).

Operation Hope flies food aid to Moscow

Giant U.S. transport planes take off loaded with supplies for the winter.

Frankfurt, Monday 10
With a deafening roar, the first giant USAF Lockheed C-5 Galaxy cargo aircraft rolled down the runway and took off from the Rhein-Main air base near here.

It was the first of 54 planned Air Force flights by C-5 and C-141 Starlifter planes from Frankfurt and Incirlik air base in southeastern Turkey. The cargo planes will carry more than 2,500 tons of surplus military food rations, mostly stock left over from the Gulf War, and pharmaceutical supplies to Moscow and to about two dozen other cities of the former Soviet Union. Because security for the aid cannot be guaranteed, Georgia is the only republic left out of the airlift. Each package of humanitarian aid carries a label in Russian and English saying: "From the American people, who assure you the fight for democracy is worth it."

U.S. Secretary of State James Baker was at Rhein-Main this morning to watch the launch of "Operation Provide Hope", an airlift lasting three weeks and financed by $100 million in Pentagon funds. He said that unlike the 1949 Berlin airlift this operation is not a long-term one. Russia and the newly-independent republics are in the grip of winter and the shelves are almost bare. Therefore, what is needed is emergency food and medical aid for schools, orphanages and hospitals, Baker added.

Ashdown admits to affair but stays cool

Attitudes to sex change in Britain.

London, Sunday 9
Having a love affair with your secretary could boost your political career. The standing of Paddy Ashdown, leader of the Liberal Democrats, has never been so high – following his admission that five years ago he had a relationship with his then secretary.

Ashdown's disclosure followed the theft of notes about the affair from his solicitor's safe. Five days ago, the Liberal Democrat leader explained that with an election looming, he decided he must come clean. His wife Jane and MPs of all parties rallied round him. Pollsters now say that his rating as a potential prime minister has risen by 13% in the last week.

Alex Haley, author of "Roots" is dead

Seattle, Monday 10
Alex Haley, the black American author whose book "Roots: The Saga of an American Family", made him the literary champion of his race, died in Seattle today. He was 70. "Roots" was a mixture of careful research and fictional detail in which he traced the history of his family from their village in Gambia, their transportation as slaves and their life in the U.S.

It had a huge impact. Made into a television series, it was seen by 130 million people. Some critics were not impressed by his factional style, however, and in 1978 he settled a lawsuit out of court, acknowledging that his book contained material from Harold Courlander's novel "The African".

Afro-Americans and their heritage.

Feb 10. Sean Connery now to fight for Scottish nationalism.

Clinton's problems with Vietnam draft

U.S., Wednesday 12
After being plagued by allegations of marital infidelity, Governor Bill Clinton of Arkansas is now having to fight off attacks on his patriotism during the Vietnam War.

Clinton, one of five major Democratic candidates for the November elections, today released a 23-year-old letter in which he thanked the head of a reserve officers training program for "saving me from the draft". Clinton said he decided to release the 1969 letter after its contents were leaked to the media. The lengthy letter was sent from Oxford University where Clinton was studying at the time. In it, he states that he was strongly opposed to the war and admired those who refused to serve in Vietnam (→ 18).

Candidate supplies musical interval.

Bush is candidate

Washington, D.C., Wednesday 12
Undaunted by plummeting polls, George Bush today officially announced his candidacy for a second term in the White House.

Addressing hundreds of cheering supporters gathered at a Washington hotel, the president said the Republican agenda would stress rebuilding the U.S. economy, restoring "decency", fighting "hatred and gloom" and reforming "our dismal welfare system". The announcement, greeted by chants of "Four more years", comes just six days before the New Hampshire primary, the nation's first (→ 18).

Ford's loss of $2.3b is the highest ever

Gloom at Dearborn plant as automobile giant goes heavily into the red.

Michigan, Thursday 13
Ford Motor Co., America's second largest automaker, was not spared by recession-hit 1991.

The company that just three years ago had a record profit of $5.3 billion today reported a $2.3 billion loss, the worst in its 89-year history. Much of this red ink is being blamed on Ford's overseas automotive operations, which last year lost $970 million compared with a $116 million profit the previous year. Before 1991, Ford's worst year was 1980, when it posted a $1.5 billion loss. Ford chairman Harold Poling said the huge 1991 loss was largely due to intense foreign competition, but added that the company's cost-cutting efforts, which include personnel reductions, will lead to a recovery.

EC and EFTA create biggest trade bloc

Brussels, Friday 14
The 12 European Community and seven European Free Trade Association nations today agreed to create the world's largest free trade zone.

With a population of 380 million, the new European Economic Area will stretch from the Mediterranean Sea to the Arctic. When it takes effect next January 1, the agreement will extend EC legislation on the free movement of people, capital and goods to the seven EFTA members. These are Austria, Finland, Iceland, Liechtenstein, Norway, Switzerland and Sweden.

Lloyd's insurance is attacked by Tories

London, Thursday 13
Two bastions of the British establishment – the Conservative Party and Lloyd's of London – are at each other's throats. Tory MPs are accusing insiders at Lloyd's, the world's best-known insurance underwriters, of creaming off the best business for themselves, dumping bad risks onto the syndicates of underwriters ("Names"), who now face substantial losses. The system at Lloyd's, where agents can draw on cash deposits made by the "Names", is open to abuse, claim the MPs. Lloyd's is supposed to minimize risks to investors by spreading it thinly. But 6,000 "Names" face losses of up to £90,000. The underwriters who lead the syndicates, by contrast, are making up to £200,000 a year.

England cricketers beat New Zealand

Christchurch, Saturday 15
England beat New Zealand by 71 runs today to win all three limited-over matches and to finish their tour unbeaten with eight wins and three draws. Ian Botham was "Man of the Match" with a rumbustious innings of 79 scored off 73 balls.

However, England have lost batsman Alan Lamb and fast bowler David Lawrence to injury, seriously affecting their chances in the World Cup which starts in Australia next week.

Feb 9. Dance legend Gene Kelly is feted by the New York City Ballet.

Feb 12. California's highways are transformed into streams.

February

1992

Su	Mo	Tu	We	Th	Fr	Sa
						1
2	3	4	5	6	7	8
9	10	11	12	13	14	15
16	17	18	19	20	21	22
23	24	25	26	27	28	29

Paris, 16
In the Five Nations Rugby Union Championship, the England XV beats France 31-13 at Parc des Princes.

Berne, 16
The Swiss vote against banning animals for medical and pharmaceutical experiments.

Antarctica, 17
Russians drilling in the ice have reached ice that is 200,000 years old.

U.K., 17
The government plans to compensate people who contracted the HIV virus through contaminated National Health blood.

Ivory Coast, 18
A demonstration, in Abidjan, against the government results in rioting with numerous arrests.

Frankfurt, 18
Germany's 1991 trade surplus fell 80% compared with the record year of 1990. The current account goes into deficit for the first time since 1981.

Punjab, 19
India's ruling Congress Party wins local elections. Abstentions were 70% due to a Sikh boycott.

Israel, 20
Veteran politician Yitzhak Rabin, former prime minister and defense minister, is elected head of the Israeli Labor Party (→ June 23).

England, 20
In soccer, England beats France 2-0, at Wembley, to end France's unbeaten 19-match run.

France, 21
Jeanne Calment, France's oldest citizen, celebrates her 117th birthday in Arles where she previously knew Vincent Van Gogh and Paul Gauguin.

Netherlands, 21
The Dutch government yields to Chinese pressure and blocks the sale of eight submarines to Taiwan.

DEATH

22. Markos Vafiades, former leader of Greece's Communist army (*1906).

U.K. growth hit by continued recession

London, Thursday 20
The United Kingdom is sinking further into its longest recession since the war.

Figures issued by the government today show that the gross domestic product fell by 0.3% in the fourth quarter of last year and ministers have been forced to concede that the underlying trend is one of steady decline.

The City is gloomy. One British banker said: "We live in hope of a recovery but I must say it is getting further and further away." The indications are that the recession will continue well into 1992.

Michael Jackson's sister Latoya stars at Paris's Moulin Rouge.

Wehrmacht abroad

Bonn, Wednesday 19
The German government today reaffirmed its intention to amend the constitution so that military units can serve abroad. At present they cannot operate outside European territory defended by NATO. The ban, introduced in 1949 in revulsion against Nazi aggression, has become an embarrassment in a world where U.N. forces are constantly involved in peacekeeping operations.

This embarrassment was highlighted by Germany's inability to provide men for the U.N. forces being sent to Yugoslavia. Defense Minister Gerhard Stoltenberg now plans to create rapid-intervention units of troops to take part in U.N. missions anywhere in the world.

Serial killer's life sentence for 15 slayings

Dahmer sits impassively in court while awaiting the murder sentence.

Milwaukee, Monday 17
One of the most gruesome criminal cases in U.S. history ended today with the sentencing of Jeffrey Dahmer to 15 consecutive life prison terms. There is no possibility of parole.

Last month Dahmer, aged 31, pleaded guilty to the murder, mutilation and dismemberment of 15 men and youths, most of them black gays. He also confessed to acts of cannibalism and necrophilia during a killing spree that lasted several years. Dahmer then pleaded not guilty by reason of insanity. However, the jury of seven men, one of them black, and five women rejected the insanity plea two days ago, ruling that the accused was not suffering from a mental disease at the time of the killings. The serial killings had increased racial tensions in Milwaukee.

Call for large U.N. force for Cambodia

New York, Thursday 20
The U.N. is to send 16,000 troops and 500 civilians to Cambodia to enforce the cease-fire in the strife-torn country. This will involve disarming the rival factions and removing tens of thousands of mines. The troops will come from all over the world. An Indonesian contingent arrives next month. It will be followed by Malaysian and Japanese units - the first soldiers to be deployed outside Japan since 1945. They will not have an easy task. Too much blood has been spilt in 13 years of civil war and the slaughter carried out by the Khmer Rouge in the "killing fields" can never be forgotten.

Feb 16. Modern-day replicas of Columbus's three ships arrive in Miami.

Bush and Tsongas beat Buchanan, Clinton

New Hampshire, Tuesday 18
The people of New Hampshire who voted today in the first primary in the 1992 presidential race have dealt George Bush's re-election hopes a unexpected blow.

Stunned New Hampshire Republicans are wondering how Bush failed to win the landslide victory he needs to stall the campaign of challenger Patrick Buchanan. In what Bush supporters concede was "the best guerrilla operation since the Vietcong", Buchanan won 37% of the vote to the president's 53%. Bush campaign managers said the poor result was due both to New Hampshire's ravaged economy and to the president's failure to use "negative" tactics against his opponent. The result has set alarm bells ringing at the White House. Worried strategists in the Bush camp have begun analyzing the New Hampshire verdict in preparation for the crucial March 3 primaries in Georgia, Colorado and Maryland and the Washington caucuses on the same day.

New Hampshire voters were not particularly kind to Bill Clinton either, although he is far from being out of the race. His chief rival for the Democratic nomination, Senator Paul Tsongas of Massachusetts, came out ahead by a narrow margin, scoring 33% of the vote, while Clinton won 25% (→ March 10).

Pope on slave island denounces holocaust

Pope sees the jetty from which the slaves sailed for the United States.

Goree Island, Saturday 22
Pope John Paul II today came to this tiny, rocky island off Senegal's capital, Dakar, in a symbolic act of remembrance of what he termed the "forgotten holocaust".

It was through here that an estimated 15 million Africans captured along the coast of West Africa, from as far south as Angola, passed on their way to slavery in America and the Caribbean. For nearly 400 years, from the mid-15th to the mid-19th centuries, Goree Island and its infamous prison, the "House of Slaves" was one of the continent's chief transit points for slaves. Thousands of African men, women and children died here while waiting in overcrowded and filthy cells to be crammed aboard French or English slave ships bound for the New World.

Church-led crowds shot in Kinshasa

Kinshasa, Sunday 16
Heavily-armed soldiers opened fire on a peaceful anti-government demonstration in the Zairian capital this morning, killing at least 13 people and wounding dozens of others.

The army went into action when thousands of the faithful left the churches after Mass and took to the streets, singing psalms and brandishing bibles. Several priests and opposition leaders among the crowd were beaten up by soldiers. The demonstrators, who quickly dispersed in panic, were protesting against the policies of President Mobutu Sese Seko of Zaire.

Democrat Tsongas comes out ahead of Clinton in New Hampshire.

Rover now adopts the Japanese style

Birmingham, Monday 17
If you can't beat 'em, join 'em. Workers at Rover's Longbridge plant are preparing to take on the Japanese on their own terms. Union leaders recommend that the workforce accept the management's offer of guaranteed jobs for life in exchange for adopting Japanese working practises. Rover hopes to match the productivity and quality standards now being set by Nissan's plant in Washington, Tyne and Wear.

Ozone layer holes create more fears

Lisbon, Saturday 22
European Community environment ministers meeting in Portugal decided today to back proposals to halt the production and use of chemicals harmful to the ozone layer. This follows data gathered by high-flying U-2 aircraft. Michael Kurylo, manager of NASA's upper atmosphere project, says: "Everybody should be alarmed about this. We are seeing conditions primed for ozone destruction. It's in a far worse way than we thought."

Feb 19. Tequila-flavored lollipops go on sale in the U.S.

Feb 16. Police now protect the girlfriend of Salman Rushdie.

1992

Su	Mo	Tu	We	Th	Fr	Sa
						1
2	3	4	5	6	7	8
9	10	11	12	13	14	15
16	17	18	19	20	21	22
23	24	25	26	27	28	29

Taiwan, 23
Over 30,000 supporters of the Democratic Progressive Party, Taiwan's primary opposition group, demonstrate for independence.

Gambia, 23
Pope John Paul II, during his visit to Gambia, urges advanced nations to help stop the spread of AIDS in Africa.

China, 23
Deng Xiaoping asserts that the new economic policy should combine Leninism with market principles.

Estonia, 24
The Baltic state parades its new army in Tallinn while waiting for the ex-Red Army to withdraw.

Washington, D.C., 24
Loan guarantees to Israel are linked to a halt to further colonization of the Occupied Territories (→ March 16).

U.S., 25
The government announces plans to sell 72 fighter aircraft (48 F15-Es, 24 F15-Hs) to Saudi Arabia. The planes are valued at $5 billion.

Virginia, 26
A group of Australian financiers and investors wins $27 million in the state lottery after placing seven million one-dollar stakes.

Moscow, 26
Mannfred Wörner, German secretary-general of NATO, discusses military cooperation with C.I.S. leaders.

Washington, D.C., 27
The Washington Post reports that Libya is operating five secret terrorist camps in the desert.

Netherlands, 27
Philips NV, the electronics giant, which fell into the red in 1990, announces $648 million net profit in 1991.

C.I.S., 28
The former Soviet army is ordered to withdraw from Nagorno-Karabakh.

DEATH

27. Samuel Ichiye Hayakawa, American politician and noted university professor (*July 18, 1906).

Alpine spectacle viewed by the world

The pride of Norway, Finn Jagge, beats Italy's star, Tomba, in the Slalom.

C.I.S. team beats its rival, Canada.

Italian idol wins the giant slalom.

Albertville, Sunday 23
There were plenty of surprises at the Winter Olympics, held in a cluster of spectacular locations in the Alps. Viktor Petrenko of the C.I.S. won the men's figure skating after the hot favorite, Canada's Kurt Browning, succumbed to injury; Bonnie Blair scooped two golds for the U.S. with a superb display of speed skating. Two more American women, who had never won an international competition before, took the gold and silver in the women's downhill skiing. Austria, too, excelled: Petra Kronberger took gold in the combined women's skiing, and Patrick Ortlieb the men's downhill gold.

America's Kristi is the Ice Queen.

Record turnover for CNN in 1991

Atlanta, Monday 24
The Gulf War was good business for the Cable News Network. In 1991 CNN had a record turnover of $479 million, a profit of $168 million and increased its roster of subscribers by 16 million. The live television coverage of Operation Desert Storm gave Ted Turner's Atlanta-based network its highest ratings ever. On the average day in 1991 about 685,000 U.S. households tuned in, but on the first night of the Gulf War the figure shot up to 5.5 million. But CNN is, of course, not only viewed in the United States: CNN International has 79 million subscribers in 129 countries.

Depots are raided during bread riots

Albania, Tuesday 25
The crisis in Albania, Europe's poorest nation, deepened today as a new spate of food riots left at least two dead and several injured.

The deaths occurred in Pogradec, a small town south-east of the capital, Tirana, when a group of starving inhabitants attacked government food depots. Local police fired into the air but failed to disperse the crowd, and the army was then called in. However, the victims were not shot but crushed to death in the stampede to get at the food stores. Similar incidents were reported at Luchje, south of Tirana. More than 40 people died in food riots last December.

Bush committed to step up drug war

San Antonio, Thursday 27
President Bush and the leaders of six Latin American nations vowed today to increase joint efforts to reduce drug production and trafficking in the Western Hemisphere. Speaking at the end of a two-day drug summit here, Bush stressed: "Make no mistake, defeat the traffickers, we will."

Bush, however, said that due to budget constraints the U.S. was not able to give Bolivia, Colombia, Ecuador, Mexico, Peru and Venezuela all the help they wanted. The leaders of these six nations had asked for increased U.S. assistance to help their farmers develop alternative crops to coca and marijuana.

Fast growth, slow democracy in Kuwait

One year later, the Emirate has regained much of its pre-war look.

Kuwait City, Tuesday 25
Kuwait celebrated the first anniversary of the defeat of Saddam Hussein's occupying army today with festivities muted in memory of the 1,000 Kuwaitis still missing in Iraq. Economically, "Kuwait Inc" has made a remarkable recovery. The oil well fires are out, the sky is blue again, Kuwait city has been cleared of debris, the airport is working, and the petrodollars are flowing.

Yet all is not well. There is anger that the ruling family, while promising democracy, has returned to feudal rule. There is antagonism between those who stayed during the occupation and the "runners". Bureaucracy thrives, and foreign workers are cruelly treated.

Liz, 60, celebrates in style at Disneyland

One star meets another in his sixties at the party while her husband looks on.

Anaheim, Thursday 27
Discretion was definitely not the order of the day.

Rarely have Californians seen a birthday bash on such a scale. The star-studded guest list reads like a Hollywood Who's Who: Shirley MacLaine, Liza Minelli, Gregory Peck, Carrie Fisher, Dustin Hoffman, Eddie Murphy, Michael Jackson, Richard Gere, Stevie Wonder, David Bowie, Robert Stack, Dennis Hopper and Michael York, to name but a few. And, of course, Mickey Mouse was there. For her 60th birthday, Liz Taylor and eighth husband Larry Fortensky, 39, had chosen Sleeping Beauty's Castle at Disneyland. Liz arrived in a white horse-drawn carriage.

Kohl seeks to bury the shame of Munich

Prague, Thursday 27
German Chancellor Helmut Kohl and President Havel of Czechoslovakia met here today to sign a treaty designed to compensate for the Nazi invasion of Czechoslovakia and the postwar expulsion of three million Sudeten Germans by the Czechs. Havel said the document marked the end of decades of lies. The treaty has been greeted with bitterness on both sides. Kohl and Havel were greeted with shouts of "Shame" and "Traitors".

Iraq non-assistance for U.N. missile team

Baghdad, Friday 28
Saddam Hussein has again slammed the door on a U.N. team sent to check Iraqi weapons systems. The Iraqi refusal to allow the team to inspect and begin destruction of equipment used to manufacture ballistic missiles violates U.N. resolutions voted after the Gulf War. The U.N. insists that Iraq declare all of its nuclear, chemical and biological missiles with a range greater than 93 miles, such as Scuds. Baghdad says it will only agree to do this if the U.N. relaxes sanctions imposed after the invasion of Kuwait in August 1990 (→ July 7).

After Ford, General Motors in turn reports a huge loss of $4.5b

A Cadillac rolls off the line, but other GM plants are closing in the U.S.

Detroit, Monday 24
Even though Wall Street and industry experts had expected bad news, the size of the 1991 losses announced today by General Motors was a shock.

The world's biggest automaker lost $4.5 billion, a world record and the largest deficit in its 84-year history. GM lost a staggering $8.5 billion in its North American automobile operations, although this was offset by profits of $4 billion in its overseas and nonautomotive operations. To make matters worse, the company announced plans to close 12 assembly plants in North America by 1995, with a loss of more than 16,000 jobs (→ April 28).

Feb 27. Europe's space rocket, Ariane, places two satellites in orbit, the 49th successful launch.

March

1992

Su	Mo	Tu	We	Th	Fr	Sa
1	2	3	4	5	6	7
8	9	10	11	12	13	14
15	16	17	18	19	20	21
22	23	24	25	26	27	28
29	30	31				

South Africa, 1
Nigel Mansell, driving a Renault-engined Williams wins the South African Grand Prix.

Libya, 1
Tripoli proposes that a neutral country judge the two Libyan suspects implicated in the Pan Am 747 bomb attack that crashed at Lockerbie in Scotland in 1988.

Moscow, 1
Metro prices are doubled as part of the policy to free prices in Russia.

Moldova, 3
Following ethnic violence, Cossacks and Russian militias from Dniester clash with Moldovan activists (→ June 20).

Miami, 3
A CIA agent tells the Miami court trying General Noriega that the former Panamanian leader served as an intermediary in numerous dealings between Washington and Fidel Castro (→ April 9).

Turkey, 4
Over 100 bodies are recovered from a coal mine in Kozlu, near the Black Sea, following a methane gas explosion.

Munich, 5
Two Russians (with German backgrounds) seeking to sell 2.6 pounds (1.2 kilos) of enriched uranium for $1.3 million are arrested.

Paris, 5
An anti-narcotics investigation affirms that Balkan drug trafficking contributes to the financing of the war in Yugoslavia.

Brussels, 6
Jean-Luc Dehaene, a Flemish Christian socialist, agrees to form Belgium's 35th post-war government.

London, 6
British Telecom announces 25,000 job cuts which is more than 10% of its workforce.

London, 7
England beats Wales (24-0) in the Five Nations Rugby Union Championship.

DEATH

1. Michael Havers, British lawyer and politician (*March 10, 1923).

Hands off French cheese, says Prince

The nation's produce is inviolable.

Paris, Monday 2
Smelly, runny French cheeses have found a new champion in the Prince of Wales. Speaking at a dinner of the Association France-Grande Bretagne, Prince Charles warned that "pettifogging" Eurocrats were threatening to impose "soulless, mechanical, clinical" production methods in the name of food hygiene. "In a bacteriologically correct society, what will become of the Brie de Meaux, the Crottin de Chavignol or the Bleu d'Auvergne?" he asked.

Tokyo crime blitz

Japan, Sunday 1
As a tough new anti-crime law went into effect today in Japan, police swooped on known hideouts of members of the dreaded *Yakuza* gangs. The nationwide operation is part of a major offensive against organized crime. The powerful and secretive *Yakuza* gangs are heavily involved in prostitution, drugs, illegal gambling and protection.

March 3. Caroline Kennedy with her child in a New York street.

Bosnian referendum ends in gun battles

Old lady votes in Sarajevo, but the fighting starts outside the polling booth.

Sarajevo, Sunday 1
Serbian gunmen began putting up barricades throughout Sarajevo and firing at civilians as soon as the result of today's referendum was announced.

Serbs, who account for 32% of the population of Bosnia-Herzegovina but who control 60% of the territory, are furious that a majority of the Muslim and ethnic Croatian communities voted in favor of the republic's independence. Serbs are opposed to independence because they do not want to be cut off from Serbia by an international border. Independence was supported by 62.6% of the voters (→ April 6).

March 3. Samba and painted bodies for Rio's four days of carnival.

President faces risk

France, Monday 2
The popularity of France's ageing Socialist president, François Mitterrand, who took over at the Elysée Palace in May 1981, is at an all-time low.

According to a national poll published today, 61% of those questioned believe he should step down if Conservative opposition parties win the legislative elections due early next year. Mitterrand was re-elected for a second seven-year term in May 1988.

Irish abortion case

Dublin, Sunday 1
Ireland has had to reconsider its ban on all abortions, following last week's lifting by the Supreme Court of an order banning a 14-year-old rape victim from traveling to England to have her pregnancy terminated. The case has caused enormous controversy, pitching conservative Catholics against the liberals who want to see contraception and abortion freely available. The girl whose misfortune caused the furore is now believed to be in London.

Baltic states form a cooperation council

Copenhagen, Friday 6
A new international organization was born here today when nine nations bordering on the Baltic Sea, plus Norway, founded the Baltic Council.

The nine Baltic signatories are the three former Soviet republics of Estonia, Latvia and Lithuania, as well as Poland, Denmark, Germany, Russia, Finland and Sweden. The Baltic Council, which will hold plenary meetings once a year, is aimed at promoting cooperation on such issues as the environment, culture, communications, transportation and the economy. The council will also seek to aid its formerly Communist members to make the transition to democracy and a market-oriented economy. At Poland's request, the Council agreed to study the problems of the region's ethnic minorities.

Screens threatened by Michelangelo virus

The deadline is zero hour on the anniversary of the great painter's birth.

Friday 6
A hacker's tribute to a great artist, a computer virus named Michelangelo, went into action today, the 517th birthday of its namesake. The virus, which travels by floppy disk, was programmed to activate itself at midnight last night. The virus hides in software, and will overwrite the memory stored on hard disks with nonsense when the machines are turned on. According to virus specialists, the bug has infected an estimated one million IBM and IBM-compatible personal computers this year. The proliferation of viruses, some more dangerous than the Michelangelo, justifies full-scale combat against this information-age plague.

Shevardnadze goes home to Georgia

Tbilisi, Saturday 7
Eduard Shevardnadze, the former Soviet foreign minister who resigned from his post and left the Communist Party, has now abandoned Moscow and returned to his homeland of Georgia. His diplomatic talents are desperately needed there following the overthrow of President Zviad Gamsakhurdia in January. The economy is in tatters, armed gunmen control the streets of Tbilisi, minority groups threaten to secede and Georgia has yet to join the Commonwealth of Independent States. On his arrival here today Shevardnadze insisted he was on a "private visit" but there is little doubt that the leadership is his for the asking. There are, however, many Georgians who remember his harsh rule when he was Moscow's Communist pro-consul and they have no love for him.

Mermaid contemplates the future.

A British study depicts changes in leisure

London, Wednesday 4
Recent impressions that Britain has become a nation of classical music lovers are given the lie by a new survey entitled *Cultural Trends*. High sales figures of classical compact discs are, it seems, largely due to music lovers upgrading their vinyl collection to CDs. Only a minute proportion are pop-lovers converted to classical music by trendy musicians such as Nigel Kennedy and Pavarotti.

Culture in general is having a bad time, it seems. Attendances at museums and art galleries are steadily dropping. The art market has suffered badly in the recession, with the total worldwide auction sales at Sotheby's and Christie's in 1990 down by 40% on 1989. People seem more interested in making their own culture. Folk dancing, amateur dramatics, brass bands and old-time barbershop quartets are all flourishing.

Is Shevardnadze Georgia's savior?

High court against trials in Hungary

Budapest, Tuesday 3
Hungary's Constitutional Court today rejected a bill that would have allowed the prosecution of Hungarian Communists for crimes committed during four decades of Party rule.

The decision is a major setback for Prime Minister Joszef Antall. Like the leaders of most of the former Communist nations of East Europe, Antall has been faced with the problem of the accountability of former officials. He had been calling for tougher penalties.

Los Angeles cops' beating trial opens

Los Angeles, Thursday 5
Four Los Angeles police officers went on trial today for the beating of a black motorist, 25-year-old Rodney King. The incident, which occurred on March 3, 1991, became front-page news after a videotape of the beating, made by a man testing his new camera, was shown on nationwide television. The trial was to be held in Los Angeles but Judge Stanley Wiesberg of the California Superior Court transferred it to Simi Valley, a mainly white enclave in Ventura County (→April 30).

Michael Jackson's wide smile for broadcasting industry award.

Azerbaijan's head Mutalibov resigns

Baku, Friday 6
Ayaz Mutalibov, the Communist boss of Azerbaijan, was forced out of office today following last week's defeat of Azeri forces and the massacre of refugees by Armenians in the disputed territory of Nagorno-Karabakh. The people accused him of failing to defend them and when his resignation was announced the demonstrators who have besieged parliament for the past two days erupted in cheers. His departure breaks the Communist hold on Azerbaijan (→May 15).

March

1992

Su	Mo	Tu	We	Th	Fr	Sa
1	2	3	4	5	6	7
8	9	10	11	12	13	14
15	16	17	18	19	20	21
22	23	24	25	26	27	28
29	30	31				

Dar es Salaam, 8
British explorers discover the first trace of Islam in Black Africa on an island off Tanzania.

London, 8
Eight hundred complaints are made against Benetton's advertising campaign featuring a photograph of a newly-born baby just after delivery.

Yugoslavia, 9
Opponents of Serbian strongman Slobodan Milosevic stage a large demonstration in the streets of Belgrade.

Paris, 10
The new third stage of the European space rocket Ariane is unveiled. It is able carry a heavier payload.

Malaysia, 10
Members of ASEAN, the Association of South East Asian Nations, express concern over Burma's repression of its Muslim Rohingyas community.

Berlin, 10
The Treuhand, responsible for privatizing former East German industry, declares that it will sell Germany's two largest Baltic shipyards.

Greece, 12
Thousands of government employees go on strike to demand higher wages.

Southern Africa, 12
Exceptional drought brings famine to the region from Zimbabwe to South Africa.

Moscow, 13
Pravda newspaper suspends publication indefinitely.

Rwanda, 13
Fighting and massacres erupt between the Hutu tribe, which holds power, and the Tutsi tribe.

New Caledonia, 14
Noumea, the capital, is the scene of violence as demonstrators burn a shopping center in protest against their living conditions.

DEATHS

9. Menachem Begin, Israeli politician, former prime minister (*Aug. 16, 1913).

11. Richard Brooks, American film writer and director (*May 18, 1912).

Bush and Clinton pull away from rivals

Super Tuesday results give a direction to the White House campaign.

Is Lenin for sale? ask the Americans

Moscow, Tuesday 10
Russia's Security Ministry is not amused. It has been flooded by mail from the U.S. ever since Forbes magazine reported last November that the corpse of Vladimir Ilyich Lenin, founder of the Soviet Union, was up for sale. Sealed bids ranging from $1,000 to an amazing $27 million have arrived here from all over the U.S. The top bid was submitted by an anonymous amateur historian in Minnesota. The corpse is still on display in a bomb-proof mausoleum in Red Square. Today, the ministry denounced the Forbes report as a tasteless hoax.

Pollution threatens sperm in West

Denmark, Sunday 8
If Danish scientists are to be believed, the sperm count of men in the West fell by half between 1940 and 1990.

After studying sperm data from nearly 15,000 Western men a research team led by Professor Niels Skakkeback says this dramatic decline could well be caused by environmental pollution. In healthy men, sperm counts vary greatly, ranging from 20 million to 150 million per milliliter of semen. A sperm count below five million means the man is infertile.

U.S., Tuesday 10
As the Super Tuesday primary elections draw to a close, two contenders already lead their respective packs. For the Democrats, Governor Bill Clinton of Arkansas established himself as a front-runner, winning in Florida, Tennessee, Mississippi, Texas, Louisiana, Oklahoma, Hawaii and Missouri. His chief rival, Senator Paul Tsongas of Massachusetts, only carried his home state, Delaware and Rhode Island. On the Republican side, President Bush won solid victories in eight primaries, while Pat Buchanan only got about a third of the vote in Florida and Rhode Island. The clearest loser was former Ku Klux Klan leader David Duke of Louisiana, whose highest score was 11% (→ March 19).

March 9. Menachem Begin, who forged peace with Sadat, dies.

Bush is "weak" on Russia, says Nixon

Washington, D.C., Wednesday 11
Former President Richard Nixon is back in the limelight. His charges that the Bush administration has provided "pathetically" inadequate aid to Russia have stung the White House.

Today, Nixon, 79, stressed there was no rift between himself and Bush, but reiterated his call for stronger U.S. support for democratic reform in Russia. Nixon has warned that if President Boris Yeltsin of Russia were to be overthrown by hard-liners, the Bush administration would be faced with the question of "who lost Russia".

Nixon speaks up on policy.

Change of status in Commonwealth

Port Louis, Thursday 12
The small Indian Ocean island nation of Mauritius, which gained its independence 80 years ago, today broke a symbolic link to the British Crown. Mauritius, which boasts a healthy economy and enjoys political stability, is no longer a constitutional monarchy with Queen Elizabeth II as its head of state, but a fully-fledged republic. The island's last governor-general, Sir Veerasamy Ringadoo, is now the nation's first president. Mauritius will, however, remain a member of the British Commonwealth.

Israel accused on Chinese arms deals

Jerusalem, Friday 13
Furious Israeli officials bowed to-day to strong U.S. pressure and agreed to allow Bush administration experts to inspect Patriot missile batteries. The move came after Washington sources claimed yesterday that Israel had exported U.S. anti-ballistic weapons technology to China.

The Patriot systems had been sent to Israel during the Gulf War as a counter to Iraqi Scud missile attacks. The Israeli government had pledged not to supply the sensitive Patriot technology to third countries.

March 13. The last issue of Pravda, once the world's largest paper, is published in Moscow.

Eastern countries sit down with NATO

Brussels, Tuesday 10
NATO and its erstwhile enemies of the Warsaw Pact sat down together here yesterday to talk peace at a remarkable meeting of the 35-nation North Atlantic Cooperation Council. U.S. Secretary of State James Baker later revealed that the Russians were "ahead of schedule" in sending thousands of former Soviet tactical nuclear weapons back to Russia to be destroyed. The meeting also discussed the war between Armenia and Azerbaijan and ways of finding new jobs for Soviet nuclear weapons scientists.

John Major names April 9 for elections

The two party leaders on the starting line. Labour's Neil Kinnock (right).

London, Wednesday 11
After months of speculation, John Major today announced that the General Election will be held on April 9. With opinion polls showing the government lagging up to three points behind Labour, the politicians are gearing up for the toughest fight since 1974 – when Edward Heath lost narrowly to Labour. Neil Kinnock looked forward to having the chance to reverse thirteen years of Thatcherism, starting on April 10. Paddy Ashdown said he was "raring to go".

Although the country is going through the worst recession since the end of the Second World War, Major must call an election before May. The country now has its first opportunity to give its verdict on the unassuming man whose meteoric rise to power seems to have surprised even himself (→April 10).

Aphrodisiac threat to the rhino's future

Kyoto, Friday 13
The meeting of the Convention on International Trade in Endangered Species has finished on a note of failure. Experts from the countries which have signed the Washington Convention have admitted that the measures taken to protect the rhinoceros have been largely ineffective.

Hunted for their horns, which are incorrectly believed to be an aphrodisiac in Asia, rhino populations have dropped sharply due to poaching. Their salvation may come from a technique tested on elephants, which are hunted for their tusks: cut off the horns before poachers can get to them.

The obvious solution is to cut off the horns before the poachers arrive.

Violent quake kills 1,000 in Turkey

Erzincan, Friday 13
Eastern Turkey was struck by a violent earthquake this evening. The city of Erzincan was partially destroyed by the quake, which registered 6.8 on the Richter scale. The collapse of a hospital and the police headquarters and the loss of electricity confounded rescue efforts. An estimated 1,000 people have died in the region, and the population fears additional tremors. In 1939 Erzincan was destroyed by the worst quake in recorded Turkish history, which led to 40,000 deaths, and a 7.1-magnitude quake in nearby Erzurum killed 1,330 in 1983.

Catherine's solo bid succeeds on Eiger

Three hours in alpine darkness.

Mount Eiger, Monday 9
Catherine Destivelle, a 31-year-old kinesipathist from Paris, has become the first woman to make a solo winter climb of the north face of this Swiss Alpine peak, considered by many alpinists as the most dangerous. Destivelle made the climb in 17 hours, having left this morning from an altitude of 6,900 feet (2,100 meters). She made it to the summit, 13,025 feet (3,974 meters) above sea level, just before 11 p.m., climbing in darkness for the last three hours. She carried only water, fruit jellies, a headlamp and replacement batteries, hooks, crampons and two 50-yard (50-meter) ropes.

March

1992

Su	Mo	Tu	We	Th	Fr	Sa
1	2	3	4	5	6	7
8	9	10	11	12	13	14
15	16	17	18	19	20	21
22	23	24	25	26	27	28
29	30	31				

Washington, D.C., 16
Moshe Arens, the Israeli defense minister, declares that colonization of the Occupied Territories will continue regardless of loan guarantees (→ July 16).

Detroit, 16
Robert Eaton, former General Motors' executive, succeeds the legendary Lee Iacocca as the head of Chrysler Corporation.

London, 17
An internal report calls for the BBC to cut its workforce by some 10,000.

Belgrade, 17
A Russian colonel is appointed commander of two U.N. battalions serving as peace-keeping forces in Yugoslavia.

Geneva, 17
The General Agreement on Tariffs and Trade (GATT) publishes its 1991 figures which shows world trade grew by only 3%.

Tokyo, 18
Citing reasons of "public hygiene" the government refuses to lift the ban on birth control pills.

London, 19
Buckingham Palace confirms that the Duchess of York, popularly known as Fergie, is seeking a divorce.

U.S., 19
The famous Connecticut-based arms manufacturer, Colt, announces its bankruptcy following a sharp drop in demand for its products.

Russia, 20
Andrei Chikatilo, the "Rostov Ripper", is charged with 53 murders. He blames the totalitarian system for his crimes.

Paris, 21
In rugby, the French team defeats Ireland with a score of 44-12.

Vancouver, 21
British Columbia police are now to use Cayenne pepper bombs in riot control.

C.I.S., 21
A French mission establishes a relief corridor within the Nagorno-Karabakh enclave in war-torn Azerbaijan.

Nikkei plunge goes beyond worst fears

Tokyo, Monday 16
It was a black Monday on the Tokyo stock market, which was once the world's healthiest.

For the first time since 1987, the Nikkei stock index dropped more than 3% today, falling below the crucial psychological threshold of 20,000. It finally closed at 19,837. Less than three years ago, the Tokyo index was flying high at nearly 40,000. The current slow-down has already hit nearly every sector of Japan's economy, from automobile manufacturing to heavy industry, computers, photo and video equipment.

Congress makes its own funny money

Washington, Tuesday 17
Defense secretary Dick Cheney has become the most prominent public figure to get caught up in the House of Representatives banking scandal. The House Bank honored 21 of the former Wyoming Congressman's checks – although he did not have funds in his account to cover them. It seems this was regular practice. The bank now faces federal investigation for giving interest-free loans.

Japan not honoring accord on U.S. chips

Washington, Wednesday 18
U.S.-Japanese trade relations have hit a new low. The two countries are at loggerheads over ... chips. American trade officials are accusing Tokyo of failing to honor an accord guaranteeing U.S. semiconductors a 20% share of the Japanese market this year. Japan pleads that it is doing its best to import chips, but with the computer hardware business suffering badly in the recession, all imports are down. The row's origins go back to the mid-1980s, when Japanese dumping of cheap chips on the U.S. market forced industry giants IBM and Texas Instruments to start manufacturing their own chips in the Far East.

Hardliners' protest draws limited support

The backlash in Moscow against Boris Yeltsin fails to shake the regime.

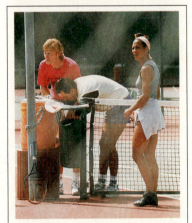

March 18. Becker relaxes with girlfriend in the Florida sun.

Moscow, Tuesday 17
Chanting "Soviet Union! Soviet Union!", 400 former deputies unfurled the Red Flag in a candle-lit hall at a state dairy farm outside Moscow today and, declaring themselves the Congress of People's Deputies, passed a series of resolutions stating that the Soviet Union was still alive and well.

"This is the happiest day of my life", declared Communist hardliner, Sazhi Umulatova, when she was elected chairman of the congress. The meeting descended into farce however, ending after 40 minutes and before journalists could find it after a wild goose chase across the snowy countryside. Political analyst, Nicolai Svanidze, said: "Today's congress took place in the best traditions of the Communist movement - in conspiracy."

No tax reductions in Labour budget

London, Tuesday 17
John Smith, who will be Chancellor if Labour wins the election, took the risky step today of presenting his party's Budget to the nation before a vote has been cast. Claiming that he was speaking for the ordinary taxpayer, he said that every employee earning up to £22,000 a year would benefit.

He believed the proposals would be seen as fair. Many of those paying more would be happy to do so in the interests of a fairer society, good public services and lower unemployment. It may not be seen that way by those earning more than £22,000. Fears are being expressed that they are going to be "squeezed until the pips squeak".

Kim Zimmer joins Cruz in Santa Barbara television series.

Ten die in blast at Israeli embassy

Buenos Aires, Tuesday 17
A suicide bomber destroyed the Israeli embassy here today with a car carrying 200 pounds of explosives. At least ten people, Israeli and Argentinian, died in the blast and it is feared others are buried in the rubble. More than 200 were injured. The bomb also damaged a school and an old people's home.

The pro-Iranian Islamic Jihad group has admitted responsibility for the bombing, claiming that it was carried out in revenge for the assassination of Sheikh Abbas Mussawi in an Israeli helicopter ambush last month.

White voters give massive approval to De Klerk's reforms

"Yes" banners are raised aloft as De Klerk addresses a big crowd.

Johannesburg, Tuesday 18
White South Africans voted in unprecedented numbers yesterday to say "Yes" to President de Klerk's plans for constitutional reforms giving legal equality to their black compatriots. The president, joyfully celebrating his 56th birthday, said the result had been "a landslide for the cause of peace and justice in the country".

"Today", he said, "will be written up in history as one of the most fundamental turning points in the history of South Africa. Today we have closed the book on apartheid. Today a deed was done which carries a powerful message of reconciliation, a powerful reaching out for justice."

Final figures show that 85.7% of the white electorate went to the polls and that 68.7% of them voted for an end to apartheid.

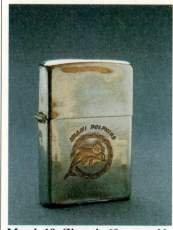

March 19. Zippo is 60 years old.

World's total will jump to 8 billion

Washington, D.C., Saturday 21
There are 5.4 billion people living on the Earth – and in 30 years' time there will be over eight billion crammed onto a planet that is already failing to feed itself. That is the alarming conclusion of the American Census Office's latest projections. Its report also shows that China alone accounts for 1.2 billion inhabitants. Despite having the worst infant death rate, African mothers produce an average of six children each: the population of the continent is expected to double by 2020. In the West, meanwhile, people are living longer, to an average of 75. We will have to start looking after the elderly – and feeding the masses.

Tsongas quits race because of money

Boston, Thursday 19
Paul Tsongas tonight announced that he was pulling out of the campaign for the Democratic Party presidential nomination – because he could not afford to fight the New York primary. Last month he looked like a winner, as he won a string of primaries in New England and Maryland, but on Super Tuesday his rival, Bill Clinton, pulled into a clear lead. Tsongas said he did not intend to stay in the race simply to "play the role of spoiler". His campaign will be remembered for his call for Americans to consume less, and invest more, to give the nation a competitive edge (→ 24).

Chinese premier for reforms in economy

Beijing, Friday 20
Prime Minister Li Peng called for sweeping economic reforms today in a report to the National People's Congress. He demanded an end to the jobs-for-life employment system and proposed a greater role for stock markets. Bolder measures, he said, were essential in order to seize a "unique opportunity" for national development.

Li, closely associated with the military crackdown on the democracy movement in 1989, made no reference to political reform. It is believed that this omission reflects the stubborn resistance to reform by the hardliners he leads.

Concorde loses bits

New York, Saturday 21
Yet again a Concorde of British Airways has lost part of its rudder. Three times part of the rudder has become detached in flight, though control has not been affected and the trouble has been detected only after landing. It was thought the problem might be moisture corrosion, but as all three incidents have affected BA and not Air France it is surmised the cause is the greater thermal cycling caused by the British airline's very dark blue paint (Air France rudders are white).

March 20. Red alert as Mexico City's pollution blackens the sky. The population is forced increasingly to wear face masks as protection.

March 21. Kim Basinger shows off her new 1992 hair style.

March

1992

Su	Mo	Tu	We	Th	Fr	Sa
1	2	3	4	5	6	7
8	9	10	11	12	13	14
15	16	17	18	19	20	21
22	23	24	25	26	27	28
29	30	31				

Bangkok, 22
Opposition parties opposed to military rule in Thailand make strong gains in parliamentary elections (→ May 17).

Moscow, 22
The Russian government fixes compensation for former dissidents at the rate of 180 rubles ($1.8) for each month they spent in prison or in a political camp.

London, 22
Margaret Thatcher comes out of "retirement" as she returns to the pre-election hustle.

Brussels, 23
The EC decides to recognize Georgia, which opted not to join the C.I.S.

Helsinki, 24
The European Security Conference calls for a special session to discuss the various wars within the Caucasus.

Washington, D.C., 25
Former President Reagan says the United States should acquire the former Soviet Union's space program.

U.S., 25
Salman Rushdie, the author condemned to death by Iran, travels to Washington, D.C.

Tokyo, 25
Union pressure forces the government to open talks on work-hour reductions.

Texas, 26
Billionaire Ross Perot wants to join the presidential race in order to present an alternative economic program (April 14).

Tahiti, 27
Greenpeace activists are taken into custody after trying to land on two Pacific atolls and penetrate the French nuclear test site at Mururoa.

Spain, 31
King Juan Carlos I and Israel's President, Chaim Herzog, attend the ceremony marking the 500th anniversary of the expulsion of the Jews.

New York, 31
The pound is quoted at $1.73.

DEATH

23. Friedrich August (von) Hayek, British economist (*May 8, 1899).

Europe's tallest building is firm, but its financiers collapse

Crisis situation threatens Europe's tallest building in London's unfinished, billion-pound Docklands office development.

Nuclear leaks are again possible

Sosnovy Bor, Tuesday 24
Alarm bells rang out at 12:30 a.m. today at the Leningrad nuclear plant, near this town of 56,000 inhabitants and just 60 miles west of St. Petersburg. A burst pressurized coolant pipe had caused a leak of radioactive iodine.

Although the leak was quickly repaired, the alarm bells are still ringing throughout Europe. The Leningrad plant is one of the 16 formerly Soviet nuclear facilities similar to the one at Chernobyl, which blew up in 1986.

London, Sunday 22
Canary Wharf, the tallest building in Europe, towers majestically over dockland but its financial foundations look increasingly precarious. Beset by rumors of bankruptcy, its owners, Olympia and York, the world's biggest property developers, announced last night that they have staved off collapse with a deal to meet short-term repayments.

A complete restructuring of the firm's huge £4.8 billion debt will now be undertaken. Canary Wharf, which cost £4 billion, initially attracted a number of blue-chip occupants for its modern offices but the recession and poor transport facilities cut demand and 40% of its offices still stand empty.

March 25. Cosmonaut Sergei Krikalev returns 300 days later.

Mike Tyson is sentenced to six years for hotel rape of model

Indianapolis, Thursday 26
The boxing career of the world's youngest heavyweight champion came to a jarring halt in a courtroom today. Five years after he won the world title, 25-year-old Mike Tyson was sentenced to 10 years in jail, with four of them suspended, after being found guilty of one count of rape and two counts of criminal deviate conduct. Tyson was convicted for the rape of a Miss Black America contestant, Desiree Washington, in his Indianapolis hotel room last year. The ex-champ, who was led off to prison after the verdict was announced, will have to serve at least three years of his term (→ April 24).

The world heavyweight boxing champion loses his biggest contest.

Jerry Brown shock in Connecticut

Connecticut, Tuesday 24
Although it was extremely narrow, Jerry Brown's victory today in the Connecticut primary has shocked the Clinton camp.

The former governor of California defeated the Arkansas governor by just 3,000 votes, winning 37% of the vote to Clinton's 36%. The Connecticut result gives Bill Clinton a total of 987 delegates to the Democratic convention, while Paul Tsongas, who withdrew from the race for nomination last week, has 439 and Jerry Brown 150. If Clinton is to be nominated at the New York Democratic convention he will need 2,145 delegates. Clinton aides attributed today's setback to recent negative publicity about the governor's personal life – his marital infidelity and draft status during the Vietnam War (→ 26).

Former governor stages comeback.

Amsterdam's anti-car poll lacks support

City hesitates whether to allow vehicles along its famous canal banks.

Amsterdam, Wednesday 25
The bicycle has long been king of Amsterdam's roads. This was confirmed today by the residents of this beautiful 17th century Dutch city of 600,000 inhabitants, dubbed the "Venice of the North".

In the capital's first-ever referendum, 52.9% of voters came out in favor of restricting motor vehicles in the city center. The nonbinding proposal includes a phased reduction of parking facilities from 17,000 to 15,000 along with higher parking fees and steps to improve public transportation. City officials were, however, dismayed at the low turnout for the poll: only about 163,000 people, or 26.6% of voters, cast their ballot.

U.K. suffers worst drought since 1745

London, Thursday 26
Britain's water reserves are at their lowest level ever, and will drop more unless the summer is ruined by heavy and sustained rain. It may not have felt like it, but the last two decades have seen much less rain than usual, and scientists fear that the drought – the worst since 1745 – could be an early sign of global warming. Last winter was particularly dry, which means that 10 million Britons now face a hosepipe ban – an unnerving prospect for a nation of gardeners.

Mr Punch closes up after 150 years run

London, Wednesday 25
Punch, the humorous magazine, is to close after 150 years of publication. Once seen in every men's club and dentist's waiting room, it has not managed to adjust to modern humor. Its sales have fallen from 175,000 in the 1940s to just 33,000 and it has been losing some £2 million a year. Failing to find a buyer, its owners, United Newspapers, have decided it has had its day. Alan Coren, a former editor, said, "There's no market for a magazine like Punch anymore." Another ex-editor, William Davis, grumbled, "It has come to be run by men in gray suits."

Pakistan victorious in World Cup final

Melbourne, Tuesday 25
Pakistan defeated England by 22 runs to win the World Cup today. It was a personal triumph for the Pakistan captain, Imran Khan, who pulled his team together when they seemed ready to disintegrate at the start of the month-long tournament. They came right on the day, while England, who had played with great professionalism throughout the tournament, could not match Pakistan's fire. Pakistan scored 249 for 6 and England were 227 all out.

Hannibal the Cannibal and the FBI lady win the 1992 Oscars

Los Angeles, Monday 30
The pundits who had tipped Oliver Stone's *JFK* or Barry Levinson's *Bugsy* to sweep the Oscars have been proved wrong. It was in fact Jonathan Demme's tale of serial cannibal murderer Hannibal Lecter, *The Silence of the Lambs*, which came up winner.

The thriller, starring Jodie Foster as the FBI agent tasked with capturing a serial killer, took the awards for best actor, best actress and best adapted screenplay. Anthony Hopkins' chilling portrayal of "Hannibal the Cannibal" earned him the best actor award. Jack Palance's role in *City Slickers* won him the best supporting actor award.

Anthony Hopkins, nicer in real life, and Jodie Foster at the ceremony.

March 31. Carol Moseley Braun seeks seat in all-male Senate.

Su	Mo	Tu	We	Th	Fr	Sa
			1	2	3	4
5	6	7	8	9	10	11
12	13	14	15	16	17	18
19	20	21	22	23	24	25
26	27	28	29	30		

Phnom Penh, 1
A cease-fire is negotiated by the U.N. and peacekeeping troops are sent to northern Cambodia to stop the fighting and monitor the area (→ 18).

London, 1
The Labour Party has a slim lead in the runup to the General Election (→ 3).

Michigan, 2
Scientists discover an enormous fungus covering more than 30 acres and weighing 100 tons. Its likely age is between 1,500 and 10,000 years old.

Tripoli, 2
Crowds demonstrating against countries that voted to impose U.N. sanctions on Libya damage the Venezuelan embassy in Libya but fail in their attacks on the Soviet embassy (→ 14).

Israel, 2
Four Palestinians die and dozens are injured in severe clashes with Israeli soldiers in the Gaza Strip.

Moscow, 2
Boris Yeltsin drops his chief economic advisor, Yegor Gaidar, from his post as the minister of finance but he remains in charge of the overall economic strategy.

Florida, 2
The space shuttle Atlantis returns to the Kennedy Space Center at Cape Canaveral after a nine-day voyage.

New York, 3
Statistics published today show that unemployment remains stagnant at 7.3%, the highest in 3 years (→ May 8).

U.K., 3
Soccer forward Gary Lineker ends his English career by being voted "Footballer of the Year" by the Football Writers Association.

London, 3
Paddy Ashdown, leader of the Liberal Democrats, improves his standing in the pre-election polls despite a proposal to raise taxes (→ 10).

London, 4
In the University Boat Race, Oxford win for the sixth successive year, defeating Cambridge by 1.5 lengths.

Murder charge sticks to 'Teflon Don' crime boss John Gotti

New York, Thursday 2
It took federal prosecutors six years and three courtroom setbacks to get their man. John Gotti, nicknamed "Teflon Don" after three earlier trials ended in acquittals, was today convicted on five counts of murder. He faces a life term and sentencing was set for June 23.

The 51-year-old Mafia boss was in particular found guilty of the 1985 murder of Paul Castellano, his predecessor as head of New York's leading crime family. Gotti's downfall was largely due to the testimony of one of his chief "lieutenants", Salvatore Gravano, who violated the Mafia code of silence to testify against his former boss (→ June 23).

New York's leading and best dressed gangster destined for prison garb.

Richest nations to give $24b to Russia

Bonn, Wednesday 1
Western nations have agreed to dig deep into their pockets to help the destitute former Soviet Union. At a meeting here of the Group of Seven industrial nations, they agreed on a $24-billion aid package to bolster the Russian economy. This includes $18 billion in aid over three years and a $6-billion fund to stabilize the ruble. The U.S. will contribute between $4.8 billion and $6 billion of the total. The Commonwealth of Independent States will also be offered full membership in the IMF and the World Bank.

April 1. Steve, Bogart's son, and Isabella, Bergman's daughter.

President's closest ally is new premier

France's new day-to-day manager.

Paris, Thursday 2
After three days of long and laborious negotiations, Pierre Bérégovoy was named French prime minister this morning, replacing the unpopular Edith Cresson. Bérégovoy, a long-time ally of President François Mitterrand, was greatly responsible for the ruling Socialist Party's adoption of market economic policies and of monetary policies similar to those of Germany. For this reason he is not well regarded by some of the other Socialist leaders; on the other hand he has an excellent image abroad, where he is viewed as the father of French economic rigor. He presented his cabinet in the evening, whose admitted objective is to improve the image of his party before legislative elections next year.

Torture allegations against Israelis

London, Wednesday 1
Palestinians arrested by the Israeli army in a swoop on suspected terrorists in the Occupied Territories on January 22 have told Amnesty International that they were systematically tortured. One man died of a heart attack. These charges follow an Amnesty report to the U.N.'s Human Rights Commission claiming the Israelis were using interrogation methods amounting to torture or ill-treatment and said the treatment of prisoners should be "consistent with the international prohibition of torture".

April 4. Party Politics, number eight, wins the Grand National.

April

1992

Su	Mo	Tu	We	Th	Fr	Sa
			1	2	3	4
5	6	7	8	9	10	11
12	13	14	15	16	17	18
19	20	21	22	23	24	25
26	27	28	29	30		

Brazil, 5
British Formula One driver Nigel Mansell wins the Brazilian Grand Prix, his third successive win in the 1992 championship (→ May 17).

Minneapolis, 6
NCAA Basketball Finals: one day after Stanford beat Kentucky, 78-62, in the women's competition in L.A., Duke's men's team defeats Michigan, 71-51.

Luxembourg, 6
The European Community officially recognizes the independence of the Yugoslav republic of Bosnia-Herzegovina (→ 8).

Tirana, 6
Sari Berisha is elected by the parliament in the capital as Albania's first non-Communist president.

Germany, 8
German authorities say that genetic tests confirm that the human remains discovered in Brazil in 1985 are those of Josef Mengele, the infamous Auschwitz doctor responsible for the deaths of more than 400,000 Jews.

New York, 8
Michael Milken, former junk bond king, agrees to testify against Drexel-Burnham-Lambert in exchange for a reduced sentence.

Washington, D.C., 9
Congressional auditors report that Secretary of State James Baker and former White House chief of staff John Sununu spent $774,000 of the taxpayers' money by using military planes for personal and political travel.

Sri Lanka, 10
Police officials report that Tamil rebels are suspected of killing 55 people, 35 civilians and 20 government officials, in several bomb explosions throughout the day.

Wigan, 11
Rugby League: Wigan beats Bradford Northern, 50-8, to win their third championship.

DEATH

6. Isaac Asimov, American biochemist and science fiction writer (*Jan. 2, 1920).

Billionaire Sam put customer first

Little Rock, Sunday 5
Sam Walton, one of the richest men in the United States, died of cancer today at the age of 74.

Sam Walton was the founder and chairman of Wal-Mart, a chain of discount stores which sell everything from jeans to popcorn to car stereos. There are 1,735 Wal-Mart stores, with an average floor-space of more than 86,000 square feet, situated in rural areas and small towns in 42 states. Friendly service, low prices and high volume sales are the bases of the Wal-Mart philosophy and success.

Since Walton opened the first Wal-Mart Discount City in 1962, the company has become the largest and most successful retailer in the United States.

Wal-Mart's founder meets the folks.

April. Thirty one years ago this month Yuri Gagarin became the first man to orbit the Earth.

Arafat escapes plane crash in Sahara

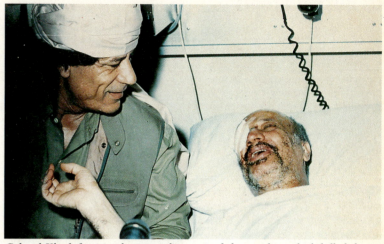
Colonel Khadafy visits the man who survived the accident which killed three.

Extreme right gains in German voting

Germany, Sunday 5
Germany's mainstream politicians suffered a major setback today as extreme right parties made stunning gains in two state parliamentary elections. In Baden-Würtemberg, the nation's most affluent state, far-right parties gained 13% of the vote. One of these, the Republican Party, headed by a former Nazi SS officer, scored 11%. In the Schleswig-Holstein poll, the neo-Fascist German People's Union won nearly 7% of the vote. The right-wing groups want to stop refugees from East European countries gaining asylum in Germany.

Libya, Wednesday 8
Yasir Arafat, the Palestinian leader, escaped death "by the will of Allah" in a crash-landing which killed the three-man crew of his Antonov-26. He was on a flight from Khartoum to inspect a PLO training base at Al Sarah, deep in the Libyan desert, when his aircraft flew into a sandstorm and was forced down. Arafat was badly knocked about but when rescuers arrived he was on his feet and tending others, more badly injured.

His escape has been greeted with joy by Palestinians throughout the Middle East who look upon it as a divine gesture of approval for his policies which have been under attack since his support for Saddam Hussein in the Gulf War proved to be so mistaken.

April 6. Liza Minelli, 46, seen with friend Billy Stritch, 27, in New York. She received an award for humanitarian work, notably for AIDS victims.

State of emergency as Bosnia erupts

Sarajevo, Wednesday 8
There are armed guards in front of every building and barricades erected by various militia groups throughout the center of Sarajevo. President of the newly-independent republic of Bosnia-Herzegovina, Alija Izetbegovic, declared a state of emergency as fighting intensified. Fighting has claimed dozens of victims the last few days, and approximately 300 people have been killed in the last month. Several thousand have fled for the Dalmation coast or for Serbia. The Serb-dominated federal army has gained control of all roads leading to the Bosnian capital (→ May 2).

Sniper in action in Sarajevo battle.

Fourth straight victory for British Tories

Enthusiastic supporters express their satisfaction following "surprise" victory.

London, Friday 10
To everyone's surprise, the little guy with the glasses has won. For weeks, the pollsters and political pundits have confidently predicted a Labour victory, or at best, a hung parliament with no party in overall control. But as the results started to roll in last night, they had to eat their words: John Major has a Tory majority of over 20 seats, and no removal men will be calling at 10 Downing Street today.

At the beginning of the week, things looked bad for Major. He had fought a lacklustre campaign in which, standing on orange crates up and down the country, shouting through battered megaphones in torrents of rain, tormented by hecklers, he looked more like the leader of the opposition than the Prime Minister. Meanwhile, Labour's Neil Kinnock rolled up in a limousine in a series of slick rallies, avoiding gaffes and becoming more leaderlike with every day. Liberal Democrat leader Paddy Ashdown, brimming with confidence, taunted both sides as he dashed around the country by helicopter.

At the last minute, however, voters shied away from the widely-predicted prospect of a Lab-Lib-Dem coalition. And they voted with their wallets: the Conservatives were the only party to pledge not to raise income tax.

Noriega trial ends with guilty verdict

Marathon trial of ex-Panama head.

Miami, Thursday 9
General Manuel Noriega, former dictator of Panama, was found guilty of drug trafficking today after a trial lasting seven months. U.S. Attorney General William Barr welcomed the verdict: "This sends an important message to the drug lords: there are no safe havens; their wealth and firepower cannot protect them forever."

Noriega, who was wearing a khaki four-star general's uniform, was found guilty of two major counts of racketeering and conspiracy and six lesser charges. The eight counts carry a maximum sentence of 120 years. His sentencing was set for July 10 (→ July 10).

April 10. Ex-tennis great Arthur Ashe reveals he is HIV-positive.

Post-poll IRA bombs rock City of London

Police say bomber is a "fanatic".

London, Friday 10
The IRA marked the Tory win in the General Election by detonating a van containing 100 pounds of Semtex explosive in the heart of the City of London this evening. Three people died and 91 were injured when the van blew up wrecking the Baltic Exchange and the Commercial Union building in St Mary Axe.

The explosion was timed to catch city workers celebrating the election. The injured ran out screaming as glass from office buildings cascaded into the streets.

A similar bomb exploded at the Staples Corner junction in north London. There were no casualties but the flyover is expected to be out of action until December (→ June 7).

Al Pacino and friend seek anonymity on Broadway.

Su	Mo	Tu	We	Th	Fr	Sa
			1	2	3	4
5	6	7	8	9	10	11
12	13	14	15	16	17	18
19	20	21	22	23	24	25
26	27	28	29	30		

Iran, 12
Supporters of President Hashemi Rafsanjani defeat anti-Western candidates in the national parliamentary elections.

Georgia, 13
Fred Couples proves to be the most talented golfer by winning the Masters Tournament in Augusta.

Warsaw, 13
Protesters demonstrate against the government's proposal to bring compulsory religious studies and ethics into state schools.

Tripoli, 14
Libya marks the sixth anniversary of American air raids, which killed 27, by staging a day of public mourning to portray itself as the victim of aggression (→ 16).

Washington, D.C., 14
Secretary of State James Baker urges Western nations to help defend Bosnia-Herzegovina from the Serbian-dominated Yugoslav army.

Milan, 16
Carlo De Benedetti, the Italian financier, is sentenced to six years in jail for involvement in the fraudulent bankruptcy of Banco Ambrosiano.

Libya, 16
Libya, in retaliation against United Nations sanctions, begins expelling foreign diplomats from countries that support U.N. action against Tripoli.

Haiti, 16
Approximately 250 Haitians, forbidden to seek refuge in the U.S., are sent back by the U.S. Coast Guard (→ May 24).

London, 17
British Muslims are outraged by the sale of shoes bearing scripture from the Koran, their holy book, on the sole.

Estonia, 17
In order to become citizens of this Baltic republic, Russians are required to pass a language exam.

Kabul, 17
The surrender of government forces as well as the creation of a new government are demanded by radical Muslim rebels (→ 18).

Euro Disney magic lights up France

Marne-la-Vallée, Sunday 12
Euro Disneyland opened its doors to the public today in the suburbs east of Paris. The opening of the $4-billion complex was celebrated last night with a show featuring stars of film, stage and song that was seen on television by 100 million people throughout the world. The show was grandiose, in line with Euro Disney's ambition to make the park the greatest and most extraordinary of entertainments. The fireworks above Sleeping Beauty's castle and the parade down Main Street were just a couple of the enticements offered to bring the crowds in for a visit.

The park opened at 8:00 a.m., and the first family to enter the gates this morning received a lifetime pass for Euro Disneyland. Only one lucky family was granted this prize, but that should not keep many more from hurrying to visit the five magic kingdoms that surround the castle. The complex can welcome an estimated 50,000 to 60,000 guests per day.

To accommodate these tourists in Wonderland, six hotels decorated in different American themes, with 5,200 rooms, have been built on the Euro Disneyland grounds. To staff this enormous complex, the largest hiring campaign ever seen in France was launched. Euro Disney hired 14,000 "cast members", efficient, smiling and clean-cut *à l'américaine* (→ June 4).

An estimated 100 million television viewers watched the opening ceremony.

Visitors to the 4,800-acre site are greeted by 12,000 "cast members".

Princess Anne arranges 'friendly divorce'

Anne and Captain Mark Phillips are pictured together in happier times.

Diminutive Perot causes a big surprise

Billionaire Ross bursts onto scene.

Dallas, Tuesday 14
Republican and Democratic campaign strategists are wishing the elfin Texas billionaire would just go away.

H. Ross Perot has not even decided yet whether he will run as an independent presidential candidate, but the latest polls credit him with 21% of the vote. The plain-talking and fiercely anti-establishment 61-year-old Texan, said to be worth about $3 billion, said last month that he was prepared to run if enough signatures are gathered to place his name on the ballot in each of the 50 states. Since then, he has received a flood of telephone calls urging him to run (→ May 26).

London, Monday 13
The Princess Royal and Captain Mark Phillips will continue to host their annual equestrian event at Gatcombe Park, but no longer as husband and wife. Buckingham Palace announced today that Princess Anne has begun the legal proceedings for a divorce from her husband of 18 years. The couple, who have been legally separated for the last two-and-a-half years, are in agreement on the decision. Their children, Zara and Peter, will live with their mother at Gatcombe, and Captain Phillips will have full visiting rights – in fact, he will continue to live at Aston Farm, part of the Gatcombe Park estate. The divorce has no effect on Anne's constitutional position: she remains eighth in line to the throne.

Labour leader steps down after defeat

London, Monday 13
Neil Kinnock resigned as leader of the Labour Party today after failing in his second attempt to oust the Conservatives. He said he was "making no excuses and expressing no bitterness", but he attacked the Tory press for helping the government "achieve a victory it could not have secured on its own".

Mr Kinnock's own victories were within his party where he defeated the hard left and, according to his colleague, Bryan Gould, "his drive to modernize the party brought us back from the precipice". He failed, however, to win the voters' trust.

Thatcher opponent is back in government

London, Sunday 12
Michael Heseltine is back. The maverick politician, who walked out of Margaret Thatcher's cabinet in 1986 only to topple her in 1990, has returned to government as minister for trade and industry. The post is, in part, a reward for his energetic contribution to the election campaign. John Major has also brought two women – Virginia Bottomley and Gillian Shephard – into his cabinet. Thatcher stalwarts Kenneth Baker and Tom King have left to make room for them. Perhaps the biggest surprise is that the unpopular and ineffective Mr Norman Lamont remains Chancellor of the Exchequer.

Man called "Tarzan" swings back.

April 13. Anti-apartheid leader Nelson Mandela and his controversial wife, Winnie, decide to separate after three decades of marriage.

Dan Maskell, veteran Wimbledon tennis commentator, retires after 40 years' service with the BBC's radio and, later, television networks.

McDonald's goes multi-national with a boom in foreign outlets

McDonald's opened a record 450 restaurants outside the U.S. last year.

New York, Friday 17
McDonald's has decided to accelerate its international expansion. The company opened more restaurants abroad than in the United States in 1991, the first time in its history to have done so, and plans to open 450 restaurants abroad this year. Foreign profits, in markets less competitive than the United States, are growing more quickly than domestic profits. The successful opening of a McDonald's in Moscow symbolizes the hamburger giant's determination to become the world's number one purveyor of fast food, from Warsaw to Jakarta.

U.N. air embargo on Libya takes effect

Tripoli, Wednesday 15
The airport of the Libyan capital is now international only in name. A U.N. air traffic embargo against Libya went into effect at 6:00 this morning. The international flight ban aims to compel Libyan leader Muammar Khadafy to hand over the two Libyans suspected of the 1988 bombing of a Pan Am Jumbo Jet which crashed in Lockerbie, Scotland, and to cooperate with an investigation into the bombing of a French UTA airliner above Niger in 1989. An arms embargo has also been put into effect. The International Court of Justice, which met last night in The Hague, rejected an appeal by Libya, as well as an offer to turn over the suspects to Malta for trial.

Tripoli Airport loses its passengers.

'Queen' Leona goes to jail for fraud

Lousville, Wednesday 15
As millions of Americans rushed to file their tax returns by tonight's deadline, hotel queen Leona Helmsley began serving a four-year sentence for tax evasion.

The 71-year-old New York millionaire, now known simply as prisoner number 15113-054, arrived here in the style to which she is accustomed. She flew in by private jet before being driven to the minimum-security women's prison. During the next four years, less if she gets time off for good behavior, the woman who was once quoted as saying that only little people paid taxes will have to make her own bed, clean her cell and mop floors.

Kabul in chaos as leader ousted

Afghan capital threatened by rebels.

Kabul, Saturday 18
Beleaguered Afghan government forces are trying to halt the advance on the capital by radical Muslim fighters led by rebel commander Ahmed Shah Masood. The overthrow two days ago of President Najibullah, who ruled the country for six years, has not put an end to the civil war. Najibullah is said to be in hiding in Kabul after failing to flee abroad. He has been replaced by a shaky interim government. Meanwhile, Masood's well-armed mujahedeen, operating from a mountain stronghold north of here, threaten a showdown with fighters of the rival Islamic Party, led by the Pakistan-based fundamentalist Gulbuddin Hekmatyar (→ 24).

U.S. military helicopter drops concrete on Etna's lava.

Metric system in return for English

Washington, D.C., Saturday 18
The U.S. administration and Congressional commissions on trade and technology are in agreement that the adoption of the metric system would improve the competitiveness of U.S. businesses. The idea of metric conversion is not a new one, but has received renewed attention because of negotiations with the European Community on international standards. But there's a catch: in exchange for metric conversion, the United States has insisted on using English as the international language of trade.

U.N. chief hopes for peace in Cambodia

Phnom Penh, Saturday 18
The arrival here today of U.N. Secretary General Butros Butros Ghali marked the official start of the United Nation's peace mission in war-torn Cambodia.

After talks with Prince Norodom Sihanouk, the former Cambodian monarch, the U.N. chief called on all sides, and particularly on the Khmer Rouge guerrillas, to cooperate in rebuilding the country. The U.N. is to deploy 20,000 troops and support personnel to oversee the disarming of the four main guerrilla groups.

North Korean dictator Kim Il Sung celebrates 80th birthday.

April

1992

Su	Mo	Tu	We	Th	Fr	Sa
			1	2	3	4
5	6	7	8	9	10	11
12	13	14	15	16	17	18
19	20	21	22	23	24	25
26	27	28	29	30		

Russia, 19
Over 50,000 people gather in central Moscow to support Yeltsin's economic reforms.

Israel, 20
Israel announces the re-opening of the West Bank Arab university, Bir Zeit, following its closure by military order.

California, 21
Despite controversy, the Supreme Court allows the execution of Robert Harris.

California, 22
An earthquake measuring 6.1 on the Richter scale strikes California. People fear stronger aftershocks will follow (→ 26).

Belgrade, 23
Serbia decides to create a Yugoslav federation with Montenegro.

Kabul, 24
Until a more permanent Grand Council can be established, rebel factions agree to form a 51-member interim government (→ 27).

Indianapolis, 24
Boxer Mike Tyson is denied bail while awaiting an appeal against his rape conviction. Authorities fear he would flee or commit another violent crime.

Warsaw, 24
More than 35,000 Poles participate in an anti-government rally protesting the lack of attention paid to the collapsing state-owned industries.

California, 25
The F-22 prototype crashes at Edwards Air Force Base. The F-22 was developed as part of a $60-million project to create a radar-evading jet.

Sheffield, 25
In soccer, Leeds United wins the race for the League Championship by beating Sheffield United 3-2.

DEATHS

19. Frankie Howerd, British comedian famous for his role in *Up Pompeii* (*1912).

21. Vladimir Romanov, pretender to the extinct Russian throne (*Aug. 20, 1917).

Stunning Seville is host to the world

Spectacular fiestas and costly international high-technology illuminate the sky above the Andalusian capital.

Seville, Monday 20
Expo 92, the first Universal Exposition in 22 years, is officially open. The 540-acre site is host to 58 national and five collective pavilions, representing 102 countries, as well as five thematic pavilions built by Spain and pavilions representing private companies, international organizations and the autonomous regions of Spain. The exposition was inaugurated today at precisely 12:16 p.m. by King Juan Carlos I; cannons fired, bells tolled, and doves and balloons filled the sky. The exposition, 10 years in the planning, is an event of great symbolic importance for Spain, the host and organizer, emphasizing its place in modern, democratic Europe. The host city has undergone a metamorphosis thanks to substantial investment prior to the exposition. A new city with bold architecture and freshly-planted gardens has been constructed on the island of Cartuja, just across the Guadalquivir River from the old town. There is a great variety of architectural styles in the pavilions: Japan's wooden structure in the style of a Buddhist temple, the open French pavilion with a glass base and sky-blue steel roof, the waterfall down the glass façade of the British pavilion. The 18 million expected visitors will arrive at the Andalusian capital's new airport, by the new high-speed rail link with Madrid, or on the new Andalusian highway network.

Native Americans and basketball are honored at the U.S. pavilion.

Great Britain shows off its achievements on a battery of television screens.

Comic genius was loved worldwide

London, Monday 20
Benny Hill, born Alfred and nicknamed "King Leer", was found dead of a heart attack at his home in London. The English comedian, born in Southampton in 1924, discovered his talent early in life and was inspired by comic masters such as Buster Keaton and Charlie Chaplin. Hill traveled England as a music hall comic before his television debut in 1951. He began producing "The Benny Hill Show" in 1969, and it was eventually seen in 80 countries worldwide. The show consisted of comic sketches and featured scantily-clad women. The show was often criticized as being in poor taste and was removed from the air in Britain in 1989, but Hill continued to produce shows for foreign markets.

His show was seen in 80 countries.

Mini Miss France contest banned

Paris, Wednesday 22
Even for the easygoing French, some things go just too far. A public outcry has forced the government to step in and ban a beauty pageant featuring girls aged four to eight.

During the contest, which was to be held at an amusement park north of here, the youngsters were to parade three times: wearing a dress, dancing costume and sportswear. The government said the event violated a 1990 law on the exploitation of children.

Russia sells space probe for $200,000

Paris, Thursday 23
Georges Lancelin, a French businessman, paid one million francs ($200,000) for a retired Photon, a Russian satellite.

The scarred spherical space probe, which weighs two tons and measures 7.5 feet in diameter, was last used in a flight in April 1990, according to Lancelin. The seller, an import-export businessman, said he was using the sale to mark the creation of a company which will market the services of Russian and Central Asian industries. The new owner intends to make the satellite part of an exposition, "Russia: from the Sputnik to today", which will tour France.

Satellite sensors confirm Big Bang theory

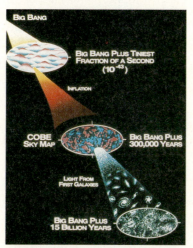
NASA's COBE looks back in time.

Washington, D.C., Thursday 23
Excited American scientists believe that they have finally found the Holy Grail of cosmology.

NASA's Cosmic Background Explorer, or COBE, satellite has found evidence of enormous, wispy clouds of matter near what could be the edge of the universe. These clouds explain how galaxies and stars were produced after the Big Bang, the cosmic explosion scientists say created the universe. The clouds date back 15 billion years, just 300,000 years after the Big Bang. COBE's findings were announced at a meeting of the American Physical Society here today.

Gas blast rips open streets, killing 200

A five-mile stretch of road is devastated in downtown Guadalajara.

Guadalajara, Wednesday 22
There has been a series of terrible explosions today in the second-largest city in Mexico, wrecking buildings in a densely-populated area of 12 square blocks. At least 200 people have been found dead; searches continue. A spokesman for Pemex, the national oil company, indicated the explosions may have been caused by the leakage of a volatile gas used by a cooking-oil company into the sewer system, while the chief of firefighters suggested a gasoline spill in the sewers might have been the cause. There were complaints yesterday of a strong gas smell coming from the sewers. Firemen had performed an inspection, but could not determine the source of the smell.

April. A futuristic fueling station for the electrical vehicles of tomorrow is officially unveiled by Diversified Technical Services of Arizona.

April 23. India's award-winning film director Satyajit Ray (*May 2, 1921) dies in Calcutta.

Su	Mo	Tu	We	Th	Fr	Sa
			1	2	3	4
5	6	7	8	9	10	11
12	13	14	15	16	17	18
19	20	21	22	23	24	25
26	27	28	29	30		

Austria, 26
Rudolf Streicher leads in the presidential race (→ May 24).

U.S., 26
The Indianapolis Colts choose Steve Emtman as the top pick at the National Football Association draft.

California, 26
Strong aftershocks, the largest measuring 6.5, cause additional damage and spark a fire.

Washington, D.C., 26
Financial officials from the seven most powerful industrial nations (G7) discuss the world economy and global growth.

U.S., 27
The Reverend Jesse Jackson claims that he should be nominated by the Democratic Party for vice-president.

Kabul, 27
Intense combat continues between all factions as the arrival of the provisional government is awaited (→ 28).

Switzerland, 27
President Rene Felber announces that the country intends to apply for European Community membership.

Syria, 27
Four thousand Syrian Jews are now free to emigrate to Israel.

Kabul, 28
Fighting abates as power is assumed by Sigbatullah Mojaddidi, leader of the coalition of Afghan Islamic resistance groups (→ May 25).

Detroit, 28
General Motors Corporation, following severe losses, reports $179.3 million profit in the first quarter.

Frankfurt, 29
On the third day of massive strikes public workers are joined by private sector employees. The demand for higher salaries is a key issue.

Maryland, 29
The National Cancer Institute announces that a breast cancer preventative drug will be tried in the U.S. and Canada.

San Diego, 30
The Italians, after beating New Zealand in the Louis Vuitton Cup, are now qualified to enter the America's Cup (May 1).

A giant of modern art dies in Madrid

Francis Bacon defied old age by continuing to paint in his London studio.

Madrid, Tuesday 28
One of Britain's greatest artists died of a heart attack here this morning. Francis Bacon, aged 82, was a self-taught genius whose powerful explorations of sex, pain and death brought him critical acclaim the world over. From Bacon's small studio in South Kensington emerged profoundly disturbing canvases evoking the dark side of the human condition with brutal candor. He will be remembered for his depiction of deformed, tormented beasts in *Base of a Crucifixion* and his series of Renaissance Popes transfixed by undefined, violent horror. Despite his gloomy themes, he was a charming man who drank champagne by the gallon.

Nine die when French Hell's Angels clash

Le Mans, Sunday 26
Daredevil stunts by drunken bikers in the streets of this racing Mecca west of Paris have cast a pall over the annual 24-hour motorcycle race. The competition was won by the Kawasaki team of Britons, Carl Fogarty and Terry Rymer, but attention focused on the off-track drama. Nine bikers died in four different pile-ups and 50 others were injured in a spate of fights and bottle-throwing incidents police were unable to prevent.

Anna, 10, aims to be world tennis champ

The girl from Moscow trains in U.S.

Florida, Thursday 30
Her coach says she has the technique of a tennis player five years her senior – not so extraordinary unless one considers that five years is half her lifetime. Ex-Muscovite Anna Kournikova is currently the top-seeded player on the Florida junior circuit. She was signed and brought to the Bollettieri Tennis Academy by Paul Theofanous, the International Management Group agent who specializes in talent from the former Soviet Union. Nick Bollettieri says she has a competitive attitude unusual for her age. "When do I want to turn pro?" she asks. "The sooner the better."

Germany's workers stage mass strike

Germany, Monday 27
Millions of Germans woke up today to find their country faced with its worst labor dispute since 1974. An estimated 2.6 million public service workers have already stopped work, crippling garbage collection, mail delivery and transportation in many parts of the country. The strike, over a bitter wage dispute, ends a lengthy period of co-operation between German labor and industry. The situation may well get worse as Chancellor Helmut Kohl has flatly refused to improve the government's offer of a 4.8% pay increase, while the unions want a 9.5% rise (→ 29).

Five rubles for the Russian NY Times

Moscow, Tuesday 28
A new paper went on sale here and in 27 other cities in the C.I.S. today. Called the *New York Times News in Review* and costing just five rubles, or about 7 cents at the official rate, the 16-page bimonthly publication had an initial print run of 100,000 copies.

It contains translations into Russian of news stories and feature articles already printed by the New York daily. Jointly produced by the *New York Times* and the Russian weekly *Moscow News*, the new paper hopes to go weekly soon.

April 27. Betty Boothroyd is first woman in six centuries to be Speaker of House of Commons.

Los Angeles burns as angry mobs seek 'revenge'

Prosecutor points to key video during the trial of Rodney King's attackers.

After the acquittal, tension starts to mount in front of the police lines.

Los Angeles, Thursday 30
A thick pall of smoke hung over much of this city this morning as badly outnumbered police continued trying to contain a terrifying wave of urban violence.

The rioting and looting erupted yesterday soon after the acquittal of four white Los Angeles police officers who had been charged with beating a black driver, Rodney King. The jury at the Simi Valley, East Ventura County, trial did not include a black.

The not-guilty verdict caused outrage among much of the city's black population. At first, only a few incidents of arson and rock throwing were reported. But, as police watched helplessly, the violence and looting quickly spread from the predominantly black South Central area to adjoining communities. Roaming gangs of youths, many of them armed, started attacking pedestrians and motorists.

One of the first to fall prey to the violence was Reginald Denny, a 33-year-old white truck driver. As television helicopters flew over South Central, Denny was pulled from his cab by a group of black youths and severely beaten. He is listed in critical condition. The dramatic incident, like many similar ones, was broadcast live, further increasing racial tensions.

Scores of businesses were looted and then torched. Looters were seen carrying away goods by the carload. Several times Fire Department crews were forced to turn back by angry crowds. By dawn,

hundreds of fires were still raging out of control. Damage is already in millions of dollars. At least 10 people, most of them black or Hispanic, are confirmed dead and the toll is certain to rise. Appeals for calm by Los Angeles Mayor Tom Bradley and Daryl Gates, the city's police chief, have so far had little or no effect. The Los Angeles riots have also sparked trouble in other cities. In Atlanta, at least four whites were beaten up by blacks, while a curfew was clamped on Las Vegas after 24 people were injured in rioting (→ May 2).

Looters begin to empty the shops in the South Central district of the city.

All the hatred and frustration of the city's ordeal are expressed in this kick destruction of a shop window.

May

1992

Su	Mo	Tu	We	Th	Fr	Sa
					1	2
3	4	5	6	7	8	9
10	11	12	13	14	15	16
17	18	19	20	21	22	23
24	25	26	27	28	29	30
31						

San Diego, 1
In preparation for the America's Cup, Bill Koch deposes Dennis Conner as the American defender (→ 16).

Sarajevo, 2
Bosnian President Alija Izetbegovic is taken hostage by Serbian forces (→ May 20).

Louisville, 2
Lil E. Tee, ridden by Pat Day, wins the Kentucky Derby. Casual Lies comes in second.

Warsaw, 3
An ethical code is adopted by physicians which strongly limits a woman's right to have an abortion.

Thailand, 4
Suchinda Kraprayoon's appointment as prime minister is protested by 50,000 people.

New York, 5
Christie's auction house sells an Andy Warhol 1962 silk-screen of stacked Coke bottles for $2.1 million.

London, 6
As parliament opens for a new term, John Major promises improved services and more money to spend for all citizens.

Tajikistan, 7
An agreement is made to share power between the Communist government and the Islamic-dominated opposition (→ Sep 7).

Virginia, 7
Dr. Cecil Jacobson, infertility specialist, is sentenced to five years in jail after impregnating some 75 patients with his own sperm.

U.S., 8
Unemployment statistics fall to 7.2% as 126,000 new jobs are created (→ July 2).

London, 8
Due to the Cold War ending, Britain's counterespionage service, MI-5, will now focus on the IRA.

Wembley, 9
Liverpool beats Sunderland, 2-0, to win the Football Association Cup.

DEATHS

2. Wilbur Mills, American politician (*May 24, 1909).

2. Lee Salk, psychologist and author (*1927).

LA seeks to recover after its trauma

Los Angeles, Saturday 2
A relative quiet has finally returned to the battered "City of Angels" where the death toll after two days of rioting stands at 37.

The toll is rising by the hour, as police and fire fighters wearing bulletproof vests continue to find charred bodies in burnt-out buildings. More than 1,500 people have been injured, dozens of them critically, and damage is estimated at $600 million.

Thousands of National Guard troops and federal law-enforcement officers are patroling the shattered streets of South Central, where the worst of the rioting took place. A dusk-to-dawn curfew is still in force, although Mayor Tom Bradley is expected to lift it soon. The White House has placed 5,000 soldiers and Marines on standby just outside city limits.

This morning black, white, Hispanic and Korean residents of the worst-hit neighborhoods began working side by side to clean up the rubble. While some worked, others distributed food and water. Food shortages have been reported in several areas, as rioters and arsonists have left hundreds of grocery stores, many of them Korean-owned, in ruins. Los Angeles International Airport is nearly back to normal after being severely disrupted yesterday by smoke from the hundreds of blazing buildings (→ 7).

National Guardsmen patrol and keep order in damaged central Los Angeles.

Angelinos work side by side to help in the massive clean-up operation.

May 4. The Inuits, Canada's Eskimos, vote in favor of a limit to their territory in exchange for political autonomy. Their land, which they call Nunavut, is claimed by others. But at least they are now full citizens.

May 6. Terry Anderson, Beirut hostage for seven years, receives the Overseas Press Club Award.

Both candidates visit the city scene and vow "Never again"

President Bush in Los Angeles talks to some of the 20,000 military and police.

Governor Bill Clinton also flew in and did his best to calm tempers.

Los Angeles, Thursday 7
"We are ashamed", President Bush said today as he toured some of the hardest hit areas of the city. The president's armored limousine was surrounded by motorcycle outriders and Secret Service agents as angry Angelinos watched the convoy sweep by. Groups of Korean-Americans demonstrated to protest the destruction of many businesses in Koreatown during the rioting.

Bush, who arrived last night, told residents of South Central their city would be rebuilt, and promised $600 million in federal loans and grants to help the victims recover from the nation's deadliest riots this century. Estimates of the damage now stand at $1 billion. A total of 5,275 buildings have been heavily damaged or destroyed by arsonists in Los Angeles County.

Latest official figures show last week's eruption of anarchy and violence has left 58 people dead and more that 2,200 injured.

The president's visit comes just two days after that of Democratic front-runner Bill Clinton. As he toured Koreatown, the Arkansas governor denied that he was playing election-year politics. But he added that last week's events manifested the need for a new president. He called for increased urban investment and lambasted the White House view that the rioting could be attributed to failed social programs of the 1970s (→ May 11).

An Irish bishop has parental problems

Dublin, Friday 8
Dr Eamonn Casey, Roman Catholic Bishop of Galway, has resigned "for personal reasons" following revelations that he is the father of a teenage boy by Annie Murphy, a 44-year-old Irish woman now living in the U.S. Friends of the 65-year-old "larger than life" bishop say that he hopes to go to South America to work as a missionary.

Senior church figures have been aware of the looming scandal for some time but their attempts to keep it quiet failed when financial negotiations broke down. Ireland's Prime Minister, Albert Reynolds, said it was a "great tragedy".

The accused Church leader resigns.

Gorbachev follows in Churchill's steps

Fulton, Missouri, Wednesday 6
Speaking from the same podium in this small town that Winston Churchill used in 1946 to warn that "an Iron Curtain has descended across Europe", Mikhail Gorbachev today delivered his own warning of "apocalyptic threats" from nationalism. He called for the reorganization of the U.N. to meet these threats, arguing that the end of East-West tension demanded a new spirit of internationalism.

Commenting on Churchill's famous speech, he criticized the limitations of Churchill's analysis which could now be evaluated "quietly and objectively".

The Blue Angel's face and Marlene's husky voice are no more

Marlene Dietrich's immortal face.

Paris, Wednesday 6
Marlene Dietrich died today in her Rue Montaigne apartment, two days before the opening of the Cannes Film Festival, the poster for which features a picture of her as she appeared in Josef von Sternberg's *Shanghai Express* in 1941. It was her work in Sternberg's *Blue Angel* that had brought her international acclaim in 1930. The Berlin native became an American citizen in 1939 and sang for Allied troops at the front in World War II. She told the story of her life and career in the 1984 documentary filmed in her apartment by Maximilian Schell, *Marlene*. Her last dramatic role was in David Hemmings' *Just a Gigolo* in 1978.

Marlene made her home in Paris.

May

1992

Su	Mo	Tu	We	Th	Fr	Sa
					1	2
3	4	5	6	7	8	9
10	11	12	13	14	15	16
17	18	19	20	21	22	23
24	25	26	27	28	29	30
31						

Hamburg, 10
Michael Stich beats Boris Becker 6-1, 6-1 in the German Open semifinal.

India, 10
The sale of home-brewed alcohol is responsible for the deaths of more than 162 people.

Brussels, 11
EC foreign ministers decide to recall their ambassadors from Belgrade (→ 16).

Los Angeles, 11
Former CIA and FBI chief, William Webster, is appointed to head inquiry into police response during L.A. rioting.

London, 12
Heathrow Airport plans to add a fifth terminal.

Lebanon, 13
Rashid Solh becomes the new, Syrian-backed, prime minister.

Switzerland, 13
In an effort to reduce the spread of AIDS, the federal government experiments with giving heroin to drug addicts.

Canada, 13
Real estate group Olympia & York files for bankruptcy as its debt surpasses $12 billion (→ 29).

Washington, D.C., 14
House of Representatives approves $800 million for businesses suffering from the L.A. riots.

Baku, 15
The Popular Front takes control of Azerbaijan's parliament (→ June 7).

London, 15
Margaret Thatcher warns that the EC is headed for severe problems unless plans for a centralized economy and political union are drastically changed (→ May 21).

Taipei, 15
Taiwan's sedition law is amended which will now allow greater freedom of speech.

Maryland, 16
Pine Bluff ridden by jockey Chris McCarron wins the Preakness.

DEATH

10. Sylvia Syms, American jazz and pop singer (*1918).

Italy's financial center is racked by a wave of kickback scandals

Milan, Sunday 10
For years the people of this prosperous industrial city in northern Italy have sneered at Rome's corrupt politicians and at Mafia-riddled Naples. Now the shoe is on the other foot: Milan is facing a huge scandal involving local businessmen, politicians, city councillors and two former Socialist mayors. Police investigating charges that city officials and politicians accepted bribes in exchange for handing out public works contracts have arrested more than 20 people. Carlo Tognoli, a former Milan mayor and close associate of Socialist Party leader Bettino Craxi, is suspected of having pocketed $500,000.

The trading floor at Milan's stock exchange has been hit by allegations.

Judith quits her cell after long injustice

London, Monday 11
Judith Ward, sentenced to life for the M62 coach bombing which killed 12 people in 1974, walked free from the Court of Appeal today after the court ruled that her convictions for the coach bombing and two other IRA attacks were unsafe and unsatisfactory.

Forensic evidence had been discredited and no reliance could be placed on her confession. She suffers from a mental disorder that causes her to fantasize. She is the eighteenth person linked to IRA cases to be freed in recent appeals. She was welcomed with cheers and flowers by her supporters. She told them: "I've waited 18 years, five days for this. It's brilliant."

A moment of joy outside the court.

Elizabeth supports the Maastricht Treaty

Queen in Royal Blue in Strasbourg.

Strasbourg, Tuesday 12
Queen Elizabeth II today became the first British monarch, and the sixth European Community one, to address the Strasbourg-based European parliament.

Reading a text that strongly reflected the pro-Europe policies of Prime Minister John Major, the Queen welcomed European integration. After quoting Winston Churchill and Jean Monnet, one of the EC's founding fathers, she told a packed chamber that the 12-member community should not be a "closed club", but should be prepared to open its doors to new nations such as those of the former Communist bloc (→ 15).

May 13. United Press purchase makes TV evangelist Pat Robertson a media tycoon.

Military-style glasses are the latest means to aid security in New York's dangerous subway.

A hand in space fixes it

Koch wins the big cup

Intelsat-6 is captured and repaired by Endeavour's three astronauts.

The America's Cup is held high in triumph by the owner of America³.

San Diego, Saturday 16

The America's Cup is the prize of the most famous regatta in the world, and the Americans like to hold on to it.

Bill Koch, skipper of *America³*, and his team succeeded today in keeping the cup in the United States by defeating the team of the Italian yacht *Il Moro di Venezia*. Before the race, the Italian boat was the one picked to win by many sailing aficionados. The series was tied after the first two races, but Koch's yacht won three straight victories to triumph in the best-of-seven competition.

The America's Cup is not only the oldest yachting competition in the world, but surely the most expensive. The Italian syndicate which backed *Il Moro di Venezia* spent $110 million, and $64 million was invested in the San Diego Yacht Club's defense of the cup, $10 million of which came out of Koch's pockets. Koch, a billionaire oil heir, criticized the sums spent on the race, and estimated that $600 million was spent by all the teams which participated.

The first race was in 1851, when an American challenged British yachtsmen to a race around the Isle of Wight. The America's Cup was presented to the winner, the *America*, by Queen Victoria. The New York Yacht Club held the cup until 1983, when it was won by Australia, and then took the trophy back in 1987; but this year San Diego was the U.S. defender.

Cape Canaveral, Thursday 14

For the first time in the history of the conquest of the heavens, three men went out into space simultaneously, in order to retrieve the Intelsat-6, a telecommunications satellite. But the spacewalk was not the most impressive feat of the mission: they captured the satellite by hand. A launching-rocket malfunction in 1990 left the satellite in too low an orbit. This problem presented NASA with an opportunity to demonstrate the utility of its shuttle, the Endeavour, by recuperating and relaunching the Intelsat-6. Without the intervention of the shuttle, the $150-million satellite would have been lost. Two attempts to capture it with a long metal bar failed on Monday and Tuesday. Another suggestion was made by the shuttle's captain, Daniel Brandenstein: "If we can't catch it with the capture bar, perhaps we can grab it." Thanks to simulations effected by computers and in a pool at NASA headquarters, the idea of the three-man repair attempt was accepted. On Wednesday Pierre Thuot, Richard Hieb and Thomas Ackers succeeded in securing the satellite after eight hours of work, affirming that a human presence is irreplaceable in space missions. The satellite was given a new rocket motor and relaunched today.

NASA billed Intelsat $93 million for the mission. The satellite, which will relay transmissions of the Barcelona Summer Olympics, will remain in space for 11 years and is expected to earn one billion dollars for the international consortium.

The winning yacht breasts the Pacific waves off the coast of California.

May

1992

Su	Mo	Tu	We	Th	Fr	Sa
					1	2
3	4	5	6	7	8	9
10	11	12	13	14	15	16
17	18	19	20	21	22	23
24	25	26	27	28	29	30
31						

Washington, D.C., 17
Greg LeMond wins the 10-day Tour Du Pont bike race by a margin of 20 seconds.

Bangkok, 17
A state of emergency is declared after more than 200,000 demonstrators demand that the prime minister step down (→ May 21).

U.S., 17
Attorney General William Barr holds gang members responsible for much of the violence during the L.A. riots.

Switzerland, 17
The country's application to join both the World Bank and the International Monetary Fund is approved.

Oxford, 18
A coroner's jury rules that American pilots are responsible for the "friendly fire" which killed nine British soldiers during the Gulf War.

U.S., 19
The two doctors who performed the autopsy on President John F. Kennedy reconfirm that both bullets were shot from behind.

Sarajevo, 20
Serbian leaders are holding around 5,000 women, children and elderly hostages until their conditions are met (→ 30).

Chad, 20
Joseph Yodoyman is appointed prime minister.

Warsaw, 20
Fiat agrees to invest $2 million in Poland to form a company with Polish carmaker FSM.

Washington, D.C., 20
CIA Director Robert Gates admits that the agency failed to predict the fall of Communism in the Soviet Union.

U.S., 20
Government reports indicate that the trade deficit widened substantially in March.

London, 21
The ratification of the Maastricht Treaty is approved by Parliament in a vote of 396 to 92.

Manila, 22
Fidel Ramos proclaims himself to be the winner of the presidential election (→ June 16).

Nazi torturer gets life prison term

Stuttgart, Monday 18
Josef Schwammberger, an 80-year-old former lieutenant in the SS and concentration camp commandant, was today sentenced to life imprisonment. He was found guilty of torturing and killing dozens of inmates of slave labor camps in Nazi-occupied Poland between 1942 and 1944.

Schwammberger was jailed in France at the end of World War II, but managed to escape and flee to Argentina, where he lived for nearly three decades. He was finally arrested in 1987 after a tip-off from an informant.

May 18. Bille August won the Palme d'Or for his film, *The Best Intentions,* **and Best Actress honors went to his wife, Pernilla, at the Cannes Film Festival.**

Paris mayor Chirac targets messy dogs

Paris, Monday 18
As millions of visitors to the French capital have found to their dismay, Paris' sidewalks have for decades been among the least salubrious in Europe. Each day the city's 200,000 pet dogs drop more than 10 tons of excrement on the public highway, and the massive cleanup operation costs over $8 million annually. As from today, dog-owners who do not get their pet to use the gutter will be liable to fines ranging from $100 to $200.

Britain's Nigel Mansell joins racing greats

The Formula One victory at Imola was Mansell's fifth in a row.

Imola, Sunday 17
Nigel Mansell seems unbeatable. His latest victory, in the Grand Prix of San Marino, has made the Briton one of the most successful drivers in racing history. He has 26 wins, which puts him in fourth place among the winningest Grand Prix drivers.

Mansell has won the first five Grand Prix races of the season, a first. Alberto Ascari won nine straight Grand Prix, but over two seasons, in 1952-53, and the record of five consecutive victories was matched by Jack Brabham in 1960 and Jim Clark in 1965.

For the fourth time this year, his teammate, the Italian, Ricardo Patrese, came in second. Mansell and Patrese both drive a Williams-Renault car and are hoping for another win in the Monaco Grand Prix on May 31 (→ June 14).

Dan Quayle takes a jab at Candice Bergen

San Francisco, Tuesday 19
Dan Quayle criticized Murphy Brown today, saying she mocked the importance of fathers and of the family. This Murphy Brown is not a liberal political foe, but a character in a television sitcom. The fictional television journalist, played by Candice Bergen, gave birth out of wedlock in Monday night's episode of the show, having decided not to marry the father. Quayle made the attack in a campaign speech in which he attributed the Los Angeles riots to a "poverty of values" in the inner cities.

Mother of illegitimate child in "Murphy Brown" series is attacked.

'Heeeere's Johnny' takes final bow

Famous U.S. talk-show host retires.

U.S., Friday 22

A page of America's television history was turned this evening as Johnny Carson hosted his very last "Tonight Show".

With tears in his eyes, the legendary 66-year-old entertainer told millions of viewers and the invited audience of friends, family and staff members: "It has just been a helluva lot of fun."

NBC's "Tonight Show" was first aired on October 1, 1962, when Carson took over from Jack Paar. The show turned its host into the highest-paid personality in the history of television, earning an estimated $2,380 per minute of airtime. The Iowa-born star's ironic, jokey monologues and irreverent interviews of celebrity guests quickly earned a huge following - on average 15 million viewers watched his show three nights a week.

May 22. The International Herald Tribune is 25. Lee Huebner, as publisher, helped build the global newspaper.

Anti-Mafia judge murdered in Sicily

All Italy is stunned as crusader Falcone dies on his way to the airport.

China tests biggest-ever nuclear device

Beijing, Thursday 21

China's Communist rulers have just sent a loud and defiant message to the West.

Chinese military scientists today carried out an underground nuclear test in Xinjiang province using a mammoth one-megaton device. Shock waves from the blast, which was 50 times larger than the bomb dropped on Hiroshima, were recorded as far away as Sweden. The test, for which experts in the West can see no military rationale, comes at a time when the U.S. and other NATO members are trying to settle the nuclear legacy of the former Soviet Union.

Bonn, Paris agree to form Euro-corps

La Rochelle, Friday 22

As the Pentagon announced further cuts in U.S. military bases in Europe, France and Germany agreed today to form a joint army corps of 35,000 to 45,000 troops.

At the end of a two-day meeting in this western France port, Chancellor Helmut Kohl and President François Mitterrand said the new Euro-corps, to be based in Strasbourg, near Germany's border, will be ready for full deployment in three to four years. They stressed the Franco-German unit should become the core of a larger corps. There would eventually be contributions from several other European nations. Italy, Spain, Belgium and Luxembourg have already shown interest, but Britain and the Netherlands have voiced opposition. For his part, Dick Cheney, the U.S. defense secretary, has given the Franco-German plan cautious approval.

Palermo, Saturday 23

Judge Giovanni Falcone, one of Italy's foremost anti-Mafia investigators, was assassinated today as his three-car motorcade headed from the Punta Raisi airport into the Sicilian capital.

More than 50 meters (164 feet) of the highway was destroyed, and there is an enormous crater, up to eight meters (26 feet) deep in some places. The bomb, set off from a remote control, had been placed in a drainage tunnel underneath the asphalt. The first car, carrying bodyguards, was thrown into the air and the passengers were killed instantly. Judge Falcone's Fiat fell into the crater, and he died on the way to the hospital. His wife survived him for only a few hours.

Judge Falcone had managed to get a confession and information which led to more than 300 arrests from Mafioso Tommaso Buscetta in 1984. The judge had already been the target of a failed assassination attempt, and in a December 1991 interview stated: "I opened an account with the Mafia. It can only close with my death" (→ June 9).

Thailand's king forces army to back down

Bangkok, Thursday 21

General Suchinda Krayaroon, the Thai prime minister, and Chamlong Srimuang, the leader of the pro-democracy movement, walked on their knees and sat on the floor before Bhumibol Adulyadej, their king. The king had summoned them to negotiate an end to violence between the army and demonstrators that has shaken the capital since last Sunday. The two affirmed this morning that they had agreed to constitutional amendments making the office of prime minister an elected position (→ Sep 13).

Bangkok's pro-democracy demonstrators in tense face-off with troops.

May
1992

Su	Mo	Tu	We	Th	Fr	Sa
					1	2
3	4	5	6	7	8	9
10	11	12	13	14	15	16
17	18	19	20	21	22	23
24	25	26	27	28	29	30
31						

Indianapolis, 24
The Indianapolis 500 race is won by Al Unser.

Tel Aviv, 24
A young Jew's assassination by a Palestinian provokes violent reactions from Israel's extreme right.

Vienna, 24
Conservative Thomas Klestil is elected president.

Washington, D.C., 24
George Bush orders that new arrivals of Haitians, fleeing to the U.S., be sent back to Haiti.

Kabul, 25
After a 7-hour meeting, guerrilla leaders Masood and Hekmatyar sign an agreement to end fighting between their forces (→ Aug 9).

Italy, 25
After a month of political gridlock, Oscar Luigi Scalfaro is elected president.

Moscow, 25
Sergei Shakhrai, aide to Boris Yeltsin, announces that the former Communist Party backed terrorists in their attacks on Western officials.

London, 26
The Body Shop which sells environmentally-friendly products announces a 26% rise in profits for 1991.

Brussels, 27
The EC forecasts 10% unemployment for 1993.

Sarajevo, 27
A mortar attack in a mall leaves more than 17 civilians dead and numerous injuries.

London, 28
David Platt becomes the most expensive soccer player, having been sold to the Italian club, Juventus, for £8 million.

U.S., 28
The number of prisoners in the nation reached the record level of 823,414. One out of every three inmates is being held for a drug-related crime.

New York, 30
The pound is quoted at $1.82.

DEATH

27. Peter Jenkins, British journalist from *The Independent* (*1934).

Security Council imposes Serbia embargo

Serbian artillery continues to pound the Bosnian capital mercilessly.

New York, Saturday 30
As Serbian-led forces launched their fiercest-ever artillery attack on Sarajevo, Bosnia's capital, the U.N. Security Council voted today to impose sanctions on Serbia and Montenegro. The sanctions, which the U.N. hopes will force Serbia to end its bloody military offensive in Bosnia-Herzegovina, include an embargo on trade and oil, and a freeze on air traffic links. Serbia and Montenegro's financial assets overseas are also to be frozen. In Belgrade, however, Serbian leaders remained defiant, vowing to pursue their policy of "ethnic cleansing" (→ June 8).

French court to reopen Bluebeard's case

Nantes, Tuesday 26
A special tribunal has agreed to re-open the case of France's Bluebeard, Field-Marshal Gilles de Rais, executed here on October 26, 1440 for the murder of 150 children. Historians now believe that De Rais, who fought against the English alongside Joan of Arc, was falsely accused by the Duke of Brittany because the latter wanted to seize his estates.

'Bomber' Harris unveiling provokes storm

Queen Mother performs ceremony.

London, Sunday 31
There were angry scenes today when the Queen Mother unveiled a statue of Marshal of the RAF Sir Arthur "Bomber" Harris at the RAF's church of St Clement Danes in the Strand. Groups of protesters shouted, "Harris was a mass murderer", while the Queen Mother spoke of the 55,000 members of Bomber Command "who died defending our country and freedom" and praised the "inspiring leadership" of the controversial Harris.

One protester sprayed a red dye at the bronze statue before being arrested. Others carried a banner reading: "Harris = Eichmann". Bomber veterans were incensed: "We had a job to do", said one, "and it was the same with Harris."

Perot still hounds Bush and Clinton

Dallas, Wednesday 26
Texas billionaire Ross Perot has emerged as a serious threat to the two established political parties in the race for the presidency of the United States. Today his supporters' petitions won him a place on election ballots in Florida and in his home state, bringing the total of states where he has qualified to eight. The businessman's ideas are changing traditional electoral strategies. Rather than relying on press conferences and short, televised political advertisements to reach the American electorate, he has appeared on talk shows, where he can more easily control the subject matter and express his views more directly. His appeal has been that of the outsider: He has claimed not to be a part of the Washington establishment – especially appealing at a time when there is widespread suspicion of, and discontentment with, incumbents and professional politicians (→ June 2).

Ireland's president charms the French

Paris, Thursday 28
The first official visit to France by Mary Robinson, president of Ireland since November 1990, has come to an end. The former lawyer went to Paris, of course, but also to Lyons, Montpellier and the picturesque village of Saint-Guilhem-le-Désert. The head of state is forbidden to participate directly in the public debate of her country, as the position is a non-political and largely symbolic one. However, her left-leaning stance, especially concerning the controversial issue of abortion, is well known.

June
1992

Su	Mo	Tu	We	Th	Fr	Sa
	1	2	3	4	5	6
7	8	9	10	11	12	13
14	15	16	17	18	19	20
21	22	23	24	25	26	27
28	29	30				

Moscow, 1
In an official visit, South African President Frederik de Klerk meets with Boris Yeltsin, marking the end of 35 years of severed relations.

Ohio, 1
American Electric Power Co. backs the E-lamp, a light bulb that should last 14 years and cost between $10 and $20.

U.S., 2
An ABC News/Washington Post poll has Perot leading the presidential preference polls with 36% to Bush's 31% and Clinton's 27% (→ 11).

New York, 2
The Dow Jones industrial average closes at over 3,400 for the first time.

Haiti, 2
Conservative Marc Bazin is appointed prime minister.

Rio de Janeiro, 3
The Earth Summit opens with representatives from around 180 nations discussing how to preserve the environment and save the planet for future generations (→ 12).

France, 4
Euro Disney reports that since the opening on April 12, it has received 1.5 million visitors: 30,000 per day.

U.S., 5
A Census Bureau study indicates that one-third of students between ages 15 and 17 have either dropped out of school or are at least one grade behind.

Washington, D.C., 5
A $270-billion military budget is approved by the House of Representatives by a vote of 198 to 168.

Warsaw, 5
Polish Peasants' Party leader Waldemar Pawlak, age 33, is named the fourth prime minister since the fall of Communism.

Canada, 5
The government announces that the 11.2% unemployment level for the month of May is the highest it has been in eight years.

DEATH

3. Robert Morley, British actor (*May 26, 1908).

Danes stun Europe with 'no' vote

Copenhagen, Tuesday 2
The Danes appear tonight to have wrecked the Maastricht Treaty by voting against its proposals in a national referendum. The vote was extremely close: 50.7% against 49.3%. There was a surprisingly large turnout: 82% of the 3.9 million electorate voted and there was a margin of only 48,000 between those against and those in favor of the Maastricht deal.

Nevertheless, unless all 12 members of the EC ratify the treaty it cannot take effect. If the strict letter of the law is applied the Danish vote means that the agreements on a single currency, a common foreign and security policy and moves towards a common defense strategy will not be put into operation.

Reaction was mixed in London. Sir Leon Brittan, Britain's senior EC commissioner, said the Danish vote was very disappointing but Norman Tebbit said: "It is a good thing for the whole of Europe. It

Danes' "Ne" wins by slim 50.7%.

Foreign minister advocated "Yes".

saves the European economic community from a disaster." He said Maastricht was dead.

His views reflect Tory unease about Maastricht. There are grow-ing demands for a renegotiation of the treaty. The forthcoming French referendum is now vital. If the French vote "Non", then Maastricht really is dead (→ Sep 20).

British actor Robert Morley dies at 84

London, Wednesday 3
Robert Morley, the great British actor, died today in London after having suffered a stroke. He de-buted on the London stage in 1929 and went on to act in 100 films and 50 plays. He was a favorite as an after-dinner speaker and also published memoirs and eight plays. His films included *The African Queen*, *Oscar Wilde*, *Cromwell* and *Those Magnificent Men in Their Flying Machines*.

A quintessential English gentleman.

Caspian Sea's caviar facing new threat

Russia, Monday 1
One of the world's most sought-after delicacies is in danger of disappearing forever. After centuries of state-controlled harvesting of sturgeon, the Caspian Sea region, home of more than 90% of the world's stocks, has been in a state of anarchy since the breakup of the Soviet Union. The quota system has broken down and the newly-independent nations bordering on the Caspian are unable to control thousands of poachers who are quickly bringing sturgeon to the brink of extinction. With an ounce of caviar selling for $50 in New York, Paris or London, illegal sturgeon catching has become big business in cash-strapped Russia.

June 4. Given a choice between the young and thin, or older and not-so-thin Elvis, Americans voted for this stamp, presented today at Graceland.

Su	Mo	Tu	We	Th	Fr	Sa
	1	2	3	4	5	6
7	8	9	10	11	12	13
14	15	16	17	18	19	20
21	22	23	24	25	26	27
28	29	30				

Paris, 7
American Jim Courier defeats Czechoslovakian Petr Korda 7-5, 6-2, 6-1 to win his second French Open title.

Newport, Rhode Island, 8
All U.S. Navy personnel are now required to attend sexual harassment seminars (→ 26).

London, 8
Around 3,000 pensioners and Maxwell company employees lobby to protest their poor financial position caused by the late Robert Maxwell's theft of their pension funds.

Paris, 8
Senior PLO official Atef Bseiso is assassinated during a routine trip to meet with French intelligence officials.

Edgbaston, 8
England and Pakistan draw in cricket's First Test (→ 21).

U.S., 8
The Big Three carmakers agree to share research on emission reduction.

Italy, 9
Over 700 people, believed to be heavily involved in Mafia crime, are held after an anti-crime decree goes into effect (→ July 19).

Los Angeles, 9
Police Chief Daryl Gates, dispelling rumors that he intends to stay with the force through July, announces plans to retire at the end of the month (→ July 1).

London, 10
A bomb explosion in Victoria Street is responsible for extensive damage but no fatalities are reported.

Boston, 11
The last survivor of the *Titanic*, Marjorie Robb, aged 103, dies.

Rio de Janeiro, 12
John Major announces that Britain will contribute an additional £100 million to protect the environment. President Bush defends the U.S. position on environmental issues.

Gothenburg, 12
In soccer, the Dutch become the first victors in the European Championships by beating Scotland 1-0.

U.N. authorizes its troops to take over vital Sarajevo airport

New York, Monday 8
This evening the U.N. Security Council agreed on a plan to open Butmir Airport, which is just outside Sarajevo and currently held by Serbian forces, for humanitarian aid. The first phase of the plan is scheduled to begin on Wednesday with the arrival in Sarajevo of a team of military observers. The operation will be carried out by 1,000 blue-helmeted troops, but is predicated upon a cease-fire. One problem in carrying out the plan is supplying the soldiers. France has already announced its intention to send forces to protect humanitarian convoys, but the U.S. and the U.K. are very reluctant to send in troops, and Germany is constitutionally restrained from doing so (→ 29).

The Security Council hopes food and medical aid can now be flown in.

Diana suicide claim causes Court storm

London, Sunday 7
A storm which is rocking the Royal Family to its foundations broke today with the publication of a book, *Diana: Her True Story*, in which the journalist, Andrew Morton, claims that she has made five attempts to commit suicide in desperation over the uncaring attitude of Prince Charles.

The book is said to be based on information given to the author by Lady Di's friends who share her distress at Prince Charles's friendship with Camilla Parker-Bowles, wife of Brigadier Andrew Parker-Bowles, Silver Stick in Waiting to the Queen. The royal marriage is now said to be a sham (→ Dec 9).

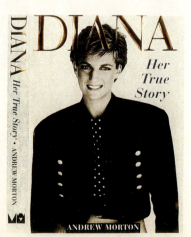
Andrew Morton's shocking book.

Japan's Nintendo buys into ball game

Seattle Mariners are the first major league team bought by Nintendo.

Seattle, Tuesday 9
Some baseball fans see the deal approved today as a ray of hope for a financially troubled team, while for others it is a final straw.

A group of overseas investors led by Hiroshi Yamauchi of Nintendo Corp. has just bought the Seattle Mariners for $125 million, of which Yamauchi will contribute $75 million. This is the first time in U.S. baseball history that ownership of a major league team has been allowed from outside North America. Commissioner Fay Vincent stressed that control of the Mariners will remain in Seattle.

IRA gunmen kill British policeman

Yorkshire, Sunday 7
A terrorist hunt is now underway after IRA gunmen shot dead one policeman and seriously wounded another. The officers had approached a red Ford Sierra on the A64, near the quiet town of Tadcaster in north Yorkshire, only to be met by a hail of bullets from a Kalashnikov rifle. Another police car gave chase, but had to retreat after being raked by fire. The dead man, 37-year-old Special Constable Glenn Goodman, leaves behind a wife and a baby son. Detectives believe the incident could be linked to the small bomb which went off on Saturday night, injuring no one, at the Royal Festival Hall in London.

Paris Open: Courier in 3 sets.

Steel corset to save Pisa's leaning tower

Pisa, Wednesday 10
A decisive step was taken today in the efforts to save one of the most famous monuments in Italy, the Leaning Tower of Pisa – its corset was tightened. The ever-increasing inclination of the tower is the cause of its fame, but could also lead to its loss, so last month a steel corset made of 16 cables was put up around the first and second floor of the tower, making the internal spine more rigid and helping to prevent its blocks from moving or forming fissures. The cables, enveloped in white teflon, are practically invisible against the marble tower. This autumn, a lead and concrete counterweight will be put in place at the tower's base to slow the rate of inclination.

It sinks at the rate of 0.3 in. per year.

Tear gas mars Bush's stopover in Panama

Panama City, Thursday 11
President Bush's carefully orchestrated stopover on his way to the Earth Summit in Brazil dissolved into fear and chaos today when police fired tear gas at left-wing demonstrators among the laughing, singing people waiting to hear the president speak in a city square. The 8,000-strong crowd panicked as the gas canisters exploded among them, and they surged towards Bush and his wife.

His bodyguards drew their guns and rushed George and Barbara Bush, their eyes streaming with tears, to their motorcade. The president suffered no ill effects and described the incident as "a little ripple". It was, however, a sign of the political turbulence in Panama.

Agents hustle Bush away to safety.

England ties with Denmark in Euro 92

Malmö, Thursday 11
England was lucky tonight to open its European Championship campaign with a goalless draw against Denmark. England promised to gain more than a single point early in the match, but as it progressed the Danes probed dangerously at England's suspect defense, and only the woodwork prevented the Danes from winning. A shot from John Jensen beat goalkeeper Chris Woods but hit the post. England's consolation is that the last time they began a major tournament 0-0 they won the World Cup (→ 26).

Clinton lashes out at black rap artist

Washington, D.C., Thursday 11
Presidential candidate Bill Clinton, in a speech before Jesse Jackson and the Rainbow Coalition, criticized the group for inviting Sister Souljah to speak the night before. Clinton cited the rapper's comments about the Los Angeles riots from a Washington Post interview: "If black people kill black people every day, why not have a week and kill white people?" The criticism was seen as a move by Clinton to distance himself from Jackson and to show his independence from core Democratic groups (→ July 10).

Yeltsin says Soviets held GIs in WWII

Washingon, D.C., Friday 12
Russian President Boris Yeltsin, in a letter to a U.S. Senate committee, revealed that 716 U.S. servicemen, mostly crew members of bombers which had made forced landings, were held prisoner by the Soviet Union during World War II, when the countries were allies. He also disclosed that nine U.S. military aircraft were shot down over the Soviet Union in the 1950s, and that there had been survivors. Senators praised Yeltsin for the letter, but some officials viewed it as a move to discredit his hardline opponents.

Falklands visit for tenth anniversary

Falkland Islands, Sunday 14
Baroness Thatcher has joined inhabitants of Britain's farthest-flung territories to mark the 10th anniversary of their liberation from Argentine occupation. Perhaps she spent some time contemplating how victory in the Falklands War helped salvage her political career – which was then flagging badly. But it was above all a day of thanksgiving and remembrance, as church services on the islands and in Britain remembered the 255 men who died to reclaim these bleak outcrops in the South Atlantic.

June 13. British actor Michael Caine is appointed Commander of the British Empire (CBE) in today's Queen's Birthday Honours list.

June 12. Elizabeth II ends her three-day state visit to France in Bordeaux, capital of the former English-held region of Aquitaine.

June

1992

Su	Mo	Tu	We	Th	Fr	Sa
	1	2	3	4	5	6
7	8	9	10	11	12	13
14	15	16	17	18	19	20
21	22	23	24	25	26	27
28	29	30				

Chicago, 14
The Chicago Bulls defeat the Portland Trail Blazers 119-106 to win the National Basketball Association finals for the second straight year.

Montreal, 14
In the Canadian Grand Prix, Nigel Mansell skids into a sand trap (→ July 5).

London, 15
The Daily Telegraph prints an apology for a previous article which unjustly accused Princess Stephanie of Monaco of demanding fees for charity events (→ 18).

London, 15
Downing Street denies that the Government Communications Headquarters (GCHQ) supplied them with information on Robert Maxwell's activities.

Washington, D.C., 16
George Bush and Boris Yeltsin announce a historic arms pact that will reduce long-range nuclear warheads.

Washington, D.C., 16
Caspar Weinberger becomes the highest-ranking member of the Reagan administration to be indicted on Iran-Contra charges.

Libya, 16
Germans Heinrich Strübig and Thomas Kemptner, the last two Western hostages in the Middle East, are freed.

London, 16
The council of the Zoological Society votes to close the London Zoo in September; the zoo opened in 1826.

Stockholm, 16
Following three nights of disturbances caused by English soccer fans, the sale of strong beer is banned in an effort to avoid further violence.

Czechoslovakia, 17
Czech and Slovak leaders meet for the third time to discuss the formation of a new government and its membership (→ July 17).

Beijing, 18
Due to the U.S. ban on importing goods made by convict labor, the Chinese government agrees to suspend exports of prison-made items to America.

Rio Earth Summit closes with many promises but little cash

Rio de Janeiro, Sunday 14
The Earth Summit on the environment, attended by more than 100 heads of state, ended here today with a ringing declaration from Canada's Maurice Strong, chairman of the conference: "This is an historic moment for humanity. It is indeed a profound human experience from which none of us can emerge unchanged."

The poorer countries were, however, not so ecstatic. They failed to get the rich nations, led by the U.S., Britain, Japan and Germany, to agree to double aid by the year 2000. All they could extract from them was a promise to reach that target "quickly".

Pro-ecology demonstrators target George Bush's environmental policies.

U.S. court backs abductions abroad

Washington, Monday 15
The Supreme Court ruled today that the United States may abduct people from foreign countries in order to bring them to trial. The decision clears the way for the trial of Humberto Alvarez-Machain, a Mexican doctor kidnapped after being accused of taking part in the murder of a U.S. drug agent.

The Mexican government argued that such abductions violate extradition treaties and contravene fundamental principles of justice. The ruling was passed by six votes to three. A dissenting opinion was entered by Justice John Stevens, who called the ruling "monstrous".

Amazon Indian chief arrested for rape

Brazil, Monday 15
The scandal could not have come at a worse time: As world leaders met in Rio to seek ways to protect the environment, a famous advocate for the Amazon's threatened rainforests has been arrested for rape, assault and cannibalism.

Chief Paulinho Paiakan of the Kaiapo tribe is accused of having brutally raped and committed acts of cannibalism on an 18-year-old white student after a wild drinking spree. Paiakan, aged 37, had become a symbol of the fight to save the rainforests. He has traveled the world and been photographed with such figures as former U.S. President Jimmy Carter and British rock star Sting.

Paiakan was a symbol for ecologists.

June 15. Claudia Schiffer signs $10-million deal with Revlon.

Lotus, owned by General Motors, stops producing its best-loved sports car, the Elan, which was first manufactured in Britain 30 years ago.

South Africa township massacre kills 39

The bloody events at Boipatong have hurt the government's peace efforts.

Johannesburg, Thursday 18

A gang of 200 men armed with guns and pangas rampaged through a squatter camp 40 miles south of here last night, killing 39 people and wounding many more. Women and children died in the massacre.

Residents, supporters of the African National Congress, blamed the attack on men from a hostel for migrant workers, a stronghold of the Zulu Inkatha Freedom Party. ANC leaders also accused the government of complicity, saying the attackers arrived in police vehicles. The government laid the blame on the ANC's campaign of mass protest saying it had pushed the political temperature unacceptably high. In this tense and ugly atmosphere survivors are plotting revenge attacks.

Anti-Russian ethnic attacks hit Moldova

Ancient hatred between Russian- and Romanian-speakers causes bloodshed.

Moldova, Saturday 20

Fighting between the Russian-speaking minority, most of whom live east of the Dniester River, and the Romanian-speaking majority has intensified. Troops of the secessionist Russians and Ukrainians are on the verge of winning control of the city of Bendery, on the eastern bank of the Dniester River. The Moldovans claim that Russian troops have intervened on the side of the secessionists, and tonight Moldovans attacked a regiment of the Russian 14th Army, which is based in Trans-Dniester. Russian President Boris Yeltsin has warned the Moldovan government that, although he would prefer to settle the conflict by negotiation, he is ready to use troops to defend the Russian community (→ July 3).

Kevin, Ian Maxwell charged with fraud

London, Thursday 18

Police made early morning raids on the homes of Kevin and Ian Maxwell, sons of the late publisher Robert Maxwell. Both men were arrested and charged with fraud offenses involving a combined total of at least £128 million. As they left the court after being released on bail Kevin Maxwell said: "After seven months of trial by rumor, of trial by innuendo, of trial by selective press leaks and prejudicial media reporting, I am really looking forward to being able to defend myself in a court of law" (→ July 20).

Fidel Ramos takes over from Cory Aquino

Manila, Tuesday 16

Cory Aquino, the woman who ousted Philippine dictator Ferdinand Marcos, is now set to bow out of power herself. Results of the apparently fraud-free elections were announced today, giving General Fidel Ramos, aged 64, the next presidency of the islands with 5.34 million votes. He beat anti-corruption campaigner Miriam Santiago by 870,000 votes. The poll was held five weeks ago, but the result has only now been announced because of the complex regulations designed to stop electoral fraud.

June 17. Superpower first ladies take time off from Bush-Yeltsin summit to study the finer points of baking the perfect cookie.

June 19. Evander Holyfield beats Larry Holmes in a 12-round contest to retain his heavyweight title at Caesar's Palace, Las Vegas (→ Nov 13).

June

1992

Su	Mo	Tu	We	Th	Fr	Sa
	1	2	3	4	5	6
7	8	9	10	11	12	13
14	15	16	17	18	19	20
21	22	23	24	25	26	27
28	29	30				

Pebble Beach, 21
Tom Kite wins the 92nd U.S. Open Golf Tournament.

Newbridge, 21
St. Jovite, ridden by jockey Christy Roche, wins the 1.5-mile Irish Derby at The Curragh and breaks the track record.

England, 21
Cricket: Pakistan beats England by two wickets in the Second Test at Lords.

New York, 23
John Gotti, Mafia godfather, involved in murder, extortion, racketeering and corruption, is sentenced to prison for life.

Germany, 23
BMW announces it will open its first U.S. car plant in South Carolina, which will assemble 300 cars per day.

Washington, D.C., 24
The Supreme Court rules that prayers or invocations at public school graduations are unconstitutional.

U.S., 24
A railroad strike puts the nation in a state of crisis. Losses in the business world reach $1 billion a day.

Isles of Scilly, 24
The Royal Navy intervenes in clashes between French and British fishing vessels.

Wimbledon, 25
John McEnroe, three-time winner of the Wimbledon championship, beats Pat Cash in tennis in a grueling five-set match.

Manchester, 27
A World War II Spitfire explodes during an air show, killing the pilot.

Lisbon, 28
The 12 members of the EC end their first summit with unanswered questions regarding the budget and new membership.

Brussels, 29
The U.N. Security Council authorizes sending 850 U.N. troops to Sarajevo.

DEATH

23. John Spencer Churchill, British painter and sculptor, nephew of Sir Winston Churchill (*May 31, 1909).

Yitzhak Rabin election win sparks hopes for Mid-East peace

Tel Aviv, Tuesday 23
New hope dawned for the Middle East peace process today with the election of Yitzhak Rabin, the Labor Party leader, as the new prime minister of Israel. His predecessor, Yitzhak Shamir, was a hardliner whose refusal to stop building Jewish settlements in the Occupied Territories brought delicate negotiations for Palestinian autonomy shuddering to a halt.

Rabin's election campaign was fought on a platform of compromise between the need for peace with the Palestinians and security in Israel. He promised to curb Jewish settlement in the West Bank, Golan Heights and Gaza Strip,

Labor supporters cheer the victory.

while insisting on no return to Israel's pre-1967 borders and no giving up of Israel's sovereignty over a united Jerusalem.

Arab leaders have welcomed the poll result, which they say improves chances for a peace agreement with Israel. U.S. officials, meanwhile, may now reconsider their offer of $10 billion in loan guarantees, withdrawn when Shamir insisted that new settlements in the Occupied Territories would continue despite President Bush's objections.

Prime Minister Rabin must now try to build a viable government. With no overall majority, Labor will have to form a coalition with at least two other parties (→ July 13).

'Queen Mary' allowed to sink into debt

The venerable luxury liner is one of Long Beach's tourist attractions.

Long Beach, Wednesday 24
The *Queen Mary*, once the pride of the North Atlantic, now a moored tourist attraction, is being scuppered by a loss of $8 million a year and, unless a buyer can be found to take her off the hands of the Disney corporation, this grand old lady is likely to end up as scrap metal.

Completed just before the war, she served as a troopship, carrying 10,000 American soldiers on each four-day crossing to England. She was handsomely fitted out after the war and carried the rich and famous in luxury between New York and Southampton.

Air travel killed off the big liners. The *United States* was scrapped, the *Queen Elizabeth*, turned into a floating university, was destroyed

by fire in Hong Kong in 1972 and the *Queen Mary*, still dignified, became the tourist center of Long Beach. Her devotees have just three months to find a new owner.

Lloyd's of London posts huge loss

London, Wednesday 24
Lloyd's of London today revealed a loss of £2.06 billion, the worst in its 300-year history. As Lloyd's accounts are presented three years in arrears the loss relates to 1989, when the insurance market was hit by huge claims from four disasters: the *Exxon Valdez* oil spill, Hurricane Hugo, the San Francisco earthquake and the Phillips Petroleum explosion in Texas.

David Coleridge, Lloyd's chairman, speaking at the annual meeting, told individual investors – known as "Names" – that the loss was "an appalling result, reflecting the extreme losses of a handful of excess of loss syndicates". This referred to syndicates which reinsure the catastrophe business of other syndicates. The Names will bear the brunt of the losses.

June 21. At Le Mans, Britain's Derek Warwick and Mark Blundell, with France's Yannick Dalmas, led in their Peugeot 905 from the second hour.

Cigarette makers' warnings are no protection from litigation

Washington, Wednesday 24
A flood of claims against cigarette companies is expected following a ruling by the U.S. Supreme Court today that the companies cannot claim protection from damages simply because their packets carry government health warnings.

The ruling, by seven votes to two, concerns the death from lung cancer of Rose Cipollone after 42 years of smoking. Her family had sued L&M, makers of her favorite cigarette, but the company successfully claimed the packet warnings meant that smokers knew the dangers they ran. Today's ruling means that the Cipollone family may now argue the cigarette manufacturers con-spired to undermine the warnings with propaganda saying smoking was not as dangerous as people thought. The case now goes back to trial in New Jersey in the light of the Supreme Court ruling.

The decision has wide-ranging implications. In the U.S. alone about 400,000 deaths a year are claimed to be smoking-related, and the potential liabilities of the ciga-rette companies are huge. Staff of one airline are suing their employer for $5 billion for damage caused by "secondary smoking". The tobacco industry is already spending some $50 million a year in legal fees. One of the lawyers involved said: "It's trench warfare out there."

Court ruling hits tobacco industry.

Danes win Euro 92

Gothenburg, Friday 26
Denmark's underrated footballers beat the World Cup holders, Germany, 2-0 here tonight to win the European Championship.

The Danes, invited to replace the banned Yugoslavs only ten days before the tournament started, over-came the three favorites, France, the Netherlands and Germany, to win their first major championship. The win on the field also had politi-cal implications. Danish Foreign Minister Uffe Ellemann-Jensen ar-rived at the EC summit in Lisbon wearing a football scarf and, linking the victory to Maastricht, said: "If we can't join them, we'll beat them."

Delors gets two more years as EC head

Lisbon, Friday 26
Britain has grudgingly endorsed Jacques Delors as president of the European Commission for a further two years despite the distrust of him expressed by Margaret Thatcher as introducing "socialism by the back Delors".

The decision was a tactical move. With Britain taking over the EC presidency next Wednesday, Prime Minister John Major did not want a lame duck in charge of the Commission, especially a resentful lame duck. Britain hopes the Danish rejection of the Maastricht treaty will curb Delors' ambition to establish an all-powerful centralized executive in Brussels.

The man Britons love to hate.

Tailhook sex scandal rocks U.S. Navy

Washington, D.C., Friday 26
At the Tailhook Association's con-vention last year, drunken male Navy and Marine Corps aviators made women run a gauntlet along a hallway in a Las Vegas hotel, touching and grabbing them in a sexually aggressive manner, ac-cording to the 26 women, half of them naval officers, who claim to be the victims. Today the Defense Department suspended the investi-gation into the sexual harassment scandal, saying that the naval of-ficers who were conducting it might be suspects themselves. Later today H. Lawrence Garrett 3d, secretary of the Navy, offered his resignation to President George Bush, perhaps under pressure from Dick Cheney, the U.S. secretary of defense. Gar-rett said that although he "neither saw nor engaged in any offensive conduct", he accepted "full re-sponsibility" and blamed himself for a "leadership failure" that led to the incident and hindered a speedy investigation. President Bush sum-moned Lieutenant Paula Coughlin, the only victim of the incident to speak out publicly, to a meeting at the White House tonight, and promised a thorough investigation. The Tailhook Association, named after the device on aircraft carriers that catches jets as they land, is a private group of active-duty and retired naval aviators (→ July 8).

June 26. The futuristic XJ220, Jaguar's 200-mph-plus two-seater road car, makes its debut in Oxfordshire. It is priced at $750,000.

June 26. Hundreds of angry French farmers mobilize 300 tractors to block access roads to the Euro Disney amusement park east of Paris.

Mitterrand in surprise Sarajevo visit

Sarajevo, Sunday 28
President François Mitterrand paid a dramatic visit to this shell-battered city today. The 75-year-old French leader walked through the dangerous streets and laid a red rose at the spot where a Serbian mortar bomb killed 14 people as they queued to buy bread. Crowds of residents, many of them in tears, shouted, "Vive la France."

Mitterrand flew to the besieged Bosnian capital from Lisbon, where he had taken part in the EC summit at which European leaders had urged the U.N. to send troops, if necessary, to break the blockade of Sarajevo's airport. Doubts about the wisdom of intervention remain, but Mitterrand was adamant. He insisted: "We are going to send humanitarian aid to the people of Sarajevo and, if necessary, it will be protected by force."

Just how difficult this might be was demonstrated when he was

The French president's trip is aimed at getting the airport reopened.

caught in a fierce exchange of fire at the airport and was forced to put on a flak jacket and take cover for 20 minutes before he could board his helicopter. Fighting round the airport later forced the diversion of two French aircraft carrying 13 tons of relief supplies. Mitterrand's courage is much appreciated, but cynics suggest his visit will do his Socialist Party no harm in the forthcoming elections (→ July 2).

Kidnapped Exxon executive killed

New Jersey, Saturday 27
Irene Seale led FBI agents to a grave in a forest preserve in southern New Jersey. There they found the body of Sidney Reso, the executive in charge of Exxon operations outside North America who had been kidnapped last April. Reso had heart problems and died shortly after his abduction. On April 29, his car had been found with the doors open and the motor running an hour-and-a-half after he had left home on his way to work. Not long after, a ransom demand for $18.5 million was received. The ransom was to be left in six different locations, on a day around June 15. Investigators spotted Irene Seale and her husband, Arthur, at several of the drop sights. The couple was subsequently arrested and charged with kidnapping, extortion and conspiracy. One or both of them will be charged with murder.

Southern California jolted by strongest quakes in 40 years

Luckily, the epicenter of the two quakes was in sparsely-populated areas.

California, Sunday 28
A child died, over 100 people were injured and half a million left without power in two strong earthquakes in the south of the state this morning. Residents of Los Angeles and San Francisco have been warned to expect another major quake along the San Andreas fault.

The first quake, centered near Joshua Tree in the Mojave Desert, 100 miles (160 km) from Los Angeles, came just before five in the morning, and was felt as far away as Denver. At 7.4 on the Richter scale – the strongest in the U.S. since 1952 – and lasting 30 seconds, it was described as being like the waves on the sea. The epicenter was in a sparsely populated area and the only death was caused by a chimney collapsing onto a child.

The second earthquake, three hours later, was televised live on CNN. Reporter Anne McDermott had to stop reading the traffic news from the cable network's Los Angeles bureau because the cameras, lights and newsdesk were swaying too much. At seven on the Richter scale, it was another warning to Californians that they are living on the brink of disaster.

Baboon liver used to save dying patient

Pittsburgh, Sunday 28
Medical history was made late tonight when surgeons at the University of Pittsburgh transplanted a baboon's liver into a human. The patient's own liver had been destroyed by the hepatitis B virus, which reinfects human livers and makes a conventional transplant impossible. Baboons, on the other hand, are thought to be immune to the disease. It is too early to say whether the 11-and-a-half-hour operation has been a success.

A baboon's liver is anatomically very similar to that of a human, but doctors are putting their hope in an experimental anti-rejection drug called FK-506. At present about one-third of all liver transplant patients die because no human organs are available (→ Sept 7).

From 'Vanity Fair' to 'The New Yorker'

New York, Tuesday 30
Stunned staff of the prestigious magazine, *The New Yorker*, learnt today that they were to be edited by the British journalist, Tina Brown, current editor of *Vanity Fair*. Wife of Harry Evans, former editor of the *Sunday Times*, Brown says she intends to preserve *The New Yorker*'s "literary and intellectual standards and to introduce it to a new generation of readers."

Britain's Tina Brown is 38.

Algerian president is assassinated

Algiers, Monday 29
Mohammed Boudiaf, president of Algeria, was assassinated at a political rally in the city of Annaba, 280 miles east of Algiers today. He was cut down by two bursts of machine-gun fire while he was making a speech at the opening of a cultural center. The assassin, dressed in police uniform, was shot by the president's bodyguard. Another man was arrested and is being questioned.

Boudiaf, 73, was one of the historic leaders of the Algerian revolt against the French. Exiled to Morocco after quarreling with his comrades, he was recalled five months ago to give respectability to the military government in its fight

Mohammed Boudiaf was aged 73.

with the powerful fundamentalist party, the Islamic Salvation Front.

Generally regarded as mild-mannered, Boudiaf showed an authoritarian streak on assuming power and defended the wholesale arrest of Islamic militants. "Respect for democracy", he argued, "must not lead to the destruction of democracy."

His stance enraged the Front which, having been deprived of victory at the polls when the election was cancelled, turned to terrorism. There is little doubt in government circles that the fundamentalists were responsible for the assassination. Boudiaf's final words were: "We are all going to die."

June 30. New Yorkers get first taste of French pay toilets.

U.S. Supreme Court ruling upholds women's abortion rights

The U.S. court's decision has outraged militant anti-abortion groups.

Washington, Monday 29
In a politically explosive decision destined to figure prominently in the presidential election campaign, the conservative-dominated U.S. Supreme Court today gave states the power to restrict women's right to have abortions. At the same time, the court stopped short of overturning its own historic 1973 ruling in the case of Roe v Wade, which enshrined abortion as a constitutional right. The vote was 5 to 4. The decision, therefore, satisfies neither side in the bitter abortion fight which has divided America for nearly 20 years. The president of the National Abortion Rights Action League, Kate Michelman, said the court's action was "devastating for women" and that it "moved them one step closer to the back alleys".

Many opponents of abortion were also unhappy. Wanda Franz, president of the National Right to Life Committee, called the ruling "a loss for unborn children and a victory for pro-abortion forces".

The battle involves both President Bush and his likely opponent, Bill Clinton. The President said he is pleased with the court's decision to uphold "reasonable restrictions on abortion", while Governor Clinton warned that a woman's right to an abortion was now "hanging by a thread". He argued that only a Democratic victory would preserve that right.

New rackets ease tennis players' agony

London, Tuesday 30
Tennis players are looking forward eagerly to the next generation of rackets to ease their aches and pains. Modern "wide-bodied" rackets, made out of metal or plastic, generate enormous power but they also generate great shock. Now, as the result of investigations into "tennis elbow", the new rackets will not be so wide and will have dampeners to absorb shock and control vibration. New stringing patterns have also been developed to improve comfort and control.

House of Lords welcomes Maggie

Westminster, Tuesday 30
Margaret Thatcher, the grocer's daughter who became Britain's first woman prime minister, and world renowned as "The Iron Lady", was today introduced to the House of Lords as Baroness Thatcher. Clad in scarlet and ermine robes, she was escorted by her sponsors, Lord Boyd-Carpenter and Lord Joseph, to swear loyalty to the House.

There can be no doubt, however, where she would rather be: in the Commons, ruling the affairs of Great Britain. She still simmers with rage at what she regards as the disloyalty of her colleagues who rebelled against her leadership. She will not be a complaisant Lady.

Baroness Thatcher of Kesteven.

Su	Mo	Tu	We	Th	Fr	Sa
			1	2	3	4
5	6	7	8	9	10	11
12	13	14	15	16	17	18
19	20	21	22	23	24	25
26	27	28	29	30	31	

Los Angeles, 1
Willie Williams replaces 14-year veteran Daryl Gates as Chief of Police of the controversial Los Angeles police force.

Vatican City, 1
The Vatican grants Caroline of Monaco an annulment of her first marriage.

London, 1
John Major agrees to match Paul McCartney's $7 million to set up a performing arts school in Liverpool modeled on the television show, *Fame*.

France, 1
France is chosen to organize the World Cup in soccer in 1998.

Bonn, 1
Germany pulls out of the $40-billion European Fighter Aircraft (EFA) project, saying its budget is strained by the need to rebuild East Germany's economy (→ Aug 4).

California, 1
California begins paying its bills with IOUs instead of regular checks. Running on no budget and an $11-billion deficit, it is "out of cash".

Northern Ireland, 2
Police find the mutilated bodies of three men that the IRA tortured and killed for being informers.

U.S., 2
The administration reports that last month's unemployment rate of 7.8% was the highest in eight years.

Virginia, 3
Senator Edward Kennedy, aged 60, marries Victoria Reggie, a Washington, D.C. lawyer.

Moldova, 3
Moldovan President Mircea Snegur and Boris Yeltsin come to an agreement to end the bloody conflict between Russians and Moldovans.

San Sebastian, 4
The Tour de France begins with France's Dominique Arnould winning the first stage (→ 26).

DEATH

4. Astor Piazzolla, Argentinian composer (*March, 3, 1921) → .

U.N. forces control Sarajevo airport

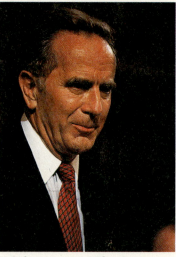
U.S. businessman Milan Panic.

Canadian U.N. troops open up the airport for emergency aid airlift.

Sarajevo, Thursday 2
Armored vehicles of a Canadian infantry battalion brushed aside a roadblock manned by drunken Serbs outside this besieged city today and then took up positions round the airport. It had taken this heavily armed U.N. force three days to cover 300 kilometers, and the men were thoroughly fed up when they were turned back at the final block by the belligerent Serbs.

Colonel Michael Jones, commander of the battalion, deployed sniper teams and ordered his armored vehicles, equipped with anti-tank missiles, to roll up to the Serb positions. He gave the Serbs half an hour to get off the road because he was going through whether they liked it or not. When he saw them calling for reinforcements instead of leaving, he cut the deadline to five minutes and then bulled his way through. There were no injuries, except to Serbian pride.

U.N. officials have now declared the airport ready to accept up to eight relief flights a day. Two landed this afternoon, one carrying French relief food and the other American-donated medicines. Both were rapidly unloaded and their cargoes hurried into the city. British and American aircraft will soon join the airlift. It remains a dangerous business, with Serbs on one side of the airport and Muslims on the other constantly engaging in firefights across the runway. (→ 14)

Over 30 tons were flown in yesterday.

July 4. Astor Piazzolla, world-famous composer of tangos, dies in Buenos Aires.

Commission in favor of renewed whaling

Glasgow, Friday 3
Commercial whaling seems likely to be resumed following a decision by the International Whaling Commission to set up a computer program enabling it to establish quotas of whales to be killed. It will come into operation next year.

Norway is not waiting. Its commissioner, Jan Arvesen, said his country had lost patience and intended to kill an unspecified number of minke whales in the northeast Atlantic. The Japanese delegate, Kazuo Shima, warned that if his country's fishermen were not allowed to hunt minke in the Antarctic their anger might force Japan to leave the I.W.C.

Greenpeace calls move a tragedy.

Cheap air fares please travelers, ruin tour firms

London, Wednesday 1

The recession has brought amazing bargains for Britain's holiday-makers but threatens many of the tour operators with bankruptcy. The problem can be traced back to the collapse of Intasun last year. Other operators, gambling that there would be a rush to get abroad to the sea and sun and cheap drink once the election was over, took up Intasun's holidays and added more of their own.

The boom never materialized. People refused to spend money, preferring to stay at home and pay off their debts. The result has been millions of unsold holidays, and the tour companies have been slashing prices, desperate to sell off seats on chartered aircraft. Just how desperate they are may be judged

from an offer by Thomson Holidays, Britain's largest operator, for seats-only deals on flights to five Mediterranean destinations for £49 return. The real size of these discounts may be judged from the fact that a one-way ticket on the London-Manchester shuttle costs £84, and it flies less than a tenth of the distance of a London-Malaga return.

It is hoped that the situation will ease with the start of the school holidays next month, and bookings for August are reported to be better. It is going to be a near-run thing for tour operators. Some may not be able to sustain the price-cutting and will go to the wall. In the meantime, if holiday-makers care to open their wallets just a fraction, the world is theirs.

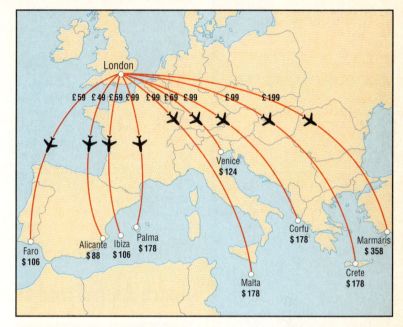

Fare war knocks out Braniff for third time

Dallas, Friday 3

The sad saga of the once-mighty Braniff airlines continued today when it ceased operations for the third time in its 64-year history. Its failure this time was blamed on a price war, begun in April by American Airlines and matched by other carriers. Some ticket prices have been slashed in half and it is feared that other weak airlines will be driven out of business. A state-

ment from Braniff's headquarters at Dallas-Fort Worth International Airport said that the airline was "considering litigation over the pricing practices that led to this unfortunate occurrence." Braniff's misfortune goes much further back, however. In the early 80s, when deregulation spurred intense fare competition, the company went bankrupt, owing a billion dollars. Since then, it has staggered along.

Belgium to drop compulsory military duty

Brussels, Friday 3

If you need further proof of the easing of military tension in Europe following the collapse of Communism in the East, look no further than Belgium. This small, low-lying country, sandwiched between France, Germany and the Netherlands, was a battlefield in both World Wars, as German troops marched over it on their way to invade France. But today Defense

Minister Leo Delcroix announced that the draft will end in 1994, halving Belgium's 86,000-strong armed forces.

Belgium will continue to honor its commitment to NATO and will continue to provide peace-keeping troops for the United Nations. But the days of conscription are numbered, and the armed forces will now be run as a voluntary, professional organization.

Romance, fantasy and suspense mark U.S. summer releases

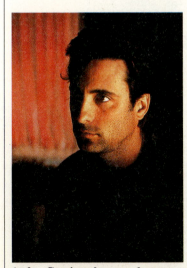

Andy Garcia plays a burnt-out cop in "Jennifer Eight".

Kim Basinger is the seductress Holli Would in Gabriel Byrne's animated fantasy adventure, "Cool World", where dreams become reality.

Eddie Murphy falls in love with his lovely boss in "Boomerang".

July

1992

Su	Mo	Tu	We	Th	Fr	Sa
			1	2	3	4
5	6	7	8	9	10	11
12	13	14	15	16	17	18
19	20	21	22	23	24	25
26	27	28	29	30	31,	

France, 5
Nigel Mansell, in his sixth victory this season, wins the French Grand Prix (→ Aug 16).

Moscow, 5
The International Monetary Fund guarantees Russia a $1-billion loan.

New York, 6
The Kirov Opera, performing for the first time in the U.S., opens at the Metropolitan.

London, 7
Sogo, the first Japanese department store in London, opens in Piccadilly.

Manchester, 7
Cricket: At Old Trafford, England and Pakistan draw in the Third Test.

U.S., 8
An investigator in the U.S. Navy Tailhook affair is removed from the case after allegations that he sexually harassed one of the victims during the investigation.

London, 8
South African cricket tour rebels have Test ban lifted because of changing political situation in South Africa.

France, 9
Organizers of the 1992 Winter Olympics announce the Albertville games posted a loss of $56 million.

Warsaw, 10
Hanna Suchocka, of the Democratic Union Party, is approved as Poland's first woman prime minister.

New York, 10
A jury finds Pam Am guilty of "willful misconduct" in the 1988 terrorist bombing over Lockerbie, Scotland (→ 23).

Mexico City, 10
For the first time in 33 years, Cuba approves constitutional changes to allow freedom of worship.

Washington, D.C, 10
Democratic presidential hopeful Bill Clinton announces his choice for running mate: Senator Al Gore from Tennessee (→ 13).

Miami, 10
General Manuel Antonio Noriega of Panama is sentenced to 40 years in prison for drug trafficking.

France's first lady escapes ambush in Iraq

Kurdistan, Monday 6
Danielle Mitterrand narrowly escaped death when bombs placed in a car were detonated as her motorcade passed by. The petite wife of French President François Mitterrand, who is also president of the humanitarian action group France-Libertés, was in Iraqi Kurdistan on a four-day visit to evaluate humanitarian need, accompanied by Bernard Kouchner, French minister for health and humanitarian action. Three Kurdish guerrillas guarding the motorcade were killed, and 19 other people were injured. Some Iraqi Kurds have placed responsibility for the attack on Saddam Hussein's Baghdad regime.

Danielle Mitterrand in Kurdistan.

Branson is wealthy, says 'Forbes'

New York, Tuesday 7
Richard Branson, owner of Virgin Atlantic Airways, has joined the ranks of the seriously rich, according to the annual list of dollar billionaires compiled by *Forbes* magazine. The British businessman, who made the first crossing of the Atlantic in a hot-air balloon and crossed it in record time in a high-powered yacht, is said by *Forbes* to be worth $1.2 billion after selling his Virgin record label – the basis of his fortune – to Thorn EMI. He shares his place at the lower end of the list with Pablo Escobar, head of the Medellin cocaine cartel.

Andre Agassi and Steffi Graf are Wimbledon singles champions

First American to win since 1984.

Wimbledon, Sunday 5
Andre Agassi, the 22-year-old American ace, dispelled all doubts about his big-match temperament today when he beat the Croat, Goran Ivanisevic 6-7 (8-10), 6-4, 6-4, 1-6, 6-4 to win the Wimbledon men's title. He won from the baseline with a string of fine passing shots to defeat the fierce serves of Ivanisevic.

The women's title was won by Steffi Graf for the fourth time in five years. The powerful German overwhelmed Monica Seles, 6-2, 6-1. Seles might have been disturbed by all the fuss made about the loud grunt she often makes when she hits the ball. She remained silent - and lost.

Graf crushes Seles 6-2, 6-1.

French army sends in tanks to rescue blocked holidaymakers

Paris, Monday 6
As the holiday season gets underway, France's truckers are up to their old tricks, blocking the roads and bringing misery and frustration to millions – because they don't like the new driving license. For just under a week, drivers who drive dangerously have stood to have points deducted from their licenses. The truckers say this isn't fair, because they drive more and therefore stand a greater chance of losing their licenses and their livelihoods. To put an end to the chaos, the French government today called in the army to clear roads.

Truckers cause chaos by demonstrating against new license-points system.

At G7 summit, Boris Yeltsin succeeds where Gorbachev failed

Munich, Wednesday 8
The Group of Seven industrial nations gave their backing today to Boris Yeltsin's reform program for Russia, a program which, he said, would be irreversible by the time his presidency ends in 1994. The leaders took care that he did not leave the "G7 plus 1" meeting empty-handed - as Mikhail Gorbachev did last year - by unlocking a billion-dollar credit from the IMF and taking a generous attitude to the deferment of the former Soviet Union's debt repayments. Chancellor Kohl, host to the meeting, spoke of a "comprehensive and lasting relationship between the G7 nations and Russia".

Group of Seven Western leaders rally behind the president of Russia.

Saddam Hussein again defies U.N.

Baghdad, Tuesday 7
Saddam Hussein continued to defy the U.N. today by refusing to allow a team of chemical-weapons experts to search the Ministry of Agriculture, which is believed to hold details of Iraq's chemical weapons program. Samir Nima, an Iraqi representative at the U.N., said there was nothing in the building and that it was a "symbol of sovereignty". But the U.N. insisted the Iraqi refusal was "unacceptable". Meanwhile the team sits outside the ministry in no doubt that the papers it seeks are being smuggled out of the back door (→21).

New Austrian leader ends Waldheim era

Vienna, Wednesday 8
Kurt Waldheim, the Austrian president who was an officer in Hitler's army, has resigned at the end of his seven-year term of office. His successor, 59-year-old diplomat Thomas Klestil, said today that Austria must deal "honestly and candidly" with its checkered history. Waldheim's presidency has not been a happy one for Austria: he was barred from the U.S. and snubbed by most Western leaders after an historical commission found that he had covered up his past as a member of a German army unit which deported Jews and others to death camps. It was never proved, however, that he had taken part in war crimes.

Thomas Klestil, elected May 24.

'Columbia' lands after its longest mission

Cape Canaveral, Thursday 9
After circling the earth 221 times, the space shuttle *Columbia* touched down at Kennedy Space Center early this morning. The seven astronauts on board had completed NASA's longest-ever shuttle mission, travelling 5.76 million miles in 14 days. NASA officials can now feel confident that the shuttle program is truly back on course after the *Challenger* disaster eight years ago. Kennedy Space Center director Robert Crippen hailed the "completion of a great mission", adding that "the vehicle has come back looking outstanding". While the Russian space program is floored by economic problems, it's full speed ahead for NASA.

Shuttle crew orbited for two weeks.

In "Mann and Machine", Yancy Butler plays a cop of the future.

Hong Kong's last governor moves in

Hong Kong, Thursday 9
Chris Patten, Hong Kong's new governor, issued a manifesto today as he took office. He wants this British colony, due to be handed back to China at the end of his tenure in 1997, to have a more accessible and democratic government. He then went walkabout in the crowded heart of his domain. Surrounded by a scrum of newsmen and guards, the grinning governor squeezed his way through the narrow streets of the Mong Kok red-light district.

Millions of square feet of office space in central London are on offer for sale or rent, but there are no takers despite plunging prices.

July

1992

Su	Mo	Tu	We	Th	Fr	Sa
			1	2	3	4
5	6	7	8	9	10	11
12	13	14	15	16	17	18
19	20	21	22	23	24	25
26	27	28	29	30	31	

New York, 13
Democrat Jerry Brown, former governor of California, refuses to support Bill Clinton (→ 16).

Sarajevo, 14
Bosnian Serbs bomb the headquarters of the U.N. forces (→ 17).

London, 14
British Airways announces plans to buy a major stake in USAir (→ 21).

Pacific, 14
A Qantas Boeing 747 en route to Los Angeles is forced to change course after the U.S. Navy uses the plane as a mock target in a military operation.

Rome, 15
Pope John Paul II undergoes an operation during which a benign tumor is removed from his intestine.

London, 15
Members of the House of Commons give themselves a 40% raise on their expense accounts.

U.S., 15
The Securities and Exchange Commission will now require more information about parent companies and affiliates from broker-dealers with more than $20 million in capital.

Algeria, 15
Abbasi Madani and Ali Belhadj, president and vice-president of the Islamic Salvation Front, are sentenced to 12 years in prison (→ Aug 26).

Jerusalem, 16
To slow down Jewish settlement in the Occupied Territories, the government suspends subsidized housing projects (→ Aug 11).

U.S., 16
American Airlines posts a record loss of $166 million for the second quarter.

India, 16
Shankar Dayal Sharma, aged 74, is appointed the new head of state.

London, 17
A 14-day cease-fire in Bosnia is agreed to by Serbs, Croats and Muslims (→ 25).

Barcelona, 17
Black-market tickets for the Olympics are being sold for up to $1,500.

Rabin proposes peace to Arab neighbors

Jerusalem, Monday 13
Yitzhak Rabin, Israel's new prime minister, presented his government to the Knesset for approval today and, pledging not to waste "precious time", offered to visit the Arab capitals "for the purpose of talking peace". The need for bold, swift strides towards peace was at the heart of Rabin's address.

The Israeli leader urged the Palestinians to listen to him: "We offer you the fairest and most viable proposal from our standpoint: autonomy, with all its advantages and limitations. You will not get everything you want, neither will we. Don't lose this opportunity that may never return" (→ 21).

Israel's premier seeks peace.

Scotsman John Smith takes over Labour

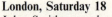

London, Saturday 18
John Smith scored a decisive victory over his only challenger, Bryan Gould, today to become the 14th leader of the Labour Party. Smith won 91% of the votes. Margaret Beckett was elected deputy leader. Smith, former "Shadow" Chancellor, faces a formidable task to revive the party after the election defeat and the resignation of Neil Kinnock. He told the election conference that he intended to democratize the opposition party and win back the support of women: "The party of change must be ready to change itself."

Smith, successor to Neil Kinnock.

Vaclav Havel quits as federation splits

Prague, Friday 17
The curtain has fallen for Vaclav Havel. The playwright-turned-president has resigned. The decision was announced just after a proclamation of Slovak sovereignty. This proclamation, approved by a large majority in the Slovak parliament, is a step toward independence for Slovakia and a "velvet divorce" by the two members of the Czech and Slovak Federal Republic. Slovak members of the federal parliament had blocked Havel's re-election as president, but his term was not to expire until October. He explained his resignation by saying that he did not want to hinder the "historic evolution" of the country and that he "could no longer fulfill, according to my convictions and my conscience, the obligations" placed on him as federal president (→ Nov 25).

Czechoslovakia is disintegrating.

July 17. More than 2,000 old vessels from all over the world came together in Brittany for the Brest 92 show.

Bill Clinton nominated by Democratic Convention

New York, Thursday 16
The Democratic Convention came to a close tonight with Bill Clinton's speech in which he accepted his party's nomination for the presidency of the United States. In fact, Clinton was already the accepted candidate, chosen in the primary elections, and had picked Al Gore, a Tennessee senator, as his running mate last week. The convention was an opportunity for Clinton to rally his party and to define the platform on which he and Gore will run. Clinton and Gore, both founding members of the centrist, pro-business Democratic Leadership Council, are positioning themselves and their party more to the political right than is traditional for Democrats. But they have not completely abandoned the liberal policies of the past. While the platform echoes traditional Republican themes, calling for "greater individual responsibility", referring to business as a "noble endeavor" and promising tax cuts for the middle class, also prominent are gay rights and abortion rights (→ Aug 13).

Delegates in New York have launched the Clinton-Gore ticket on the long, hard road to the White House.

Independent Ross Perot abandons drive for the White House

Dallas, Thursday 16
Ross Perot has announced that he is leaving the race for the White House. George Bush and Bill Clinton had kind words for the Perot movement and sought to attract his supporters. The supporters themselves were not quite so happy to hear the news, expressing anger and bitterness over the decision. The "temperamental tycoon", as Vice President Dan Quayle has called him, said he was dropping out because the Democratic Party had "revitalized" itself, and he no long-er felt he had a chance of winning. Recent polls show a significant lead for Clinton. Two weeks ago Perot had a small lead over the other two candidates. The diminutive Texas billionaire said that a close three-way race could throw the election into the House of Representatives, and that he did not want to "disrupt" the process in this way. Perot could, in fact, remain a choice for voters in the 24 states where he has qualified: most states require a written request to take his name off the ballot (→ Sept 18).

Convention fashions...

July
1992

Su	Mo	Tu	We	Th	Fr	Sa
			1	2	3	4
5	6	7	8	9	10	11
12	13	14	15	16	17	18
19	20	21	22	23	24	25
26	27	28	29	30	31	

Vietnam, 19
The Communist Party wins the general election.

Bristol, 19
In Hartcliff, 50% unemployment fuels intense anger on the third day of violent riots.

Scotland, 19
Britain's Nick Faldo wins his third U.K. Golf Open.

Amsterdam, 20
The World Health Organization reports that women are now infected with AIDS as often as men.

London, 20
Kevin Maxwell is ordered to pay $800 million in fines.

Washington, D.C., 20
An experimental tilt-rotor Osprey V-22 aircraft crashes, killing all seven people aboard.

Cairo, 21
For the first time in 15 years, Egyptian President Mubarak accepts Israeli Prime Minister Rabin's invitation to visit Israel.

U.N., 21
The U.S., U.K. and France warn Iraq of serious consequences if U.N. weapons inspectors are hindered. Iraq is refusing to allow U.N. inspectors into a building suspected of holding missile documentation (→Aug 27).

U.S., 22
The administration announces a second "green card" lottery. It will enable 40,000 foreigners to obtain permanent U.S. residency.

New York, 23
Pan Am is ordered to pay $9.25 million to the family of a passenger killed in the 1988 Lockerbie bombing.

U.K., 23
Following riots in Bristol and Carlisle, 62 youths are arrested during violence in Blackburn, Burnley and Huddersfield.

Sicily, 24
Ten thousand people attend the funeral of anti-Mafia judge Paolo Borsellino (→27).

DEATH

19. Victor Louis, Soviet journalist (*Feb. 5, 1928).

Sicilian killers murder second anti-Mafia judge in two months

Palermo, Sunday 19
Two months after the assassination of Judge Giovanni Falcone, the Mafia has struck again. Falcone's friend and designated successor, Judge Paolo Borsellino, was at the door of his mother's apartment house when a car bomb was detonated by remote control, killing him and five bodyguards. Fifth-floor windows were shattered and 200 meters (650 feet) of the suburban street was destroyed. The judge was to have headed an anti-Mafia agency composed of members of Italy's three police forces. Italian Mafia experts have suggested the killing was meant to prevent the establishment of this agency (→24).

The Cosa Nostra has again proved its power in downtown Palermo.

British Airways announces USAir takeover

USAir operates a fleet of more than 400 aircraft, including the Fokker 100.

London, Tuesday 21
Lord King, chairman of British Airways, has brought off a deal with the USAir group by which BA will inject a much-needed $750 million into the American company in return for a 44% stake and four seats on the board. More important, from Lord King's point of view, it will give BA a gateway into USAir's short-haul routes.

Announcing the deal today, the delighted Lord King said: "Our opportunity here is traffic. This gives us more people to fly, and that is how we earn our living." He said that USAir, the fourth-largest U.S. carrier, was "an ideal partner" because its catchment area covered a large portion of the United States,

while BA drew its passengers mainly from "one little island". For USAir the alliance will provide cash to offset its $2-billion-dollar debts and the international reach which will enable it to compete with its bigger American rivals. USAir's vice president, Tom Lagow, said the deal will "create a fourth major competitor in the U.S. with a global scope."

Company officials pointed out today that USAir and BA carried a combined total of nearly 80 million passengers last year and claimed they would form the world's biggest airline alliance. The initial reaction from the alliance's rivals was to demand greater access to the British market for U.S. carriers.

Mystery killer virus scares AIDS experts

Amsterdam, Thursday 23
Health officials at the international AIDS conference today responded to reports of AIDS-like illnesses in patients that have tested negative for HIV, the virus believed to be the cause of AIDS. Is there another, mystery, virus? Officials said that they believed this fear to be unwarranted. Nevertheless, James Curran of the U.S. Centers for Disease Control said that the study of such cases was "an extremely important priority", and Michael Mearson, head of the World Health Organization's AIDS program, said that a "worldwide follow-up" was needed.

Liz Taylor at the conference.

Luxury prison fails to keep drug lord in

Pablo Escobar's hilltop jail.

Medellin, Wednesday 22
Pablo Escobar, the most powerful of South American drug lords, has escaped from a ranch-style prison in the mountains just outside the city that is the headquarters of his drug cartel. Escobar surrendered in June 1991, after being promised that he would not be extradited to the United States. The government decided to transfer Escobar to a higher-security military prison because of reports that he was continuing to run his drug business from inside the jail. There was a shoot-out yesterday when guards attempted to move him, and two government officials were taken prisoner. Military reinforcements attacked this morning and retook the prison, but Escobar had slipped away during the fighting.

A bedroom fit for a prince.

Former U.S. Navy man is first to pedal across Atlantic Ocean

Plymouth, Friday 24
A Connecticut property agent has become the first person to pedal across the Atlantic. Dwight Collins, 34, arrived here today 41 days after setting out from St John's, Newfoundland. He has pedaled his 23-foot boat, *Tango*, 1,950 nautical miles through 40-knot gales, fogs and high seas. Collins, who is a former member of the U.S. Navy's elite Seal division, pedaled his two-blade propeller for up to 24 hours a day, listening to tapes and working out riddles to stave off boredom. At one point he was nearly run over by a ship. No doubt his wife Corinne, who greeted him at Plymouth Harbour, will give his tired legs a massage tonight.

Dwight Collins reaches Plymouth just 41 days after leaving Newfoundland.

Castro the odd man out at Madrid summit

Madrid, Friday 24
The Ibero-American summit was the occasion for Fidel Castro's first official visit to Western Europe since he came to power in Cuba in 1959. Cuba is the only one of the countries represented at the summit with a government that was not chosen in free elections. Addressing the leaders of Spain, Portugal and 15 Latin American states, Castro expressed a desire for Latin unity and cooperation, but used most of his speech to attack the United States. Felipe Gonzalez, the prime minister of Spain, condemned authoritarian regimes which imprison its citizens for political reasons, but did not mention Cuba by name.

It is the first official visit to Western Europe for Cuba's ageing leader.

Alpine iceman may be 5,300 years old

Remains found in September 1991.

Innsbruck, Friday 24
The Stone Age iceman found last September in the Alps near Italy's border with Austria could be 5,300 years old. The mummified corpse, the oldest ever discovered in Europe, is stored in conditions simulating the glacier in which he was found. Scientists have suggested the man might have been a shepherd, a hunter or even a shaman, as the markings on his body would suggest. The clothes he wore and the equipment he carried – a copper axe and a bow, quiver and arrows – is a treasure trove of clues about life in the Stone Age.

Great Britain calls for Yugoslav talks

London, Saturday 25
The British government announced today that it will call an international conference on Yugoslavia in order to seek an end to the war which is ravaging Bosnia-Herzegovina. The conference, to be held in the last half of August, will bring together representatives of the belligerent nations and of members of the European Community and the United Nations. In Bosnia the fighting continues, notably in Dobrinja, the suburb of Sarajevo which has been under relentless shelling by Serbian forces for the last three months (→ Aug 3).

July 23. French movie star Arletty dies at age 94.

Barcelona Summer Games open in blaze of glory

Barcelona, Saturday 25

An archer let fly a flaming arrow, lit from the torch that had been carried from the waterfront to the stadium on Montjuic, to kindle the Olympic flame and open the Summer Games. The ceremonies featured dancers and drum corps, flamenco and opera, characters in costumes that honored Spanish master painters and a Roman galley ship. The athlete's parade featured 10,000 competitors from 172 countries, including South Africans for the first time in 32 years, and Bosnians competing under their own flag. King Juan Carlos gave the inaugural speech before 70,000 spectators in the stadium and 3.5 billion television viewers (→ 27).

Opening ceremony organizers picked Hercules' voyage across the ocean as a symbol of epic achievement.

From opera to avant-garde theater, artists such as Placido Domingo, Montserrat Caballe and Flamenco queen Cristina Hoyos welcome the world.

Members of the U.S. Olympic team stride proudly into Montjuic Stadium.

Cheered by tens of thousands of spectators, Britain's athletes march by.

July
1992

Su	Mo	Tu	We	Th	Fr	Sa
			1	2	3	4
5	6	7	8	9	10	11
12	13	14	15	16	17	18
19	20	21	22	23	24	25
26	27	28	29	30	31	

Headingley, 26
Cricket: England beats Pakistan by six wickets in the Fourth Test.

Paris, 26
Spaniard Miguel Indurain wins his second Tour de France.

Iraq, 27
Oil experts assert that Iraq has almost restored its oil-refining capabilities.

Sicily, 27
Mafia violence continues as Giovanni Lizzio, anti-Mafia police inspector, is murdered.

Barcelona, 27
The U.S. brings in two more gold medals: Pablo Morales wins the 100-meter butterfly; Nicole Haislett wins the 200-meter freestyle (→ 31).

Afghanistan, 28
Women, even wearing veils, are no longer allowed to be viewed on television.

Washington, D.C., 28
The Bush administration announces it plans to sell aircraft, missiles and ammunition worth $1 billion to South Korea.

Spain, 28
Fidel Castro finishes his tour of Spain by visiting Galicia, where his father was born.

Vatican City, 29
Israel and the Vatican announce they are to negotiate the forging of bilateral diplomatic relations.

Berlin, 30
Former East German leader Erich Honecker is held on charges of manslaughter and corruption (→ Aug 15).

London, 30
The *Sun* newspaper is ordered to pay £25,000 to British comedian John Cleese for printing articles about his sex drive.

Barcelona, 31
Gold medals are won by Americans Mike Stulce in the shot-put and Summer Sanders in the 200-meter butterfly.

New York, 31
The pound is quoted at $1.92.

DEATH

31. Lord Cheshire, British war pilot (*Sept. 7, 1918).

British and American athletes begin to harvest gold medals

Barcelona, Friday 31
British and U.S. athletes had a successful first week. The "Dream Team", featuring Magic Johnson and Michael Jordan, humiliated the Angolan basketball team in their first game, winning 116-48. Nelson Diebel won the first of the U.S. swim team's 11 gold medals in the 100-meter backstroke. British cyclist Chris Boardman won the gold in the 4,000-meter race, riding a specially-built carbon-fiber-frame Lotus. But there was bad news as well for the British: Three athletes were sent home after tests revealed the presence of steroids in their blood (→ Aug 8).

China's 13-year-old wonder girl, Fu Mingxia, wins gold in platform diving.

Chris Boardman speeds to victory and gold atop his new hi-tech bicycle.

Swimmer Diebel celebrates victory.

All 291 people aboard stricken TWA Tristar escape inferno

Kennedy Airport, Friday 31
TWA Flight 843 to San Francisco began its take-off roll shortly after 5:30 p.m.

Seconds later, the 275 passengers and 16 crew aboard the Lockheed L1011 felt the aircraft lurch violently to one side, as dense smoke filled the cabin. The pilot was aborting take-off. With its rear engine ablaze, apparently because of a ruptured fuel line, the speeding jetliner crashed through a runway barrier and skidded to a stop. The flight attendants then went into action, leading the passengers to the two escape chutes behind the cockpit. In less than two minutes, all aboard the blazing Tristar were safely on the tarmac. The near-catastrophe left 67 people with minor injuries.

The flight crew's quick actions saved their passengers, but not the aircraft.

August

1992

Su	Mo	Tu	We	Th	Fr	Sa
						1
2	3	4	5	6	7	8
9	10	11	12	13	14	15
16	17	18	19	20	21	22
23	24	25	26	27	28	29
30	31					

New York, 2
Pitchers Tom Seaver, Rollie Fingers and Hal Newhouser are inducted into baseball's Hall of Fame.

Croatia, 2
The first presidential and legislative elections are organized since the country's independence.

Germany, 2
Police say neo-Nazi skinheads attacked foreigners residing in five eastern German towns, and in Nuremberg in western Germany, over the weekend (→ 29).

Moscow, 3
A Russian-Ukrainian accord is signed that will place the Black Sea Fleet under the joint command of the two states.

Paris, 3
France ratifies the nuclear non-proliferation treaty.

Bonn, 4
The Constitutional Court suspends a law liberalizing abortion.

Washington, D.C., 6
George Bush announces the establishment of diplomatic relations with Slovenia, Croatia, and Bosnia-Herzegovina and calls on the U.N. to use force against the Serbs.

L.A., 6
The four Los Angeles Police Department officers acquitted of the Rodney King beating, in 1991, are ordered to surrender today to face civil rights charges.

Haiti, 6
A wave of terrorist bomb and shooting attacks leaves 10 dead in three days.

Hollywood, 7
Actor Harold Russell sells Oscar he won in 1946 for *The Best Years of Our Lives* for $60,000.

Cape Canaveral, 8
The space shuttle *Atlantis* returns from its eight-day mission.

DEATHS

3. Wang Hongwen, Chinese political leader (*1934).

4. Sir Edward Chilton, British Air Marshal (*Nov. 1, 1906).

U.S. forces begin maneuvers in Kuwait

U.S. Marines deploy around Kuwait City, but this time it's a drill.

Kuwait, Monday 3
An advance guard of U.S. Marines landed here today to prepare for joint maneuvers in the desert with Kuwaiti forces. Some 5,000 American troops will take part in the exercises which will last two weeks. There can be little doubt that, while they will give the soldiers useful desert experience, the exercises are primarily designed to warn the increasingly belligerent Saddam Hussein not to do anything rash.

He has stepped up his war of words. On Sunday, the second anniversary of his invasion of Kuwait, Iraqi television once again laid claim to this oil-rich country. The program was entitled *Mirage and Reality*.

EFA too expensive

Madrid, Tuesday 4
Britain, Germany, Italy and Spain, the nations involved in the Eurofighter Aircraft project, agreed today on a plan to save the EFA. Bonn pulled out of the program last week, saying it was too expensive. A trimmed-down version of the fighter, costing $55-$70 million each instead of $100 million is now to be built.

August 1. Amy Kleinhaus, 24, is crowned Miss South Africa.

Concentration camp horror in Bosnia

Washington, D.C., Monday 3
The U.S. State Department has independent information confirming reports of torture and killings in Serb-run prison camps in Bosnia, a department spokesman said today. Respected news organizations have reported that the Serbian policy of "ethnic cleansing", removing members of other ethnic groups from Serbian-dominated areas, has led to the establishment of Nazi-style concentration camps where detainees are starved, tortured and shot. The spokesman added that Washington has also had reports of Bosnian and Croatian detention centers, but said there was no evidence of abuse in those camps. Serbian officials have refused requests by the International Red Cross to inspect the camps. He expressed opposition to "the detention of innocent people" and to "the forcible expulsion of people from their homes", but refused to say whether the U.S. was prepared to intervene militarily (→ 15).

Atlantis aborts tethered satellite launch

Earth orbit, Wednesday 5
Astronauts aboard the space shuttle *Atlantis* retrieved a satellite that was connected to the shuttle by a wire-and-fiber tether 20 kilometers (12.4 miles) long. The cord, attached to a tower in the shuttle's cargo bay, had developed a snag and the satellite was stuck 230 meters (750 feet) above the bay. The crew was unable to extend the cord to its full length or reel it in. At first they tried popping the clutch of the motor that guides the tether, but the cord did not budge. The astronauts, using controls inside *Atlantis*, then dipped and raised the tower, pulling out the snag. The satellite was reeled back in. The Italian space agency, owner of the satellite, and NASA have spent $379 million on the system.

August 7. At 10:20 p.m. New York time, the majestic cruise liner QE2 runs aground off Cuttyhunk Island, Mass., and passengers are evacuated.

ANC general strike hits South Africa

Johannesburg, Tuesday 4

A two-day general strike called by the African National Congress ended today. The nationwide strike was part of its "mass action" campaign to pressure the South African government to agree to ANC demands for resuming the constitutional negotiations which it had broken off in June. The ANC estimated that 4 million people stayed away from work, but estimates by business and government leaders put the number at half that. There have been 40 to 50 deaths by violence since Sunday, at least 10 of which were strike-related.

Mozambique foes sign peace deal

Rome, Friday 7

An agreement to end the civil war in Mozambique, which has lasted for 17 years and cost a million lives by bullet and starvation, was signed here today by President Joaquim Chissano and Afonso Dhlakama, leader of the Renamo rebels.

The war, which has been fought with great brutality, broke out after Mozambique received its independence from Portugal in 1975. Apart from the villagers who died, millions have been made homeless. The breakthrough in the peace talks was welcomed by Italy's Foreign Minister, Emilio Colombo, who said: "From far-off Africa a message of peace meant also for Europe has arrived" (→ Oct 4).

Ex-U.S.S.R. still Olympic superpower

Magic Johnson, Michael Jordan and their fellow U.S. Dream Team players have fulfilled their promises.

Barcelona, Saturday 8

The Unified Team, athletes representing the countries that made up the now-disintegrated Soviet Union, enters the final weekend of the 25th Olympic Games leading at the medal table, with 42 gold medals, 35 silver and 23 bronze, well clear of the United States, which has 31 golds.

They are making a glorious farewell, for when these Games end so will the Unified Team. The next time its members compete they will be wearing the colors of their own states. Their performance has been surprising given the political turmoil in which they had to train.

There would seem, however, to be good economic rather than nationalistic reasons for them to perform well: a gold medal could be a passport to lucrative contracts and the good life in the West. Vitaly Scherbo, who has won six gym-

Sally Gunnell is first British woman to win an Olympic track event since '64.

nastic golds, explained: "We all knew the higher we ranked, the higher the earnings might be."

Wvgeni Sadovyi, who won three swimming golds, believes that the £3,000 being offered to each gold medalist in the team will be the last state help the Olympic athletes can expect: "Now everything has to be done by your own efforts."

Carl Lewis takes the 4x100-meter relay and beats the world record.

Britain's Linford Christie grabs the gold in the historic 100-meter race.

August

1992

Su	Mo	Tu	We	Th	Fr	Sa
						1
2	3	4	5	6	7	8
9	10	11	12	13	14	15
16	17	18	19	20	21	22
23	24	25	26	27	28	29
30	31					

Montreal, 9
Rioting, after a Guns N' Roses concert is cut short, leaves 13 wounded.

U.K., 9
The Italian yacht *Destriero* wins the Virgin Atlantic Challenge Trophy by crossing the Atlantic in 58 hours, 34 minutes and 4 seconds.

C.I.S., 9
Armenia asks for Russian aid to help defend itself from Azerbaidjan's "aggression".

Kabul, 9
Thousands of Afghans flee after the government fails to stop combat between guerrilla factions.

Brazil, 10
President Collor is accused of making $270 million in illegal profits (→ Sept 29).

C.I.S., 10
The Soyuz space vehicle lands after 15-day mission.

Minnesota, 11
The biggest mall in America opens in Bloomington. It cost $625 million to build and it has more than 300 stores covering 4.2 million square feet.

U.S., 11
Fifteen central banks worldwide intervene to support the falling dollar (→ 21).

London, 11
De Beers, the diamond monopoly, announces a strong fall in the market and significant profit loss.

Sarajevo, 12
U.N. troops evacuate more than 300 women and children.

Berlin, 15
A lawyer for the former East German leader Erich Honecker declares that his client suffers from liver cancer.

DEATHS

9. Lord Devlin, former British High Court judge (*Nov. 25, 1905).

14. John J. Sirica, American judge, made famous by the Watergate hearings (*March 19, 1904).

14. Tony Williams, American singer with the Platters group (*April 15, 1928).

Goodbye Barcelona, see you in Atlanta in 1996

Pakistan XI wins Fifth Test and series

The Oval, Sunday 9
Pakistan thrashed England by ten wickets here today to win the Test series by two matches to one with two drawn. Their victory was won by the devastating ability of their fast bowlers, Wasim Akram and Waqar Younis, to make the ball swing. The English batsmen could not cope with them, and the English bowlers could not match them.

However, while the triumphant Pakistanis, who won the World Cup earlier this year, rejoice in the title of the "best cricketing team in the world", controversy has arisen over accusations that they tamper with the ball to make it swing. England's captain, Graham Gooch, would make no excuses for his defeat. He insisted: "They were too good for us."

England batsman David Gower tries to score past Mushtaq Ahmed.

World's wealthiest trade bloc born

Washington, D.C., Wednesday 12
Ending months of negotiations, the United States, Canada and Mexico today concluded an historic pact aimed at creating the world's largest and wealthiest trading bloc. President Bush said the accord, known as the North American Free Trade Agreement, or NAFTA, is "the beginning of a new era" for economic cooperation between the three nations.

The agreement, also welcomed by Canadian and Mexican leaders, will span a zone stretching from the Yukon to the Yucatan, totaling 360 million people and a $6-trillion economy. The three nations have agreed to do away with barriers to the movement of money, goods and services over the next 15 years. The NAFTA pact must, however, be approved by the legislatures of the three states. The U.S. Congress will vote on it next year. Several leading Democrats and labor unions have already voiced strong opposition, saying the pact will mean thousands of lost jobs in the U.S.

Bush backs Rabin with $10-billion loan

Kennebunkport, Tuesday 11
U.S. President George Bush and Israeli Prime Minister Yitzhak Rabin appeared together before Bush's vacation home in Maine to announce a U.S. repayment guarantee on $10 billion in loans for Israel. Rabin promised to restrict Israeli settlements in occupied Arab lands to those important for Israel's security, prohibiting all "political" settlements. The press conference was interrupted by a question from a CNN journalist about an allegation that Bush had had an extramarital affair in 1984. Bush was visibly angry and said, "I'm not going to take any sleazy questions like that from CNN." He denied the charge.

Two leaders on the road to peace.

Death camps stun world

In Bosnia's camps, some victims of Serbian "ethnic cleansing" policy.

Ailing GOP campaign calls Baker for help

Washington, Thursday 13
Secretary of State James Baker has been appointed White House chief of staff in an attempt to put life into President Bush's lackluster election campaign. As senior aide to the president, his task will be to design a broad new agenda that will "integrate" domestic and foreign policies. Baker, 62, is a Houston lawyer who has been a friend of Bush for 35 years. He is credited with masterminding the president's successful campaign in 1988, but he has much to do to make inroads into Bill Clinton's 25-point lead in the polls (→ 20).

Foreign policy boss to the rescue.

Zagreb, Saturday 15
The appalling images of emaciated, cowed prisoners held in Serbian prison camps have raised the specter of Nazi death camps and shocked the world. Stories of brutality, murder and rape have been emerging for weeks, but now they have been confirmed by television pictures seen around the world.

One Muslim told investigators how he had been held for 15 days and had his hands bound with wire: "One day a drunk guard tried to throw a hand grenade at us but he was restrained by the others. He started calling for a Muslim prisoner he had been to school with because he wanted to kill him. Then he just shot a man in the back of the neck as he ate."

A woman who had been in another detention centre described how she and her husband were beaten by young Serbian guards: "He was a teacher and many of them had been his pupils. Some of them had got bad marks so they made him wear a woman's wig. They beat him every day." She had been exchanged for a Serbian officer. She was unaware of her husband's fate.

Others told of prisoners being machine-gunned when they rioted after being deprived of water at the notorious Prijedor camp. One man, made to carry out the dead, counted 160 bullet-ridden corpses.

These stories are supported by a Red Cross report which tells of "innocent civilians being arrested and subjected to inhumane treatment as part of a policy of forced population transfers carried out on a massive scale and marked by the systematic use of brutality" (→ 18).

Industrial pollution threatens Lake Baikal

Siberia, Saturday 15
A group of students and scientists sent by the Ushuaia foundation, a French environmentalist group, to study the Siberian Lake Baikal has finished its mission. This natural wonder, whose banks and waters are home to unique flora and fauna, has always intrigued scientists. The world's largest fresh-water reservoir, and deepest lake at 5,369 feet (1,637 meters), is the object of an ecological controversy. Is pollution from the paper-pulp factory on its bank killing the lake? Russian scientists do not agree, neither do they have viable figures on pollution levels. Assessments range from reassuring to predicting catastrophe.

Ecological disaster on a huge scale.

A dramatic scene that brings back tragic memories of World War II.

1992 Barcelona

Men's Athletics

100 m
1. Christie GBR 9.96
2. Fredericks NAM 10.02
3. Mitchell USA 10.04

200 m
1. Marsh USA 20.01
2. Fredericks NAM 20.13
3. Bates USA 20.38

400 m
1. Watts USA 43.50
2. Lewis USA 44.21
3. Kitur KEN 44.24

800 m
1. Tanui KEN 1:43.66
2. Kiprotich KEN 1:43.70
3. Gray USA 1:43.97

1 500 m
1. Cacho Ruiz SPA 3:40.12
2. El Basir MOR 3:40.62
3. Sulaiman QAT 3:40.69

5 000 m
1. Baumann GER 13:12.52
2. Bitok KEN 13:12.71
3. Bayisa ETH 13:13.03

10 000 m
1. Skah MOR 27:46.70
2. Chelimo KEN 27:47.72
3. Abebe ETH 28:00.07

110 m Hurdles
1. McKoy CAN 13.12
2. Dees USA 13.24
3. Pierce USA 13.26

400 m Hurdles
1. Young USA 46.78
2. Graham JAM 47.66
3. Akabusi GBR 47.82

3 000 m Steeple
1. Birir KEN 8:08.84
2. Sang KEN 8:09.55
3. Mutwol KEN 8:10.74

High Jump
1. Sotomayor CUB 2.34
2. Sjoeberg SWE 2.34
3. Partyka POL 2.34
Forsythe AUS 2.34
Conway USA 2.34

Long Jump
1. Lewis USA 8.67
2. Powell USA 8.64
3. Greene USA 8.34

Triple Jump
1. Conley USA 18.17
2. Simpkins USA 17.60
3. Rutherford BAH 17.36

Pole Vault
1. Tarassov CIS 5.80
2. Trandenkov CIS 5.80
3. Garcia Chico SPA 5.75

Shot Put
1. Stulce USA 21.70
2. Doehring USA 20.96
3. Lykho CIS 20.94

Hammer
1. Abduvaliev CIS 82.54
2. Astapkovitch CIS 81.96
3. Nikuline CIS 81.38

Discus Throw
1. Hubertas LIT 65.12
2. Schult GER 65.94
3. Moya Sandoval CUB 64.12

Javelin
1. Zelezny CZS 89.66
2. Raty FIN 86.60
3. Backley GBR 83.38

Decathlon
1. Zmelik CZS 8 611 pts
2. Penalver SPA 8 412 pts
3. Johnson USA 8 309 pts

Marathon
1. Hwang Young-cho KOR 2 h 13:23
2. Morishita JAP 2 h 13:45
3. Freigang GER 2 h 14:00

4 x 100 m Relay
1. USA 37.40 (Marsh, Burrell, Mitchell, Lewis)
2. NGA 37.98 (Kayode, Imoh, Adeniken, Ezinwa)
3. CUB 38 (Simon Gomez, Lamela Loaces, Isasi Gonzalez, Aguilera Ruiz)

4 x 400 m Relay
1. USA 2:55.74 (Valmon, Watts, Johnson, Lewis)
2. CUB 2:59.51 (Martinez Despaigne, Herrera Ortiz, Tellez, Hernandez Prendez)
3. GBR 2:59.73 (Black, Grindley, Akabusi, Regis)

20 km Walk
1. Plaza Montero SPA 1 h 21:45
2. Leblanc CAN 1 h 22:05
3. De Benedictis ITA 1 h 23:11

Women's Athletics

100 m
1. Devers USA 10.82
2. Cuthbert JAM 10.83
3. Privalova CIS 10.84

200 m
1. Torrence USA 21.81
2. Cuthbert JAM 22.02
3. Ottey JAM 22.09

400 m
1. Pérec FRA 48.83
2. Bryzgina CIS 49.05
3. Restrepo Gaviria COL 49.64

800 m
1. Van Langen NET 1:55.54
2. Nurutdinova CIS 1:55.99
3. Quirot Moret CUB 1:56.80

1 500 m
1. Boulmerka ALG 3:55.30
2. Rogacheva CIS 3:56.91
3. Q. Yunxia CHN 3:57.08

3 000 m
1. Romanova CIS 8:46.04
2. Dorovskikh CIS 8:46.85
3. Chalmers CAN 8:47.22

10 000 m
1. Tulu ETH 31:6.02
2. Meyer SAF 31:11.75
3. Jennings USA 31:19.89

100 m Hurdles
1. Patoulidou GRE 12.64
2. Martin USA 12.69
3. Donkova BUL 12.70

400 m Hurdles
1. Gunnell GBR 53.23
2. Farmer-Patrick USA 53.69
3. Vickers USA 54.31

High Jump
1. Henkel GER 2.02
2. Astafei ROM 2.00
3. Quintero CUB 1.97

Long Jump
1. Drechsler GER 7.14
2. Kravets CIS 7.12
3. Joyner-Kersee USA 7.70

Shot Put
1. Kriveleva CIS 21.06
2. Huang CHN 20.47
3. Neimke GER 19.78

Discus Throw
1. Marten CUB 70.06
2. Khristova BUL 67.78
3. Costian AUS 66.24

Javelin
1. Renk GER 68.34
2. Shikolenko CIS 68.26
3. Forkel GER 66.86

Heptathlon
1. Joyner-Kersee USA 7 044 pts
2. Belova CIS 6 845 pts
3. Braun GBR 6 649 pts

Marathon
1. Yegorova CIS 2 h 32:41
2. Arimori JAP 2 h 32:49
3. Moller NZE 2 h 33:59

4 x 100 m Relay
1. USA 42.11 (Ashford, Jones, Guidry, Torrence)
2. CIS 42.16 (Bogoslovskaya, Malchugina, Trandenkova, Privalova)
3. NGA 42.81 (Utondu, Idehen, Opara Thompson, Onyali)

4 x 400 m Relay
1. CIS 3:20.20 (Ruzina, Dzhigalova, Nazarova, Bryzgina)
2. USA 3:20.92 (Kaiser, Torrence, Miles, Stevens)
3. GBR 3:24.23 (Smith, Douglas, Stoute, Gunnell)

10 km Walk
1. Chen CHN 44.32
2. Nikolaeva CIS 44.33
3. Li CHN 44.41

Linford Christie of Britain.

Men's Rowing

Sculls
1. Lange GER 6:51.40
2. Chalupa CZS 6:52.93
3. Broniewski POL 6:56.82

Coxless Pairs
1. GBR 6:27.72 (Redgrave, Pinsent)
2. GER 6:32.68 (Hoeltzenbein, Von Ettinshausen)
3. SLO 6:33.43 (Cop, Zvegelj)

Double sculls
1. AUS 6:17.32 (Hawkins, Antonie Peter)
2. AUT 6:18.42 (Jonke, Zerbst)
3. NET 6:22.82 (Zwolle, Rienks)

Coxed Pairs
1. GBR 6:49.83 (Searle, Searle; coxswain: Herbert)
2. ITA 6:50.98 (Abbagnale, Abbagnale; coxswain: Di Capua)
3. ROM 6:51.58 (Popescu, Taga; coxswain: Raducanu)

Coxless Fours
1. AUS 5:55.04 (Cooper, McKay, Green, Tomkins)
2. USA 5:56.68 (Burden, McLaughlin, Bohrer, Manning)
3. SLO 5:58.24 (Klemencic, Mirjanic, Jansa, Mujkic)

Quadruple Sculls
1. GER 5:45.17 (Willms, Hajek, Volker, Steinbach)
2. NOR 5:47.09 (Bjonness, Thorsen, Undset, Saetersdal)
3. ITA 5:47.33 (Farina, Galtarossa, Corona, Soffici)

Coxed Fours
1. ROM 5:59.37 (Talapan, Ruican, Popescu, Taga, Raducanu)
2. GER 6:0.34 (Kellner, Brudel, Peters, Finger, Reiher)
3. POL 6:3.27 (Streich, Jankowski, Tomiak, Lasicki, Cieslak)

Eights
A. CAN 5:29.53
2. ROM 5:29.67
3. GER 5:31.00

Women's Rowing

Sculls
1. Lipa ROM 7:25.54
2. Bredael BEL 7:26.64
3. Lauman CAN 7:28.85

Coxless Pairs
1. CAN 7:6.22 (McLean, Heddle)
2. GER 7:7.96 (Werremeier, Schwerzmann)
3. USA 7:8.11 (Seaton, Pierson)

Double sculls
1. GER 6:49.00 (Koeppen, Boron)
2. ROM 6:51.47 (Cochelea, Lipa)
3. CHN 6:55.16 (Gu, Lu)

Coxless Fours
1. CAN 6:30.85 (Barnes, Taylor, Monroe, Worthington)
2. USA 6:31.86 (Donohoe, Eckert, Fuller, Feeney)
3. GER 6:32.33 (Frank, Mehl, Siech, Hohn)

Quadruple Sculls
1. GER 6:20.18
2. ROM 6:24.34
3. IOP 6:25.07

Eights
1. CAN 6:2.62
2. ROM 6:6.26
3. GER 6:7.80

Basketball

Men
1. United States – 2. Croatia – 3. Lithuania

Women
1. CIS – 2. China – 3. United States

Boxing

– 48 kg (Light Flyweight)
1. Marcelo Garcia CUB
2. Bojinov BUL
3. Velasco PHI
Quast GER

– 51 kg (Flyweight)
1. Chol Su Choi PRK
2. Gonzalez Sanchez CUB
3. Austin USA
Kovacs HUN

– 54 kg (Bantamweight)
1. Casamayor Johnson CUB
2. McCullough IRL
3. Sik Li PRK
Achik MOR

– 57 kg (Featherweight)
1. Tews GER
2. Reyes Lopez SPA
3. Soltani ALG
Paliani CIS

– 60 kg (Lightweight)
1. De La Hoya USA
2. Rudolph GER
3. Bayarsaikhan MON
Sik Hong-sung KOR

– 63.5 kg (Light Welterweight)
1. Vinent CUB
2. Leduc CAN
3. Goeran Kjall FIN
Doroftei ROM

– 67 kg (Welterweight)
1. Carruth IRL
2. Hernandez Sierra CUB
3. Chenglai THA
Santiago PUR

– 71 kg (Light Middleweight)
1. Lemus Garcia CUB
2. Delibas NET
3. Mizsei HUN
Reid GBR

– 75 kg (Middleweight)
1. Hernandez CUB
2. Byrd USA
3. Johnson CAN
Seng Bae-lee KOR

– 81 kg (Light Heavyweight)
1. May GER
2. Zaoulitchnyi CIS
3. Beres HUN
Bartnik POL

– 91 kg (Heavyweight)
1. Felix Savon Fabre CUB
2. Izonritei NGA
3. Tua NZE
Van Der Lijde NET

More than 91 kg (Super Heavyweight)
1. Balado Mendez CUB
2. Igbineghu NGA
3. Nielsen DEN
Aldinov Roussinov BUL

Men's Canoeing

Slalom C1
1. Pollert CZS 113.69 pts
2. Marriott GBR 116.48 pts
3. Avril FRA 117.18 pts

Slalom C2
1. Strausbaugh-Jacobi USA 122.41 pts
2. Simek-Rohan CZS 124.25 pts
3. Adisson-Forgues FRA 124.38 pts

Slalom K1
1. Ferrazzi ITA 106.89 pts
2. Curinier FRA 107.06 pts
3. Lettmann GER 108.52 pts

Kayak K1 (500 m)
1. Kolehmainen FIN 1:40.34
2. Gyulay HUN 1:40.64
3. Holmann NOR 1:40.71

Kayak K2 (500 m)
1. GER 1:28.27 (Bluhm, Gutsche)
2. POL 1:29.84 (Freimut, Kurpiewski)
3. ITA 1:30 (Rossi, Dreossi)

Canadian C1 (1 000 m)
1. Bulkhalov BUL
2. Klementjevs LAT
3. Zala HUN

Canadian C2 (1 000 m)
1. GER (Papke, Spelly)
2. DEN (Nielsson, Frederiksen)
3. FRA (Hoyer, Boivin)

Kayak K1 (1 000 m)
1. Robinson AUS
2. Holmann NOR
3. Barton USA

Kayak K2 (1 000 m)
1. GER (Bluhm, Gutsche)
2. SWE Olsson, Sundqvist)
3. POL (Kotowicz, Bialkowski)

Kayak K4 (1 000 m)
1. GER (Von Appen, Kegel, Reineck, Wohllebe)
2. HUN (Csipes, Gyulay, Fidel, Abraham)
3. AUS (Graham, Rowling, Wood, Andersson)

Women's Canoeing

Slalom K1
1. Micheler GER 126.41 pts
2. Woodward AUS 128.27 pts
3. Chiadek USA 131.75 pts

Kayak K1 (500 m)
1. Schmidt GER 1:51.60
2. Koban HUN 1:51.96
3. Dylewska POL 1:52.36

Kayak K2 (500 m)
1. GER 1:40.29 (Portwich, Von Seck)
2. SWE 1:40.41 (Gunnarsson, Andersson)
3. HUN 1:40.81 (Koban, Donusz)

Kayak K4 (500 m)
1. HUN (Donusz, Czigany, Meszaros, Koban)
2. GER (Borchert, Schmidt, Von Seck, Portwich)
3. SWE (Olsson, Haglund, Rosenqvist, Andersson)

Men's Cycling

100 km Team Time Trial
1. GER 2 h 1:39 (B. Dittert, C. Meyer, U. Peschet, M. Rich)
2. ITA 2 h 2:39 (F. Anastasia, L. Colombo, G. Contri, A. Peron)
3. FRA 2 h 5:25 (H. Boussard, D. Faivre-Pierret, P. Gaumont, J. Harel)

Team Pursuit
1. Germany – 2. Australia – 3. Denmark

Speed
1. Fiedler GER
2. Neiwand AUS
3. Harnett CAN

1 000 m Sprint
1. Moreno SPA 1:3.342
2. Kelly AUS 1:4.288
3. Hartwell USA 1:4.753

Individual Road Race
1. Boardman GBR
2. Lehmann GER
3. Anderson NZE

Points Race
1. Lombardi ITA 44 pts
(50 km in 1 h 0:59.213. Average Speed: 49.190 km/h.)
2. Van Bon NET 43 pts
3. Mathy BEL 41 pts

Road Race
1. Casartelli ITA 4 h 35:21
(Average Speed: 42.360 km/h.)
2. Dekker NET 4 h 35:21
3. Ozols LAT 4 h 35:21

Women's Cycling

Individual Road Race
1. Rossner (GER) – 2. Watt (AUS) – 3. Twigg (USA)

Speed
1. Salumae (EST) – 2. Neumann (GER)
3. Haringa (NET)

Road Race
1. Watt AUS 81 km in 2 h 04:22
(Average Speed: 38.973 km/h.)
2. Longo-Ciprelli FRA 2 h 05:02
3. Knol NET 2 h 05:03

Equestrian Sports

Individual Jumping
1. Beerbaum GER "Classic Touch"
2. Raymakers NET "Ratina Z"
3. Dello Joio USA "Irish"

Jumping Team
1. NET 12 pts (Raymakers, "Ratina Z"; Tops, "Top Gun"; Lansink, "Egano")
2. AUT 16,75 pts (Muntzner, "Graf Grande"; Simon, "Apricot D"; Fruhmann, "Genius")
3. FRA 25,75 pts (Godignon "Quidam de Revel"; Bourdy, "Razzia du Poncel"; Robert, "Nonix"; Navet, "Quito de Baussy")

Individual Dressage
1. Uphoff GER "Rembrandt" 1 626 pts
2. Werth GER "Gigolo" 1 551 pts
3. Balkenhol GER "Goldstern" 1 515 pts

Team Dressage
1. GER 5 224 pts (Uphoff-"Rembrandt", Theodorescu-"Gruno x", Werth-"Gigolo")
2. NET 4 742 pts (Van Grunsven-"Olympic Bonfire", Sanders-"Olympic Montreux", Bartels-"Olympic Courage")
3. USA 4 643 pts

Grand Prix Individual Jumping
1. Ryan/"Kibach Tic Toc" AUS 70 pts
2. Blocker/"Feine Dame" GER 81.30 pts
3. Tait/"Messiah" NZE 87.60 pts

Grand Prix Team Jumping
1. AUS 288.80 pts (Rolton, Hoy, Ryan)
2. NZE 290.80 pts (Nicholson, Latta, Tait)
3. GER 300.30 pts (Baumann, Mysegaes, Ehrenbring, Blocker)

Men's Fencing

Individual Foil
1. Omnès FRA
2. Golubitski CIS
3. Gregory Gil CUB

Individual Sabre
1. Szabo HUN
2. Marin ITA
3. Lamour FRA

Individual Epée
1. Srecki FRA
2. Kolobkov CIS
3. Henry FRA

Team Foil
1. GER – 2. CUB – 3. POL

Team Sabre
1. CIS – 2. HUN – 3. FRA

Team Epée
1. GER – 2. HUN – 3. CIS

Women's Fencing

Individual Foil
1. Trillini ITA
2. Hui Feng CHN
3. Sadovskaia CIS

Team Foil
1. ITA – 2. GER – 3. ROM

Soccer

1. SPA – 2. POL – 3. GHA

Men's Gymnastics

All-round Individual Competition
1. Chtcherbo CIS
2. Misiutine CIS
3. Belenki CIS

Combined Exercises Team
1. CIS 585.450 pts (Chtcherbo, Belenki, Misiutine, Korobtchinski, Vorpaev, Charipov)
2. CHN 580.375 pts (X.-Li, C.-Li, Guo, J.-Li, D.-Li, G.-Li).
3. JAP 578.250 pts (Iketani, Hatakeda, Chinen, Nishikawa, Aihara, Matsunaga)

Horizontal Bar
1. Dimas USA 9.875 pts
2. Misiutine CIS 9.837 pts
3. Wecker GER 9.837 pts

Parallel Bars
1. Stcherbo CIS
2. JingLi CHN
3. Korobtchinski CIS
Linyao Guo CHN
Matsunaga JAP

Floor Exercises
1. Xiao Li CHN 9.925 pts
2. Misiutine CIS 9.787 pts
3. Iketani JAP 9.787 pts

Rings
1. Stcherbo CIS 9.937 pts
2. Li CHN 9.875 pts
3. Xiaosahuang Li CHN 9.862 pts
Wecker GER 9.862 pts

Pommel Horse
1. Stcherbo CIS 9.925 pts
Pae PRK 9.925 pts
3. Wecker GER 9.887 pts

Horse Vault
1. Chtcherbo CIS 9.856 pts
2. Misjoutine CIS 9.781 pts
3. Ok Ryul Yoo KOR 9.762 pts

Women's Gymnastics

Individual Competition
1. Gutsu CIS 39.737 pts
2. Miller USA 39.725 pts
3. Milosovici ROM 39.687 pts

Team Competition
1. CIS 395.666 pts (Boginskaia, Lyssenko, Galierva, Gutsu, Grudneva, Tchussovitina)
2. ROM 395.079 pts (Bontas, Milosovici, Gogean, Hadarean, Neculita, Pasca)
3. USA 394.704 pts (Miller, Okino, Zmeskal, Strug, Dawes, Bruce)

Floor Exercices
1. Milosovici ROM 10 pts
2. Onodi HUN 9.950 pts
3. Gutsu CIS 9.912 pts
Bontas ROM
Miller USA

Horse Vault
1. Onodi HUN 9.925 pts
2. Milosovici ROM 9.925 pts
3. Lyssenko CIS 9.912 pts

Asymmetric Bars
1. Lu CHN 10 pts
2. Gutsu CIS 9.975 pts
3. Miller USA 9.962 pts

Beam
1. Lyssenko CIS 9.975 pts
2. Lu CHN 9.912 pts
3. Miller USA 9.912 pts

Rhythmic Competition
1. Timoshenko CIS 59.037 pts
2. Pascual Garcia SPA 58.100 pts
3. Straldina CIS 57.912 pts

Weightlifting

52 kg
1. Ivanov BUL 265 kg
2. Lin Qisheng CHN 262.5 kg
3. Ciharean ROM 252.5 kg

1992 Barcelona

56 kg
1. Byung-kwan KOR 287.5 kg
2. Liu Shugin CHN 277.5 kg
3. Luo Jianming CHN 277.5 kg

– 60 kg
1. Suleymanoglu TUR 320 kg
2. Peshalov BUL 305 kg
3. Yinggiang CHN 295 kg

– 67.5 kg
1. Militossain CIS 337.5 kg
2. Yotov BUL 327.5 kg
3. Behm GER 320 kg

– 75 kg
1. Kassapu CIS 357.5 kg
2. Lara Rodriguez CUB 357.5 kg
3. Myong Nam PRK 352.5 kg

– 82.5 kg
1. Dimas GRE 370 kg (167.5 + 202.5)
2. Siemion POL 370 kg (165 + 205)
3. Bronze Medal not awarded.

90 kg
1. Kakhiachvili CIS 412.5 kg
2. Syrtsov CIS 412.5 kg
3. Wolczaniecki POL 392.5 kg

100 kg
1. Tregubov CIS 410 kg
2. Taimazov CIS 402.5 kg
3. Malak POL 400 kg

110 kg
1. Weller CIS 432 kg
2. Ahoev CIS 430 kg
3. Botev BUL 417.5 kg

+ 110 kg
1. Kurlovitch CIS 450 kg
2. Taranenko CIS 425 kg
3. Nerlinger GER 412.5 kg

Handball

Men
1. CIS – 2. SWE – 3. FRA

Women
1. KOR – 2. NOR – 3. CIS

Hockey Field

Men
1. GER – 2. AUS – 3. PAK

Women
1. SPA – 2. GER – 3. GBR

Men's Judo

Extra-Lightweight (less than 60 kg)
1. Gusseinov CIS
2. Yoon KOR
3. Koshino JAP
Trautmann GER

Half-Lightweight (less than 65 kg)
1. Sampaio BRA
2. Csak HUN
3. Quellmalz GER
Planas CUB

Lightweight (less than 71 kg)
1. Koga JAP
2. Hjtos HUN
3. Smaga ISR
Chung KOR

Half-Middleweight (less than 78 kg)
1. Yoshida JAP
2. Morris USA
3. Byung-Joo KOR
Damaisin FRA

Middleweight (less than 86 kg)
1. Legien POL
2. Tayot FRA
3. Gill CAN
Okada JAP

Half-Heavyweight (less than 95 kg)
1. Kovacs HUN
2. Stevens GBR
3. Meijer NET
Sergeev CIS

Heavyweight (more than 95 kg)
1. Khakhaleichvili CIS
2. Ogawa JAP
3. Douillet FRA
Csosz HUN

Women's Judo

– 48 kg
1. Nowak FRA
2. Tamura JAP
3. Savon CUB
Senyurt TUR

– 52 kg
1. Martinez SPA
2. Mizoguchi JAP
3. Rendle GBR
Li CHN

– 56 kg
1. Blasco SPA
2. Fairbrother GBR
3. Tateno JAP
Morales CUB

– 61 kg
1. Fleury FRA
2. Arad ISR
3. Zhang CHN
Petrova CIS

– 66 kg
1. Reve CUB
2. Pierantozzi ITA
3. Rakels BEL
Howey GBR

72 kg
1. Mi-Jung KOR
2. Tanabe JAP
3. Meignan FRA
De Kok NET

+ 72 kg
1. Xiaoyan CHN
2. Rodriguez CUB
3. Lupino FRA
Sakaue JAP

Greco-Roman Wrestling

Light-Flyweight (48 kg)
1. Kutcherenko CIS
2. Maenza ITA
3. Amita CUB

Flyweight (52 kg)
1. Ronningen NOR
2. Ter-Mkretchian CIS
3. Kyung Kap KOR

Bantamweight (57 kg)
1. Han-Bong KOR
2. Yildiz GER
3. Zetian CHN

Featherweight (62 kg)
1. Pirim (TUR) – 2. Martinov (CIS) – 3. Delis (CUB)

Lightweight (68 kg)
1. Repka HUN
2. Dugutchiev CIS
3. Smith USA

Welterweight (74 kg)
1. Iskandarian CIS
2. Tracz POL
3. Kornbakk SWE

Middleweight (82 kg)
1. Farkas HUN
2. Stepien POL
3. Turlykhanov CIS

Light Heavyweight (90 kg)
1. Bullmann GER
2. Basar TUR
3. Koguachvili CIS

Heavyweight (100 kg)
1. Perez CUB
2. Koslowski USA
3. Demiachkievitch CIS

Super Heavyweight (130 kg)
1. Karelin CIS
2. Johansson SWE
3. Grigoras ROM

Freestyle Wrestling

48 kg
1. Kim Il KOR
2. Jong Shin-kim KOR
3. Orudjov CIS

52 kg
1. Li (KOR) – 2. Jones (USA) – 3. Jordanov (BUL)

57 kg
1. Diaz PRK
2. Smal CIS
3. Sik Kim KOR

62 kg
1. Smith USA
2. Mohammadian IRA
3. Martinez CUB

68 kg
1. Fadzaev CIS
2. Dotchev Getzov BUL
3. Akkaishi JAP

74 kg
1. Jang Soon KOR
2. Monday USA
3. Azghadi GER

82 kg
1. Jackson USA
2. Jabraijlov CIS
3. Azghadi IRA

90 kg
1. Khadartsev CIS
2. Simsek TUR
3. Campbell USA

100 kg
1. Khabelov CIS
2. Balz GER
3. Kayali TUR

130 kg
1. Baumgartner USA
2. Thue CAN
3. Gobedjichvili CIS

Men's Swimming

50 m Freestyle
1. Popov CIS 21.91
2. Biondi USA 22.09
3. Jager USA 22.30

100 m Freestyle
1. Popov CIS 49.02
2. Borges BRA 49.43
3. Caron FRA 49.50

200 m Freestyle
1. Sadovyi CIS 1:46.70
2. Holmertz SWE 1:46.86
3. Kasvio FIN 1:47.63

400 m Freestyle
1. Sadovyi CIS 3:45.00
2. Perkins AUS 3:45.16
3. Holmertz SWE 3:46.77

1 500 m Freestyle
1. Perkins AUS 14:43.48
2. Housman AUS 14:55.29
3. Hoffmann GER 15:2.29

100 m Backstroke
1. Tewksbury CAN 53.98
2. Rouse USA 54.04
3. Berkoff USA 54.78

200 m Backstroke
1. Lopez Zubero SPA 1:58.47
2. Selkov CIS 1:58.87
3. Battistelli ITA 1:59.40

100 m Butterfly
1. Morales USA 53.32
2. Szukala POL 53.35
3. Nesty SUR 53.41

200 m Butterfly
1. Stewart USA 1:56.26
2. Loader NZE 1:57.93
3. Esposito FRA 1:58.51

100 m Breaststroke
1. Diebel USA 1:1.50
2. Rozsa HUN 1:1.68
3. Rogers AUS 1:1.76

200 m Breaststroke
1. Barrowman USA 2:10.16 (World Record)
2. Rozsa HUN 2:11.23
3. Gillingham GBR 2:11.29

200 m Medley
1. Darnyi HUN 2:0.76
2. Burgess USA 2:0.97
3. Czene HUN 2:1

400 m Medley
1. Darnyi HUN 4:14.23
2. Namesnik USA 4:15.57
3. Sacchi ITA 4:16.34

4 x 100 m
1. USA 3:16.74 (Hudepohl, Biondi, Jager, Olsen)
2. CIS 3:17.56 (Khnykin, Prigoda, Bashkatov, Popov)
3. GER 3:17.90 (Troeger, Richter, Zesner, Pinger)

4 x 200 m
1. CIS 7:11.95 (Lepikov, Pychnenko, Taianovitch, Sadovyi)
2. SWE 7:15.51 (Wallim, Holmertz, Werner, Frolander)
3. USA 7:16.23 (Hudepohl, Stewart, Olsen, Gjertsen)

4 x 100 m Medley
1. USA 3:36.93 (Rousse, Diebel Morales, Olsen), World Record equaled
2. CIS 3:38.56 (Selkov, Ivanov Khnykine, Popov)
3. CAN 3:39.66 (Tewksbury, Cleveland, Gery, Clarke)

Women's singles: Capriati.

Women's Swimming

50 m Freestyle
1. Yang CHN 24.79
2. Zhuang CHN 25.08
3. Martino USA 25.23

100 m Freestyle
1. Zuhang CHN 54.64
2. Thompson USA 54.84
3. Van Almsick GER 54.94

200 m Freestyle
1. Haislett USA 1:57.90
2. Van Almsick GER 1:58
3. Kieglas GER 1:59.67

400 m Freestyle
1. Hase GER 4:7.18
2. Evans USA 4:7.37
3. Lewis AUS 4:11.22

800 m Freestyle
1. Evans USA 8:25.52
2. Lewis AUS 8:30.34
3. Henke GER 8:30.99

100 m Backstroke
1. Egerszegi HUN 1:0.68
2. Szabo HUN 1:1.14
3. Loveless USA 1:1.43

200 m Backstroke
1. Egerszegi HUN 2:7.06
2. Hase GER 2:9.46
3. Stevenson AUS 2:10.20

100 m Butterfly
1. Qian CHN 58.62
2. M. Ahmann-Leighton USA 58.74
3. Plewinski FRA 59.01

200 m Butterfly
1. Sanders USA 2:8.67
2. Wang CHN 2:9.01
3. O'Neill AUS 2:9.03

100 m Breaststroke
1. Rudkovskaia CIS 1:8
2. Nall USA 1:8.25
3. Riley AUS 1:9.25

200 m Breaststroke
1. Iwasaki JAP 2:26.65
2. Lin CHN 2:26.85
3. Nall USA 2:26.88

200 m Medley
1. Lin CHN 2:11.65 (World Record)
2. Sanders USA 2:11.91
3. Hunger GER 2:13.92

400 m Medley
1. Egerszegi HUN 4:36.54
2. Li Lin CHN 4:36.73
3. Sanders USA 4:37.58

4 x 100 m Freestyle
1. USA 3:39.46 (Haislett, Torres, Martino, Thompson)
2. CHN 3:41.60 (Zhuang, Lu, Yang, Le)
3. GER 3:41.60 (Van Almsick, Osygus, Hunger, Stellmach)

4 x 100 m Medley
1. USA 4:2.54 (Loveless, Nall, Ahmann-Leighton, Thompson)
2. GER 4:5.19 (Hase, Doerries, Van Almsick, Hunger)
3. CIS 4:6.44 (Jivanevskaia, Rudkovskaia, Kiritchenko, Mechtcheriakova)

Men's Diving

Spring Board Diving 3 m
1. Lenzi USA 676.530 pts
2. Tan CAN 645.570 pts
3. Saoutin CIS 627.780 pts

Platform Diving
1. Shuwei Sun CHN 677.310 pts
2. Donie CIS 633.630 pts
3. Ni Xiong CHN 600.150 pts

Women's Diving

Spring Board Diving 3 m
1. Gao CHN 572.400 pts
2. Lachko CIS 514.140 pts
3. Baldus GER 503.070 pts

Platform Diving
1. Mingwia Fu CHN 461.430 pts
2. Mirochina CIS 411.630 pts
3. Clark USA 401.910 pts

Modern Pentathlon

Individual
1. Skrzypaszek POL 5 559 pts
2. Mizser HUN 5 446 pts
3. Zenovka CIS 5 361 pts

Team
1. POL 16 018 pts
2. CIS 15 924 pts
3. ITA 15 760 pts

Tennis

Men's Singles
1. Rosset SWI
2. Arrese SPA
3. Ivanisevic CRO
Cherkasov CIS

Men's Doubles
1. Becker-Stich GER
2. Ferreira-Norval SAF
3. Ivanisevic-Prpic CRO
Frana-Miniussi ARG

Women's Singles
1. Capriati USA
2. Graf GER
3. Sanchez SPA
Fernandez USA

Table Tennis

Men's Singles
1. Waldner SWE
2. Gatien FRA
3. Ma Wenge CHN
Taek Soo-kim KOR

Men's Doubles
1. Lu Lin-Wang Tao CHN
2. Fetzner-Roskopf GER
3. Kang Hee-Lee Chul KOR
Kim Taek-Yo Nams KOR

Women's Singles
1. Deng Yaping CHN
2. Qiao Hong CHN
3. Hyun Jung KOR
Li Bun PRK

Women's Doubles
1. Den Yaping-Qiao Hong CHN
2. Chen Zihe-Gao Jun CHN
3. Li Bun-Yu Sun PRK
Hong Cha-Huyn Jung KOR

Men's Shooting

Rapid-Fire Pistol
1. Schumann GER 789 pts
2. Kuzmins LAT 785 pts
3. Vokhmianin CIS 786 pts

Free Pistol
1. Loukachik CIS 658 pts
2. Wang CHN 657 pts
3. Skanaker SWE 657 pts

Pistol, 10 m
1. Wang Yifu CHN 684.8 pts
2. Pyjianov CIS 684.1 pts
3. Babii ROM 684.1 pts

Rifle, 10 m
1. Fedkin CIS 593 pts
2. Badiou FRA 591 pts
3. Riederer GER 590 pts

Rifle, prone
1. Eun-Chul KOR 702.5 pts
2. Stenvaag NOR 701.4 pts
3. Pletikosic IOP 701.1 pts

Rifle, 3 x 40
1. Petikian CIS 1 267.4 pts
2. Foth USA 1 266.6 pts
3. Koba JAP 1 265.9 pts

Moving Target
1. Jakosits GER 673 pts
2. Asrabaev CIS 672 pts
3. Racansky CZS 670 pts

Women's Shooting

Pistol, 10 m
1. Logvinenko CIS 486.4 pts
2. Sekaric IOP 486.4 pts
3. Grusdeva BUL 481.6 pts

Pistol, 22 caliber
1. Logvinenko CIS 684 pts
2. Duihong Li CHN 680 pts
3. Munkhbayar MON 679 pts

Airgun
1. Kab-Soon Yeo KOR 498.2 pts
2. Letcheva BUL 495.3 pts
3. Binder BOS 495.1 pts

Rifle, 3 x 20
1. Meili USA 684.3 pts
2. Matova BUL 682.7 pts
3. Ksiazkiewicz POL 681.5 pts

Men's Archery

Individual
1. Flute FRA
2. Chung KOR
3. Terry GBR

Team
1. SPA – 2. FIN – 3. GBR

Women's Archery

Individual
1. Y. Cho (KOR) – 2. S. Kim (KOR)
3. Valeeva (CIS)

Team
1. KOR – 2. CHN – 3. CIS

Men's Yachting

Finn Class
1. SPA Garcia 33.40 pts
2. USA Ledbetter 54.70 pts
3. NZE Monk 64.70 pts

470 Class
1. SPA (Calafat, Sanchez) 50 pts
2. USA (Reeser, Burnham) 66.70 pts
3. EST (T. Toniste, N. Toniste) 68.70 pts

Flying Dutchman Class
1. SPA 29.70 pts
2. USA 32.70 pts
3. DEN 37.70 pts

Soling Class
1. DEN – 2. USA – 3. GBR

Tornado Class
1. FRA (Loday, Hénard) 40.40 pts
2. USA (Smyth, Notary) 42 pts
3. AUS (Booth, Forbes) 44.40 pts

Star Class
1. USA (Reynolds, Haenel) 31.40 pts
2. NZE (Davis, Cowie) 58.40 pts
3. CAN (McDonald, Jespersen) 62.70 pts

Windsurfing
1. David FRA
2. Gebhardt USA
3. Kleppich AUS

Women's Yachting

470 class
1. SPA (Zabell, Guerra) 30.70 pts
2. NZE (Egnot, Shearer) 39.70 pts
3. USA (Isler, Healy) 42.40 pts

Europ
1. NOR Andersen 48.70 pts
2. SPA Via Dufresne 57.40 pts
3. USA Trotman 62.70 pts

Windsurfing
1. NZE 47.80 pts
2. CHN 65.80 pts
3. NET 68.70 pts

Volleyball

Men
1. BRA – 2. NET – 3. USA

Women
1. CIS – 2. CUB – 3. USA

Final Country Standings

Country	G	S	B	T
Commonwealth of Independent States(CIS)	45	38	29	112
United States (USA)	37	34	37	108
Germany (GER)	33	21	28	82
China (CHN)	16	22	16	54
Cuba (CUB)	14	6	11	31
Spain (SPA)	13	7	2	22
South Korea (KOR)	12	5	12	29
Hungary (HUN)	11	12	7	30
France (FRA)	8	5	16	29
Australia (AUS)	7	9	11	27
Italy (ITA)	6	5	8	19
Canada (CAN)	6	5	7	18
Britain (GBR)	5	3	12	20
Romania (ROM)	4	6	8	18
Czechoslovakia (CZS)	4	2	1	7
North Korea (PRK)	4	0	5	9
Japan (JAP)	3	8	11	22
Bulgaria (BUL)	3	7	6	16
Poland (POL)	3	6	10	19
Netherlands (NET)	2	6	7	15
Kenya (KEN)	2	4	2	8
Norway (NOR)	2	4	1	7
Turkey (TUR)	2	2	2	6
Indonesia (INA)	2	2	1	5
Brazil (BRA)	2	1	0	3
Greece (GRE)	2	0	0	2
Sweden (SWE)	1	7	4	12
New Zealand (NZE)	1	4	5	10
Finland (FIN)	1	2	2	5
Denmark (DEN)	1	1	4	6
Morocco (MOR)	1	1	1	3
Ireland (IRL)	1	1	0	2
Ethiopia (ETH)	1	0	2	3
Algeria (ALG)	1	0	1	2
Estonia (EST)	1	0	1	2
Lithuania (LIT)	1	0	1	2
Switzerland (SWI)	1	0	0	1
Jamaica (JAM)	0	3	1	4
Nigeria (NGA)	0	3	1	4
Latvia (LAT)	0	2	1	3
South Africa (SAF)	0	2	0	2
Austria (AUT)	0	2	0	2
Namibia (NAM)	0	2	0	2
Belgium (BEL)	0	1	2	3
Croatia (CRO)	0	1	2	3
Iran (IRA)	0	1	2	3
Independent Olympic Participants* (IOP)	0	1	2	3
Israel (ISR)	0	1	1	2
Mexico (MEX)	0	1	0	1
Peru (PER)	0	1	0	1
Taiwan (TAI)	0	1	0	1
Mongolia (MON)	0	0	2	2
Slovenia (SLO)	0	0	2	2
Argentina (ARG)	0	0	1	1
Bahamas (BAH)	0	0	1	1
Colombia (COL)	0	0	1	1
Ghana (GHA)	0	0	1	1
Malaysia (MAL)	0	0	1	1
Pakistan (PAK)	0	0	1	1
Philippines (PHI)	0	0	1	1
Puerto Rico (PUR)	0	0	1	1
Qatar (QAT)	0	0	1	1
Surinam (SUR)	0	0	1	1
Thailand (THA)	0	0	1	1
Total	259	258	298	815

* Serbia, Montenegro, Macedonia.

August

1992

Su	Mo	Tu	We	Th	Fr	Sa
						1
2	3	4	5	6	7	8
9	10	11	12	13	14	15
16	17	18	19	20	21	22
23	24	25	26	27	28	29
30	31					

St Louis, 16
Nick Price of Zimbabwe wins the Professional Golfers' Association Championship.

Estonia, 16
The International Monetary Fund allocates $40 million to Estonia.

Boston, 18
Ending a 13-season career in pro basketball, Larry Bird retires from the Boston Celtics.

U.S., 18
Accumulated losses of $3.5 billion over the past three years cause Wang Laboratories Inc., the former computer giant, to file for bankruptcy.

Alaska, 18
For the second time this year, Mount Spurr volcano, west of Anchorage, erupts.

London, 18
Britain announces that 1,800 troops are ready to be sent to Bosnia-Herzegovina to help U.N. relief efforts (→ 27).

Sukhumi, 18
After five days of violent fighting, Georgian troops take control of the Abkhazian capital.

Spain, 19
A tour bus, carrying visitors from Barcelona to the Seville Expo, crashes, killing 45 people.

Germany, 19
Hundreds of homosexual couples demand the right to official marriages.

U.S., 19
The magazine *Fortune*, in its annual list of billionaires, names the Sultan of Brunei, worth $37 billion, the world's wealthiest person.

Baghdad, 20
Paul Ride, a Briton, is sentenced to seven years in prison for crossing the Iraqi border illegally.

Miami, 23
As Hurricane Andrew nears, one million people are urged to evacuate the area (→ 25).

DEATH

18. John Sturges, American film director. Famous for *The Magnificent Seven* and *Gunfight at the O.K. Corral* (*Jan. 3, 1911).

Woody Allen at war with Mia Farrow

New York, Tuesday 18
In the latest round of a custody battle between Woody Allen and his former companion and leading lady, Mia Farrow, the filmmaker denied charges by Farrow's lawyer that he had sexually abused one of her adopted children. Connecticut police confirmed that they were investigating Allen, but said no charges had been filed and refused to indicate the nature of the investigation. Allen admitted yesterday that he was romantically involved with 21-year-old Soon-Yi Farrow Previn, the daughter adopted by Farrow when she was married to conductor Andre Previn (→ Sept 21).

Woody and Mia in happier times.

Aug 16. Tall ship at Liverpool for Columbus anniversary regatta.

Unlucky Nigel Mansell a winner at last

Mansell's Williams-Renault came in behind Senna's McLaren-Honda.

Budapest, Sunday 16
Nigel Mansell, so often unlucky, today became the Formula One motor racing champion of the world and so achieved the ambition he set himself 30 years ago.

He did it not by winning, but by coming second to his great rival and the current Formula One champion, Ayrton Senna, in 77 uncompromising laps in the Hungarian Grand Prix.

Fifteen laps from the end it seemed that his bad luck still dogged him when he had to take his Williams-Renault into the pits with a puncture, but nine seconds later he roared away to work his way through the field and gain enough points to get an unbeatable lead in the championship with five of the 16 races remaining (→ Sept 13).

A new world champion celebrates.

August 22. Groups of Germany's racist hoodlums again attack hostels housing foreign asylum-seekers at Rostock, in former East Germany.

President Bush goes into tough campaign mode

Houston, Thursday 20

The Republican Convention has set the stage for a more energized, and more aggressive, presidential campaign. "I can feel it", said President George Bush, "I can feel it building in my blood." If the prominent themes of the convention continue to be stressed throughout the rest of the campaign, and Republican strategists say they will be, Americans will be hearing a lot about "family values". The convention featured speakers from the party's right wing, for whom these social issues are especially important. Patrick Buchanan, a political columnist and presidential candidate in the primaries, attacked Democratic candidate Bill Clinton's agenda as "abortion on demand, a litmus test for the Supreme Court, homosexual rights, discrimination against religious schools, women in combat units", all unacceptable "in a nation we still call God's country". Televangelist Pat Robertson accused Clinton and his wife, Hillary, of proposing "a radical plan to destroy the traditional family". Not all Republicans were comfortable with the strident and uncompromising tone, particularly on the controversial issue of abortion. Despite the platform plank which supports a constitutional ban, both George Bush and Vice President Dan Quayle have said that they would support a daughter

Bush tries to rally his troops.

First Lady Barbara Bush won much acclaim at the Houston convention.

or granddaughter who chose to have an abortion. Barbara Bush called abortion "a personal thing" that had no place in the platform.

Although the Republicans emphasized what the religious right calls "Judeo-Christian ethics", foreign policy and economic issues were not forgotten. In his acceptance speech Bush said that he would cut taxes and reduce government spending, and stressed his experience in matters of state, opening his speech by implying that he had helped to bring about the fall of the Berlin Wall, the decline of Soviet Communism and the moves toward peace between Israel and its Arab neighbors (→ Sept 4).

Dan Quayle and wife join in the rejoicing as convention draws to a close.

Dollar hits record low against the Mark

New York, Friday 21

The dollar fell to a record low of 1.4250 Deutsche marks today. The central banks of 18 countries, led by the U.S. Federal Reserve, have intervened several times since July, buying greenbacks in an effort to stop the plunge. Although the drop in the U.S. currency makes its exports more competitive, it is dangerous because it devalues foreign owners' American assets, tempting them to sell. The decline could not have come at a worse time for President George Bush: He is behind in a presidential campaign in which the American voters are focused on the economy (→ Sept 1).

August 20. Pictures in the British tabloid paper, the "Daily Mirror", showing a topless Duchess of York relaxing in private with her American financial advisor, John Bryan, cause a storm of protest in Great Britain. Buckingham Palace tried and failed to block publication of the photos and criticized invasion of the Royal Family's privacy by reporters.

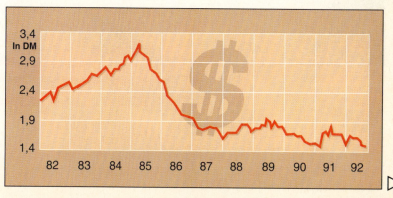

Hurricane Andrew batters Florida

Florida, Tuesday 25

After ripping through southern Florida and destroying much of Dade County south of Miami, Hurricane Andrew is on its way through the Gulf of Mexico to the Louisiana coast. At least 15 people have been killed, and damage estimates range from $15 billion to $20 billion, more than for any other natural disaster in U.S. history. The town of Homestead, where the storm hit Florida's Atlantic coast, was almost entirely destroyed by winds which reached speeds of 160 miles per hour, and almost the whole of its population was left homeless. Andrew wrenched trees from the ground, mowed down houses and picked up boats, cars and planes and flung them into the air. A spokesman for Florida Power and Light said that 825,000 homes and businesses were without electricity, and that it may be weeks before the service is restored.

Miami and Coconut Grove were virtually under martial law, as riot-equipped police and 15,000 National Guard troops patroled the city to prevent looting.

Weather forecasters predict that the hurricane will hit the south-central coast of Louisiana, west of New Orleans. About 1.7 million people have been advised to evacuate, including the entire population of New Orleans (→ Sept 1).

August

1992

Su	Mo	Tu	We	Th	Fr	Sa
						1
2	3	4	5	6	7	8
9	10	11	12	13	14	15
16	17	18	19	20	21	22
23	24	25	26	27	28	29
30	31					

Israel, 23
The government decides to free 800 Palestinian prisoners, as Middle East peace talks resume in Washington, D.C.

Maryland, 24
Baseball star Cal Ripken signs richest guaranteed contract in the sport's history.

Manchester, 24
England cricketers beat Pakistan by six wickets to win the Texaco Trophy series.

Beijing, 24
Diplomatic relations are restored between China and South Korea (→ Sept 30).

Jordan, 24
King Hussein's doctors say he is being treated for cancer, adding they expect a quick recovery.

Brno, 26
Vladimir Meciar, the Slovak premier, announces that on January 1 Czechoslovakia will split (→ Nov 25).

Rome, 27
Giovanni Falcone is succeeded by his former chief aide, Judge Liliana Ferraro (→ Sept 6).

Japan, 28
In an unprecedented plan to help the economy, Japan announces that 10.7 trillion yen ($84.5 billion) will be used to help spur growth.

Jerusalem, 28
Prime Minister Rabin warns that Israel will respond to any missile threat from Iraq.

Russia, 28
An Aeroflot Tupolev 134 crashes north-east of Moscow killing all 82 people aboard.

Belgium, 30
German Michael Schumacher wins the Belgian Grand Prix.

Alsace, 31
Two hundred Jewish tombs are desecrated in a cemetery in eastern France.

London, 31
A young Swede who looks after a British couple's children is to be deported due to a law allowing only women to be au pairs (→ Sept 1).

DEATH
27. Daniel Ludwig, American shipping tycoon (*1897).

Air exclusion zone in southern Iraq to protect Shiite Muslims

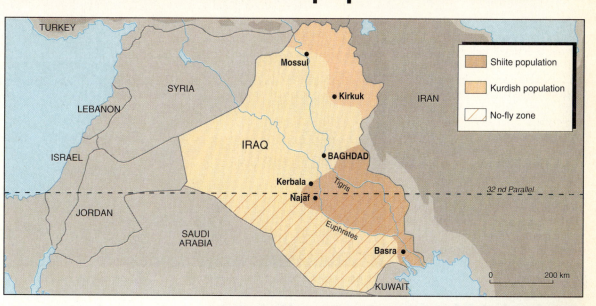

Iraq, Thursday 27

"No Iraqi planes. We saw a lot of American planes," commented one of the first USAF pilots to return from a sortie in Operation Southern Watch, the establishment by the Gulf War allies of a "no-fly" zone over Iraq south of the 32nd parallel. The enforcement of the air exclusion zone, which began today, is the allies' response to Iraqi attacks against Shiite civilians and insurgents in southern Iraq, and will be carried out by U.S., British and French aircraft.

President George Bush said that the no-fly zone "will remain in effect until the coalition determines it is no longer necessary."

RAF Tornados ready at Marham, Norfolk, to fly to Dhahran, Saudi Arabia.

Hundreds rescued from sinking liner

Malaysia, Sunday 23

Over 500 passengers have been rescued from the Greek cruise liner *Royal Pacific*, which sank in the Malacca Straits following a collision with a Taiwanese fishing boat in the middle of the night. The crash left a hole "big enough for two buses to pass through". The liner on "a cruise to nowhere" began to sink immediately, and many passengers were thrown into the debris-littered sea. Two people are known to have died and seven are missing. Susan Hopley, a British passenger, said of her rescue: "It's a miracle. I thought I was dying. I couldn't breathe."

Sterling survives huge share fall

London, Monday 24

Sterling survived a stiff test today as the dollar continued to plunge. The pound's steadiness against the Deutsche mark on a day when the French franc and the Italian lira lost ground is seen as vindication of the government's tactic of combining central bank intervention with a staunch commitment to the pound's parity within the ERM.

However, while the pound remained steady, more than £10 billion was wiped from share values as the London stock market suffered its biggest one-day fall in more than a year with fears growing that bank base rates will be raised.

Nine die in Algiers airport bombing

Algiers, Wednesday 26

A bomb exploded in Houari Boumedienne Airport here, killing nine people and injuring more than 100. The bomb, hidden in a flowerpot near the Air France counter, wrecked most of the terminal. Witnesses said the force of the explosion was so strong that a body was stuck to the ceiling. This is the first attack not directly aimed at government forces, in a wave of violence that began in January when the government cancelled general elections after the Islamic Salvation Front's victory in the first round. The fundamentalist group was outlawed in February.

Hugh McKibben is 3,000th victim of Northern Ireland conflict

Belfast, Thursday 27

A grim milestone was reached in Northern Ireland today when 19-year-old Hugh McKibben became the 3,000th victim of the sectarian violence which has claimed a life every three days in the past 23 years since John Gallagher, a 30-year-old Catholic, was shot dead by the now-disbanded B Specials during riots in Armagh.

McKibben's death is thought to stem from a dispute between rival factions of the Irish People's Liberation Organisation, a republican splinter group. The security forces were not involved, and the IRA denies responsibility. It was just another killing.

The first victim in Ulster, John Gallagher, was killed on August 14, 1969.

London conference on Yugoslav peace

London, Thursday 27

A step-by-step path to peace was agreed here tonight after a two-day conference involving 30 nations and the former republics of Yugoslavia. The agreement, an apparent triumph for international diplomacy, was announced by Prime Minister John Major and U.N. Secretary General Butros Ghali.

It involves a swift end to the fighting, U.N. supervision of heavy weapons, the recognition of the borders of Bosnia-Herzegovina, the return of refugees and the closing down of detention camps.

Negotiations between the leaders

U.S. food airlift to starving Somalia gets underway at last

American and U.N. aircraft are rushing in tons of food and medicine.

Belet Uen, Friday 28

Four Hercules transport planes bearing the emblem of the Red Cross landed in this desert town 250 miles north of Mogadishu, beginning an airlift which is a co-operative effort between the Pentagon and the International Red Cross. The U.S. planes carry food, but no armed personnel. The effort to feed the Somalis, 1.5 million of whom face death by starvation, according to Red Cross estimates, is a dangerous undertaking. For the rival gangs fighting each other in this starving country, food is power. As much as half of the food brought in by relief organizations has been stolen by gangs (→ Nov 16).

Serb leader under U.N. pressure.

of the three Bosnian communities will be held in Geneva under the chairmanship of U.N. envoy Cyrus Vance and former British Foreign Secretary Lord Owen, although there were reservations about Lord Owen because of his support for air strikes against artillery positions.

Aware of scepticism about the warring parties' sincerity, Major said that, if necessary, sanctions would be tightened and that he had warned Radovan Karadzic, the Bosnian Serb leader, that the international community was determined to end the fighting.

As Major was speaking, the Serbian president, Slobodan Milosevic, stormed out in a fury and, when asked about the talks, replied: "Talks, what talks?" (→ Sept 3)

Germans demonstrate against extreme-right thugs in Rostock

Nazi salute against immigrants.

Rostock, Saturday 29

After a week of attacks against foreign asylum-seekers in this Baltic Sea port and throughout eastern Germany, 13,000 people marched in protest against racist violence. The demonstration was largely peaceful, but there were fights and 90 people were arrested. According to German police, foreign television crews offered to pay children to give the banned Nazi salute. Officials quoted residents as saying the offending crews were from France and the United States. The crews could be indicted for inciting a pro-Nazi demonstration, illegal in Germany (→ Sept 4).

Anti-Nazi citizens take to streets.

September
1992

Su	Mo	Tu	We	Th	Fr	Sa
		1	2	3	4	5
6	7	8	9	10	11	12
13	14	15	16	17	18	19
20	21	22	23	24	25	26
27	28	29	30			

New York, 1
The dollar reaches a record low at 1.3885 DM. The close against sterling was $2.002.

England, 1
Keith Fletcher, former England cricket captain, replaces Mickey Stewart as England's new team manager.

Czechoslovakia, 1
Alexander Dubcek, aged 70, former leader of the Prague Spring, is badly injured in a car accident (→ Nov 7).

Florida, 1
President Bush announces to state authorities that they will be reimbursed 100% for hurricane recovery operations.

London, 1
Britain is to reconsider its law allowing only unmarried women, between ages 17 to 27, to be au pairs.

New York, 1
More than one million gallons of water flood the Wall Street district after a 41-year-old main bursts.

U.S., 2
President Bush allocates $1.1 billion to aid American farmers.

U.S., 3
The Census Bureau reports that poverty levels in the U.S. climbed to 14.2% in 1991.

Bulgaria, 4
Former Communist leader Todor Zhivkov is sentenced to seven years in prison for crimes committed during his 35 years in power.

Bonn, 4
Forty-four Romanian and Bulgarian refugees narrowly escape injury after German rightist extremists firebomb their shelter (→ Oct 3).

London, 5
Ferrari announces that its Formula One division will be designing and manufacturing cars in Britain.

DEATHS

2. Barbara McClintock, American scientist (*June 16, 1902).

5. Fritz Leiber, American science-fiction writer (*Dec. 25, 1910).

U.N. plane downed as peace talks open

A missile attack on the U.N. aircraft has halted the airlift to Sarajevo.

Sarajevo, Thursday 3
At 1:37 p.m. the pilot of an Italian cargo plane which was part of the U.N. airlift to the Bosnian capital made a routine contact with the control tower in Zagreb, giving his location as 30 kilometres (19 miles) west of Sarajevo. Tonight the wreckage of the plane was found outside the city. First reports indicate the plane was shot down by missile fire.

Other pilots have reported being focused on by anti-aircraft radar. All humanitarian flights into Sarajevo have been suspended.

This was hardly a good omen for the opening today in Geneva of the U.N.-sponsored international conference on Yugoslavia. The first session will focus on Bosnia and methods of tightening the embargo on Yugoslavia (→ 7).

U.S. economy in trouble as election nears

Washington, Friday 4
It has been business as usual today for the battered economy of the U.S. News that 83,000 jobs were lost here last month sent the dollar plunging two pfennigs against the Deutsche mark. Almost as a reflex

action, the Federal Reserve Board dropped its interest rates by one-quarter of 1%. President Bush tried to put a brave face on it. But the U.S.'s continued economic problems can only cloud his hopes of re-election next month (→ Oct 1).

Sept 3. Kevin Maxwell, owing £406 m, is declared bankrupt.

Sept 3. 3,200 athletes attend start of the Barcelona Paralympics.

Bush backs sale of F-16s to Taiwan

Washington, Wednesday 2
President Bush has approved the sale of 150 Fighting Falcon F-16 warplanes to Taiwan. The deal, worth some $4 billion, reverses an agreement that Bush, then vice president, helped to negotiate ten years ago under which the U.S. promised to restrict and eventually phase out arms sales to Taiwan.

The change in policy is said to be due to China's recent purchase of advanced Sukhoi-27 fighters from Russia, a sale which fundamentally changed the balance of power between the Communist mainland and the Nationalist island. Until that purchase, China and Taiwan were flying obsolescent aircraft.

There are also domestic political reasons for the sale. The F-16 deal has pre-empted French attempts to sell Mirages to Taiwan, and it was hardly a coincidence that the president made the announcement of the F-16 sale while on his way to an election meeting in Fort Worth, Texas, where General Dynamics builds the fighter.

Bobby Fischer spits venom at U.S.

Svetni Stefan, Tuesday 1
Chess genius Bobby Fischer will again confront the Russian Boris Spassky. At a press conference today, Fischer held up a letter from the U.S. Treasury Department and said that he had been ordered not to play the match, which carries $5 million in prize money, because it violates the U.N. embargo on Yugoslavia. Fischer's response was to spit on the letter (→ Nov 11).

September
1992

Su	Mo	Tu	We	Th	Fr	Sa
		1	2	3	4	5
6	7	8	9	10	11	12
13	14	15	16	17	18	19
20	21	22	23	24	25	26
27	28	29	30			

Spain, 6
Italy's Gianni Bugno keeps his title, for the second year, as the world champion in cycling.

London, 6
The IRA claims responsibility for a bomb explosion in the Hilton Hotel. No injuries are reported (→ Oct 9).

Italy, 6
Sicilian Mafioso Giuseppe Madonia, suspected of involvement in the murders of two anti-Mafia judges, is arrested.

Philippines, 7
Heavy rains cause mud slides on Mount Pinatubo, leaving 55 people dead.

Kabul, 7
The first public hanging in over 20 years takes place with about 3,000 spectators.

Tajikistan, 7
President Rakhman Nabiyev resigns (→ 28).

Sarajevo, 7
Serbian gunfire on U.N. forces leaves two dead (→ Oct 9).

Toyko, 8
The government authorizes soldiers to be sent to Cambodia as part of the U.N. peacekeeping force (→ 20).

Hamburg, 8
The Cunard liner *Queen Elizabeth 2* arrives at Blohm & Voss shipyard, after crossing the Atlantic, for hull repairs.

Sweden, 9
In an effort to protect its currency, the krona, Sweden raises its bank lending rate to 75% (→ 13).

Washington, D.C., 10
The University of Pittsburgh Medical Center reveals that the Pittsburgh man who died after having had a baboon-liver transplant was infected with the AIDS virus.

Los Angeles, 12
A parking-control officer tickets a Cadillac without noticing that the driver inside is dead: he had been shot in the back of the head 13 hours earlier.

DEATH
12. Anthony Perkins, American film actor (*April 4, 1932).

At Farnborough Air Show, Russians ready to sell everything

A Russian MIG-29 high-performance fighter goes through its paces.

Farnborough, Monday 7
The Farnborough Air Show was a chance for Russia, the Ukraine and Uzbekistan to drum up some hard currency. One crew member was even charging £5 ($8.50) to look inside the cockpit of a previously top-secret MIG fighter. The Yakovlev Yak-141 was on display: It had never been seen in the West before, except in fuzzy photographs. Another first-time showing was that of the Kamov Ka-50 helicopter, which sported a Werewolf logo in an attempt at marketing the craft. The flying-display highlight was the incredible aerobatics performance by world champ Yurgiz Karlis in a new Su-29T.

Ciskei soldiers open fire on ANC demonstrators, killing 28

ANC supporters scramble for safety under a hail of bullets near Bisho.

Ciskei, Monday 7
At least 28 people were killed and some 200 wounded today when soldiers opened fire on an African National Congress march. The demonstrators, 70,000 strong, were seeking to occupy Bisho, capital of this nominally independent "homeland", and were heading for a stadium where, they said, they had permission to hold a rally.

Soldiers loyal to Brigadier Joshua Gqozo, who seized power in Ciskei two years ago, opened fire with sustained bursts from automatic weapons, and soon the dry earth of the veldt was soaking up the blood of the dead and wounded.

Outrage as Gower left out of cricket tour

Ready to play, nowhere to go.

London, Monday 7
David Gower, that most elegant of batsmen, who has scored more runs in Test matches than any other English player, has been left out of the England cricket team which will tour India this winter. "I hoped the team would have been selected on quality and experience, but it seems those qualities are not important any more," he said.

There was outrage among his admirers who pointed out that among those selected were three players, Mike Gatting, John Embury and Paul Jervis, whose five-year ban for taking part in the "rebel" tour of South Africa was prematurely lifted two months ago.

Baboon-liver man dies of a stroke

Pittsburgh, Monday 7
A 35-year-old man who received a transplant of a baboon liver in June died yesterday of a stroke. Doctors said that according to the autopsy the liver had not been rejected by the patient, but that the cause of the stroke would not be known until the autopsy was completed. In fact, the doctor who is performing the autopsy stated that the liver "looked pretty good", and that it had "adjusted nicely". The team of surgeons at the University of Pittsburgh said that they planned to perform another baboon-liver transplant (→ 10).

First man and wife team in space

Houston, Saturday 12
Those who fear that marriage is an endangered institution will take heart from today's launch of the space shuttle *Endeavour*. Two of the astronauts, Mark Lee and Jan Davis, are the first married couple to go into space. They are part of a seven-strong crew that will perform special experiments on metal vaporization, fruitfly larvae and frogs. Lee and Davis have denied speculation by the seamier newspapers that they will be doing any extra research into the problems, or pleasures, of making love under weightless conditions.

The starry-eyed couple.

End of the road for Shining Path leader

Abimael Guzman's guerrillas are responsible for the deaths of 25,000 people.

Lima, Saturday 12
Abimael Guzman Reynoso, the "fourth sword of Marxism", as he is known by his followers, was arrested today in a middle-class district of the Peruvian capital. The former philosophy professor is the leader of *Sendero Luminoso*, or Shining Path, the Maoist guerrilla organization he founded in 1970. Guzman has been in hiding since 1980, when the Shining Path began its campaign of armed insurgency. The death toll of violence by the Shining Path and another guerrilla group has exceeded 25,000.

President Alberto Fujimori has made defeating the Shining Path the government's main goal. In April he suspended parliament and the judiciary to rule the country single-handedly with the backing of the military. The government had offered a $1-million reward for information leading to the capture of Guzman. The 57-year-old guerrilla leader faces charges of treason and a life sentence.

Police said that Guzman's arrest was a result of their investigative work, not information from another source. It is hoped that the capture of the head of the Shining Path is the beginning of the end for the organization, but the police and the army are preparing for retaliatory attacks by the group and for attempts to free Guzman.

Rabin sends peace signal to Syrians

Jerusalem, Thursday 10
Public signals expressing a willingness to make peace have been exchanged by the leaders of those formerly intransigent enemies, Israel and Syria. In a radio interview today Prime Minister Yitzhak Rabin spelt out his country's readiness to withdraw from unspecified parts of the Golan Heights.

President Hafez Assad of Syria sent his signal by telling a delegation of Druze from the Golan Heights, which Israel captured in 1967 and annexed in 1981, that Syria seeks "the peace of the brave" with the people of Israel (→ 16).

Sept 12. Clint Eastwood is guest of honor at Deauville film fest.

Sept 12. Hurricane Iniki ravages Kauai Island, in Hawaii.

Sept 11. RAF bandswomen, ending a 155-year tradition, practice for tomorrow's Changing of the Guard ceremony at Buckingham Palace.

Sept 12. Actor Anthony Perkins (*Apr 4, 1932) dies of AIDS.

September

1992

Su	Mo	Tu	We	Th	Fr	Sa
		1	2	3	4	5
6	7	8	9	10	11	12
13	14	15	16	17	18	19
20	21	22	23	24	25	26
27	28	29	30			

Europe, 13
The Italian lira is devalued by 7% against all other currencies in the EC's exchange-rate mechanism (→ 18).

Thailand, 13
The four political parties that obtained 185 votes out of 360 in the parliamentary elections agree to set up a new coalition government.

Somalia, 13
The U.N. begins air-lifting food to small towns in an effort to stop Somalians from fleeing to cities (→ Nov 16).

Strasbourg, 15
The European Parliament celebrates its 40th anniversary.

St. Louis, 15
Police search for John Vincent, who could face misdemeanor charges for using suction cups to scale the city's 630-foot historic gateway before parachuting to the ground.

Israel, 15
A rape-crisis center reports that a Haifa man, aged 30, is seeking help after being raped by three women.

Virginia, 15
With 3.8 billion copies sold and 486 million in annual sales, the *USA Today* newspaper celebrates its 10th birthday.

U.S., 16
Israeli and Syrian negotiators indicate that progress was made between the two countries during talks at the State Department.

Quebec, 17
Quebec celebrates its parliament's bicentennial.

Budapest, 17
Hungarian soccer officials file complaints after uniformed masked men beat fans at the Club Champions' Cup match.

U.S., 18
Petitions help place Ross Perot on the ballot in all 50 states (→ Oct 1).

DEATHS

14. Paul Martin, Canadian politician (*June 25, 1903).

16. Millicent Fenwick, noted American politician and diplomatist (*Feb. 25, 1910).

Kodak launches innovative compact disc photograph system

Families are now able to view their snapshots at home on television.

U.S., September
Inviting relatives or neighbors to view family snaps will never be the same again.

The Kodak company this month put on sale its CD Photo system, which allows users to view normal photographs on existing television sets. Photographic prints or slides are first digitalized before being transferred onto a compact disc. It is then simply a matter of inserting this disc into the special player, which is linked to the television set. Among its many advantages, the CD Photo system makes for easy, safe storage and retrieval of hundreds of snapshots. Kodak predicts a $5-billion market worldwide for its system by 1995.

Pakistan flood catastrophe: more than 2,000 dead in one week

Stricken flood victims carry stones to try to rebuild washed-out roads.

Islamabad, Monday 14
More than 2,000 people have died in the floods and landslides which have devastated northern India and Pakistan following three days of torrential rain. Millions of people have been made homeless and thousands of square miles of crops have been washed away by the floods, the worst this century.

Pakistani and Indian troops have mounted a massive relief operation, using helicopters to lift stranded villagers to safety and dropping parcels of food and medicine. Whole towns have been inundated and roads swept away. Now there is fear of famine and pestilence in the coming months.

Nigel Mansell quits Formula One racing

Monza, Sunday 13
Nigel Mansell, the world champion, announced his retirement from Formula One racing today, hours before the Italian Grand Prix, after failing to agree terms with his successful team, Williams. He said at a press conference: "To say I have been badly treated is, I think, a gross understatement. Due to circumstances beyond my control, I have decided to retire from Formula One at the end of the season." He took part in today's race, but gearbox trouble forced him to quit.

Sept 13. Sweden's Stefan Edberg (right) wins his sixth Grand Slam title at Flushing Meadow, defeating Pete Sampras, hit by a stomach virus.

Dutch handicapped get call-girl aid

The Netherlands, Friday 18
State-subsidized sex is the focus of a report in the current issue of *Elsevier*, the Dutch weekly. A handicapped man from Noordoostpolder had been trying to get government aid to pay for his monthly visit to a prostitute. He brought his case before the Dutch government's top advisory agency, putting forward a psychologist's report that lack of sex can lead to depression and anti-social behavior. The advisory agency ruled that the town must pay 65 guilders ($39) per month to defray his expenses.

Sept 16. At just 17, Niki Taylor of Florida becomes the youngest model for Cover Girl Cosmetics.

Sept 16. Lifetime Achievement accolade for Ol' Blue Eyes at the American Cinema Awards.

Monetary chaos sweeps over Europe

As the Bundesbank throws its weight around, weaker currencies, such as sterling and the Italian lira, tumble.

London, Friday 18
European diplomacy has been thrown into disarray by Britain's announcement Wednesday that it is to leave the European exchange rate mechanism and allow sterling to float. The admission of defeat by Prime Minister John Major and Chancellor Norman Lamont, after a battle against speculators which is estimated to have cost Britain £15 billion, has led to harsh words between Britain and Germany and confusion in the markets.

The rift with Germany opened after Lamont blamed Bonn's economic policies for the fall of the pound and "many of the tensions within the ERM", and Major said Britain would not resume its membership until the mechanism was run "in the interests of all the countries of Europe".

An obviously angry Chancellor Kohl hit back at Lamont, saying his remarks were childishly simplistic and "inappropriate for a minister". Giuliano Amato, the Italian prime minister, whose currency was devalued last week, supported Kohl, saying it was naïve to blame the Germans as the Italian and British press had done. Meanwhile, the speculators look for their next victim.

French president has operation for cancer

Paris, Wednesday 16
President François Mitterrand has left a Parisian hospital after undergoing prostate surgery to remove a cancer. In Western countries prostate cancer is second only to lung cancer in deaths caused by the disease. But medical experts say that if it is caught early enough, the cure rate is nearly 100%.

Nevertheless, the announcement confirming the reason for the president's five-day hospital stay has led to speculation that Mitterrand might resign before his term ends in 1995. The 76-year-old leader responded to reporters' questions as to whether he might retire by saying: "There is no reason for that. I don't think they gave me a lobotomy, because it's not at that end that this happened."

A shaky François Mitterrand leaves Cochin Hospital in central Paris.

September

1992

Su	Mo	Tu	We	Th	Fr	Sa
		1	2	3	4	5
6	7	8	9	10	11	12
13	14	15	16	17	18	19
20	21	22	23	24	25	26
27	28	29	30			

Cape Canaveral, 20
The space shuttle *Endeavour* returns to Earth from its second mission.

Spain, 21
After crossing more than 2,500 miles, the first transatlantic balloon race is won by a Belgian team.

Vatican City, 21
The Vatican and Mexico resume diplomatic relations following 130 years of severed ties.

U.S., 21
Box-office statistics from the first weekend of Woody Allen's latest film, *Husbands and Wives*, shows earnings estimated at $3.5 million.

Bristol Channel, 22
Two Irish fishermen are feared drowned after their vessel collides with a French trawler.

Zurich, 22
Soccer midfielder Diego Maradona receives his desired transfer from the Italian team Napoli to the Spanish team FC Sevilla.

Florida, 23
A teenager mistakenly given to the wrong parents at birth, nearly 14 years ago, is awarded more that $5 million in damages.

Hatfield, 23
British Aerospace announces the closing of its Hatfield aeronautical factory where Tiger Moths, Mosquitos and other aircraft were manufactured.

Florida, 23
Manon Rheaume, aged 20, of the National Hockey League's Tampa Bay Lightning, makes history as the first woman to play in one of the four U.S. professional sports leagues.

Moscow, 25
Russia and the U.S. agree to lift decades-old travel restrictions for journalists and business people.

Germany, 25
The last link in the 2,180-mile-long North Sea to Black Sea inland waterway is opened.

DEATH

23. James Van Fleet, American general (*March 19, 1892).

A timid French 'Yes' vote for Europe

Paris, Sunday 20
The people of France gave grudging approval to the Maastricht treaty in a referendum today which, with most of the votes counted, shows that 51% approve of closer European unity. This approval, even one given so timidly, saved President Mitterrand from an embarrassing repudiation of his pro-European policy.

However, the closeness of the vote, in the country which has been at the core of the European movement, reinforces the view that the EC must loosen its plans for the community. Prime Minister Paul Schluter of Denmark, which rejected Maastricht in June, said it shows "certain elements of the treaty are unacceptable to the citizens of France and Denmark and other countries, and that understanding for the Danish rejection has grown." The official reaction in Paris, more in relief than conviction, is that the "Yes" vote is just as binding as the equally close "No" vote by the Danes.

British golfer wins Lancôme Trophy

France, Sunday 20
Britain's Mark Roe has seen off Nick Faldo and Vicente Fernandez to win golf's Lancôme Trophy and pick up a check for $148,000. He finished the 6,661-yard (6,177 meter) course at St-Nom-la-Bretèche 13-under-par at 267. Roe's victory was more or less assured in the first three holes, which he achieved with three birdies. He stroked in three more at the 8th, 10th and 16th holes, and had a stroke of luck at the 14th when his ball hit a spectator's thigh and bounced back onto the fairway instead of deep into the woods. He put his win down to improved concentration.

Japan sends first troops to Cambodia

Phnom Penh, Sunday 20
The first Japanese soldiers to be deployed abroad since World War II, arrived here today to join the U.N. peacekeeping force trying to restore Cambodia's stability after 13 years of civil war. The eight officers, led by Lieutenant Colonel Yusuke Fukui, an affable man who likes to sing, are the advance guard of several hundred Japanese troops who will arrive over the next month.

John Major mired in Maastricht revolt

London, Monday 21
Prime Minister John Major, facing a growing rebellion within his party by the "Euro-sceptics" following the close French vote to approve the Maastricht treaty, sought today to defuse the revolt by promising a "profound look" at the future of the EC. The olive branch was spurned by opponents of the treaty who promised "trench warfare" against it in the Commons (→ Oct 1).

Mark Roe's second European title.

Sept 22. Noblesse oblige: Princess Diana has to give up her $152,000 Mercedes roadster after an outcry from "Buy British" enthusiasts.

British minister resigns over sex scandal

David Mellor, dubbed "Minister for Fun", admits affair with an actress.

Gregory, aged 12, divorces his parents

A very determined Gregory Kingsley being escorted to court in Orlando.

London, Thursday 24

David Mellor, the heritage secretary and one of John Major's closest friends, resigned tonight, blaming his departure from the cabinet on a "constant barrage of stories about me in certain tabloid newspapers". Mellor's problems began with the revelation in July of his affair with actress Antonia de Sancha.

Supported by his wife and Major, he survived that scandal, but a libel case brought by Mona Bauwens, daughter of a PLO official, against *The People* newspaper finished him off. Mona Bauwens, who had invited the Mellor family to holiday with her in Spain, argued that *The People* had suggested she was not fit to be seen in decent company. The jury did not agree and Mellor's wisdom – or lack of it – in accepting a free holiday from Bauwens was so fiercely questioned that his resignation became inevitable.

Germany to expel Romanian Gypsies

Bucharest, Thursday 24

Germany is to repatriate 50,000 Romanians, most of them nomadic Gypsies, under an agreement signed by the two countries here today. Since their arrival in Germany without papers, following the collapse of Communism in 1989, most of the Gypsies have faced racial persecution and have been forced to live in holding camps for their own security. Rudolf Seiters, German Interior Minister, and Victor Babiuc, his Romanian counterpart, who signed the agreement, said they were studying the best way to carry out the deportation. Herr Seiters said Bonn will allocate £12 million to create jobs for the Gypsies in Romanian towns.

Former Vietcong is elected president

General Le Duc Anh is a hardliner.

Hanoi, Wednesday 23

The Vietnamese National Assembly unanimously elected General Le Duc Anh, the sole candidate, to the presidency. General Anh is a veteran of the wars against France and the U.S., and led the Vietnamese intervention in Cambodia in 1978-1979. Last year he participated in negotiations with China which led to a normalization of the countries' relations in November, ending a rift which had resulted from the invasion of Cambodia. General Anh was the minister of defense and is the second-ranking member of the Politburo.

Orlando, Friday 25

Gregory Kingsley, a 12-year-old Florida boy, has won a "divorce" from his biological parents. For the first time in U.S. judicial history, a child has initiated a court action to separate himself from his biological family. The judge approved Gregory's adoption by his foster parents, George and Elizabeth Russ. His foster father is a lawyer and, although Gregory had hired his own lawyer, gave his advice throughout the case. "Let the law protect real families", said Russ, "not families in name only."

The judge said that the evidence had shown that Gregory's mother had neglected and abandoned her son. Gregory had lived with his mother for only seven months in the last eight years, and he testified that for two years while he was in a foster home she never wrote, called or visited him.

Sept 24. Workers in New York dismantle the huge sign on the Pan Am building, now owned by the insurance company Metropolitan Life.

Sept 26. The Swiss firm, Swatch, makes its 100-millionth watch.

September

1992

Su	Mo	Tu	We	Th	Fr	Sa
		1	2	3	4	5
6	7	8	9	10	11	12
13	14	15	16	17	18	19
20	21	22	23	24	25	26
27	28	29	30			

Nigeria, 27
A military C-130 plane crashes near Lagos killing more than 200 people.

Geneva, 27
Swiss citizens approve a project to build a high-speed rail system that will cut through the Alps.

Chile, 28
Pictures taken by astronomers confirm that a 10th planet exists 3,700 million miles from the Sun. The planet was originally discovered by University of Hawaii students.

Romania, 28
Presidential elections show former Communist and current president Ion Iliescu with a strong lead (→ Oct 11).

Moscow, 28
Russia says it will send troops to Tajikistan to defend Russians and stop the spread of civil war.

California, 29
Magic Johnson announces his return to the Los Angeles Lakers. He had retired after making public that he is HIV positive.

Germany, 29
A survey of Germans between ages 16 and 24 indicates a rise in racism: more than 28% have racist views (15% in 1990).

Luanda, 29
Following 16 years of civil war and hundreds of years of colonial rule, the first democratic Angolan elections take place in the presence of U.N. observers (→ Oct 6).

Beijing, 30
China and South Korea sign a historic agreement to end hostility and promote cooperation between the two countries.

U.K., 30
The British Mint introduces a new 10-pence (18-cent) coin which is lighter and smaller than the previous coin.

New York, 30
The pound is quoted at $1.78.

DEATH

28. William Douglas-Home, British playwright (*June 3, 1912).

Brazilian president impeached for graft

Brasilia, Tuesday 29
Fernando Collor de Mello, Brazil's first freely elected president for 29 years, was impeached tonight by the Chamber of Deputies on charges of receiving $6.5 million from a slush fund run by his former campaign treasurer, Paulo Cesar Farias, and lying to cover up the payments. The scandal has practically paralyzed Brazil. Massive anti-Collor rallies have been held throughout the country, and tonight tens of thousands of demonstrators gathered in front of the congress, cheering as the deputies cast their votes for impeachment. Collor will now be suspended for 180 days and tried by the senate.

"Out", demands this protester.

Turkish army blasts Kurdish separatists

Fierce fighting leaves 203 dead.

Ankara, Monday 28
Turkish troops are conducting a full-scale security sweep against Kurdish separatist guerrillas in the rugged country along the Iraqi border. Some reports say the Turks have crossed the border and that aircraft have been bombing the Kurdish strongholds in Iraq.

Twenty-nine soldiers and 174 guerrillas of the Kurdistan Workers Party died in a 12-hour battle around Semdinli where the borders of Iran, Iraq and Turkey converge. Prime Minister Suleyman Demirel, again rejecting the Kurdish demand for a separate state, said: "We have to defeat them, we can defeat them and we will defeat them."

Sept 30. After 94 years of U.S. naval presence at Subic Bay, the U.S. Navy formally hands over the 62,000-acre base to the Philippines.

Britons outraged at German V2 homage

Bonn, Monday 28
The celebrations planned to mark the fiftieth anniversary of the V2 rocket, which the Germans used to bombard London in the closing stages of the war, have been called off. Billed as a commemoration of "man's first step into space" the event ran into a barrage of criticism from Britons with long memories and German politicians already concerned about the strained relations between the two countries.

However, Karl Dersch, president of the aerospace federation, regretted that Germany's scientific achievement in building the V2 could not be honored: "It remains the foundation for worldwide space technology."

Remains of a V2 rocket engine.

Cricket great Imran retires from game

London, Monday 28
Imran Khan, the handsome athlete who inspired the Pakistani cricket team first as a player and later as a captain, is to retire. In a career illuminated by great feats on the field none was greater than the way he, although injured, led his team to victory over England in the final of the World Cup last March. "I am fortunate", he said today, "that God has allowed me to leave cricket with so much dignity." He now plans to concentrate on the cancer hospital he has founded in memory of his mother.

October

1992

Su	Mo	Tu	We	Th	Fr	Sa
				1	2	3
4	5	6	7	8	9	10
11	12	13	14	15	16	17
18	19	20	21	22	23	24
25	26	27	28	29	30	31

Tokyo, 1
Japanese nuclear experts deny that a malfunctioning reactor near here was ever in danger of a core meltdown.

U.S., 2
IBM announces that it is to lay off 40,000 people, 25% of its workforce (→ 15).

Italy, 4
A cease-fire agreement is signed in Rome between the Mozambique government and rebel forces (→ 7).

Estonia, 5
Lennart Meri, aged 63, is elected president of this Baltic nation.

Dublin, 6
The government decides to hold a referendum which will focus on the issue of abortion rights in Ireland (→ Nov 5).

France, 6
Customs officials in Le Havre block the entry of Madonna's controversial book, *Sex*.

Virginia, 7
Six people are killed when a USAF C-130 crashes near a residential zone of Berkeley Springs.

Amsterdam, 8
Dutch authorities drastically lower the toll of the El Al Boeing 747 cargo aircraft crash to 50 dead.

U.S., 8
A $27-billion tax bill, covering urban assistance and Individual Retirement Accounts, is passed by Congress and sent to President Bush for approval.

Paris, 8
French Agriculture Minister Jean-Pierre Soisson says that the European Community will not make further concessions in GATT negotiations with the United States (→ 16).

U.K., 9
Two bombs explode in London. Police believe that they were planted by the IRA to protest the Conservative Party's annual conference.

DEATHS

6. Denholm Elliott, British actor (*May 31, 1922).

8. Willy Brandt, German statesman (*Dec. 18, 1913).

Perot leaps back into election fray

Dallas, Thursday 1
Texan billionaire Ross Perot today reversed his decision of 11 weeks ago and declared himself an independent candidate in the presidential election. Announcing his change of mind at a chaotic press conference, he said, "Volunteers in all 50 states have asked me to run."

He squabbled with reporters, accusing them of being "hostile, negative, yelling and screaming like three-year-olds", and attacked the administration for being "a mess". He said he was rejoining the race because "neither political party had effectively addressed the issues that concern the people" (→ 15).

The Texas billionaire and running-mate, retired admiral Jim Stockdale.

Brazil's military police kill 111 prisoners in Sao Paulo riot

Sao Paulo, Friday 2
The Sao Paulo House of Detention, South America's largest prison, erupted in violence today. The riot, the worst prison violence ever in South America, claimed the lives of 111 prisoners. No police officers were killed, and reports of the number of police injured ranged from 22 to 35. The 300 riot police sent into the prison to put down the uprising were authorized to shoot in self-defense, but the state security director of Sao Paulo said that most of the deaths were at the hands of the inmates. The state governor called for an investigation into the riot and the reponse by the security forces.

Prisoners and human rights groups blame authorities for the massacre.

Racist violence mars Kohl call for unity

Neo-Nazi youths take to the streets.

Schwerin, Saturday 3
Tens of thousands of people gathered here today in what should have been a joyful celebration of the second anniversary of Germany's "Day of Unity", but this is a city beset by unemployment and racism and there was little joy.

Chancellor Kohl was jostled and pelted with eggs. He turned on the chanting militants and shouted: "Look at their faces, that is downright Nazi hate." Later, in a TV speech, he said: "I know that many people in the new federal states view the future with worry and fear but I am sure that we are going in the right direction" (→ Nov 5).

Gorbachev barred from travel abroad

Moscow, Friday 2
Mikhail Gorbachev has joined the long list of Russians who have been prohibited from leaving the country by the government in power. The Russian Constitutional Court is conducting hearings on the legality of President Boris Yeltsin's August 1991 decision to ban the Communist Party. Gorbachev has refused to testify, calling the process a "political game". The court has ruled that as long as the former president refuses to appear before the court, he will not be allowed a diplomatic passport (→ 19).

El Al Boeing 747 crashes into Amsterdam apartment blocks

The cargo jet, loaded with 100,000 liters of fuel, devastated two crowded buildings at the Bijlmermeer complex.

Amsterdam, Sunday 4
A Boeing 747-200F crashed in a working-class district of the Dutch capital tonight, 15 minutes after take-off from Schipol Airport. The impact demolished two nine-story buildings, inhabited mostly by immigrants from Suriname and the Antilles. Estimates put the number of deaths at 150 to 200. The flight had left at 6:21 p.m. for New York, and only a few minutes later the Israeli pilot, Isaac Fuchs, radioed the control tower, reporting a fire in one of the jet's engines. Almost immediately after, he reported a second engine fire. He tried to turn around and go back to the airport, but the loss of at least one of the engines caused him to lose control of the plane (→ 8).

Angolan guerrillas reject election results

Angola, Tuesday 6
The fragile truce between the government and UNITA guerrilla forces seemed close to breaking down tonight after a group of senior UNITA officers left the national army, newly created from the warring forces, in protest against what they said was fraud in last week's national election. With most of the votes counted President dos Santos has a 51 to 39% lead over UNITA's leader, Jonas Savimbi. People fear the civil war, which lasted 16 years, will erupt again (→ 31).

UNITA leader Jonas Savimbi.

Pentagon apology for missile error

Aegean Sea, Friday 2
At least one of two Sea Sparrow missiles fired from the U.S. aircraft carrier *Saratoga* hit a Turkish warship, killing five Turkish sailors. The craft were participating in NATO naval exercises. The firing was accidental, but the cause is not yet known. The U.S. Navy has begun an investigation, and apologies were offered by NATO's top military commander, U.S. General John Shalikashvili, and the acting U.S. secretary of state, Lawrence Eagleburger.

Major faces uphill struggle on Europe

Brighton, Thursday 8
Prime Minister John Major will address the Conservative Party conference at this windswept seaside town today in an attempt to boost confidence following a week in which his determination to push the Maastricht Treaty through parliament has been savagely attacked by Lady Thatcher, Lord Tebbit and other "Euro-sceptics".

His task was not eased by a lame speech from Chancellor Norman Lamont yesterday. Speaker after speaker accused Lamont of failing to put British interests first. One said the government was lost in a fog with "no captain or navigator and a purser who sounds unsure how he is going to finance the trip home" (→ 16).

Rainforest warning issued by U.N.

New York, Monday 5
The United Nations has published a startling study on the state of the world's tropical rainforests. Rainforests are valued for the diversity of plant and animal life which is found there and for their effect in regulating the Earth's climate. The three-year study, which used aerial and satellite photography, found that more than an acre of rainforest is being destroyed each second, 40 million acres each year.

October 8. Nobel Peace Prize winner Willy Brandt, who died today, with Kennedy during the president's historic 1963 visit to the Berlin Wall.

Oct. 8. A visibly ailing Rudolf Nureyev at the Paris Opera.

Premier tries to rally Tories.

Mozambique truce threatened by fighting

The Rome peace accord is aimed at ending a brutal 16-year conflict.

Maputo, Wednesday 7

The Mozambique Army has accused the Mozambican National Resistance Movement, know by its Portuguese acronym, Renamo, of violating the cease-fire agreement signed in Rome on Sunday. The accord was the result of two years of negotiations and is meant to end the 16-year war, which has claimed a million lives. Western officials feared that the truce might be ineffective, as neither the government nor Renamo has full control over their troops. The U.N. World Food program predicts that continued fighting, which prevents effective food-aid distribution, could lead to a famine on the level of the one in Somalia.

The 'Crazy Cajun' loves 'Bloody Mary'

Mary Matalin works for Bush, James Carville backs Clinton.

Washington, D.C., Saturday 10

Politics makes strange bedfellows, and this seems to be especially true in an election year. Consider the case of Chicago-native Mary Matalin and Louisianan James Carville. She is the political director of the Bush campaign, and he holds the same position in the Clinton camp. This unlikely couple supposedly put their relationship on hold for the duration of the presidential race, but the *New York Times* has reported seeing them grocery shopping and dining together in the nation's capital, and house-hunting in Virginia. Hopefully for them the Republican-Democrat rivalry will not lead to as tragic an end as that of the Montagues and Capulets.

West Indian author gets Literature Nobel

Derek Walcott of Trinidad.

Stockholm, Thursday 8

Derek Walcott was awarded the Nobel Prize for Literature today. The poet and dramatist from Trinidad is the first Caribbean writer to receive the prize, worth $1.2 million (£710,000) this year. Walcott is best known for *Omeros*, which remakes the Homeric epics as the story of an itinerant West Indian. The 325-page poem, published in 1990, has sold tens of thousands of copies. The choice of Walcott for the honor is especially significant in the year of the 500th anniversary of Christopher Columbus' landing in the West Indies.

Bosnia no-fly zone imposed by U.N.

New York, Friday 9

The United Nations today imposed an air exclusion zone over Bosnia to stop Serbian planes attacking Muslim targets but, for the time being, it stopped short of sanctioning aerial patrols and the shooting down of Serbian aircraft breaking the "no-fly" zone rules.

The Security Council, which passed the measure by 14 votes to 0 with China abstaining, said it would urgently consider "further measures necessary to enforce the ban" in case of violations. The ban goes into effect immediately (→ 29).

Oct. 9. One of 800 works loaned to Spain by Baron Thyssen.

October 10. In Washington, D.C., a quilt is formed of more than 20,000 panels, each one remembering the life of a victim of the AIDS epidemic.

October

1992

Su	Mo	Tu	We	Th	Fr	Sa
				1	2	3
4	5	6	7	8	9	10
11	12	13	14	15	16	17
18	19	20	21	22	23	24
25	26	27	28	29	30	31

Romania, 11
Ion Iliescu is elected president with 60% of the vote.

France, 11
Despite the fact that airline companies are in the red, roundtrip tickets L.A.-Paris are being sold for $679.

Seville, 12
The World's Fair closes its doors after having received 15 million visitors.

Stockholm, 12
The Nobel Prize for Medicine is awarded to Americans Edmond Fisher and Edwin Krebs of the University of Washington. American Gary Becker of the University of Chicago receives the Nobel Prize for Economy.

Washington, D.C., 13
Thirteen Komodo dragons are born at the National Zoo. It is the first time any have hatched outside Indonesia.

Munich, 13
Police seize 2 kilograms (4.4 pounds) of radioactive uranium which originated in the former Soviet Union.

U.K., 14
England open their campaign to enter the finals of the soccer World Cup at Wembley by drawing 1-1 with Norway.

Stockholm, 14
American Rudolph Marcus receives the Nobel Prize for Chemistry.

Toronto, 14
The Blue Jays win the American League pennant, becoming the first baseball team outside the U.S. to play in the World Series (→ 24).

Sri Lanka, 15
Tamil separatist guerrillas massacre more then 160 Muslims.

London, 15
The Pentland group decides to drop its plans to buy the French sportswear company Adidas.

Moscow, 16
A 100% tariff on imported alcohol is imposed to protect domestic vodka producers.

DEATH

16. Shirley Booth, American actress (*1898).

Columbus celebration stirs passions

America, Monday 12

The 500th anniversary of Christopher Columbus' landing in the West Indies is the occasion for celebrations, protests and the launching of a modern effort to discover new worlds.

Columbus has long been hailed as a hero for his "discovery" of the New World, but recently there has been a reappraisal of the man and his mission. For nearly every celebration there has been a protest, pointing out the disastrous effects of European colonization on Native American populations. Nevertheless, an Associated Press opinion poll taken just before the anniversary celebrations showed that

Near Santo Domingo, a huge lighthouse projects a cross into the heavens.

NASA launches a $100-million program to seek intelligent life in space.

64% of U.S. citizens still consider him a "hero". Only 15% viewed him as a "villain".

NASA has launched an effort to find extra-terrestrial Columbuses. A 10-year, $100-million program will use sophisticated electronics, highly sensitive radio receivers and powerful telescopes to look and listen for evidence of civilizations from other planets.

One of the most lavish of the tributes is Philip Glass' opera, *The Voyage*, at the New York Metropolitan. The $2-million spectacle explores the themes of discovery and confrontation between different cultures. The first act shows aliens landing on Earth in the Ice Age, the second the landing of Columbus, and the third the discovery of intelligent life in space.

Oct. 12. Ridley Scott's film "1492" is released today.

Native Americans demonstrate in Denver against Columbus hoopla.

Quake kills hundreds in Egypt's capital

The tremor lasted only one minute but devastated much of the city center.

Bush, Clinton, Perot square off in debates

Can time be running out for Republican incumbent George Bush?

Cairo, Monday 12
A powerful earthquake hit Cairo this afternoon, killing at least 340 people and injuring 4,000. The center of the quake, which registered 5.9 on the Richter scale, was thirty kilometers (19 miles) outside of the city. Tremors were felt as far away as Jerusalem, 250 miles (400 kilometers) to the northeast. The ensuing panic led to traffic accidents and many people were trampled to death in the chaos. As many as 160 buildings were demolished or badly damaged. The results could have been much worse. The Sphinx, pyramids and other national monuments escaped damage, as did the Azwan High Dam in southern Egypt, which holds back Lake Nasser, the largest artificial lake in the world.

French play tough in crucial GATT talks

World trade faces heavy weather.

Brussels, Friday 16
Last-ditch attempts will be made by U.S. and European Community negotiators today to strike a deal which could avoid a trade war and boost world trade by £140 billion a year. Ray MacSharry, the Irish EC farm commissioner, said that "some progress has been made".

However, even this cautious optimism was contradicted by the obdurate French foreign minister, Roland Dumas, who insisted that the talks "have not made it possible to advance positively". France wanted a deal, he said, but not one that risked its vital interests. "French agriculture absolutely cannot be sacrificed" (→ Nov 5).

Richmond, Thursday 15
The second of the three presidential debates, held at the university here tonight, saw the candidates exchanging ideas rather than insults, a tactic which suited Governor Clinton well. Ross Perot, the independent, won laughs with his folksy one-liners but his maverick novelty has begun to wear thin.

President Bush played the experience card, asking the voters which man they would want in the White House "if a major international threat erupted". His was a lackluster performance, however, and it is generally agreed that by concentrating on domestic issues Bill Clinton won the debate. A CBS poll found that 54% of viewers thought he had won, 25% voted for the president and 20% for Perot (→ 26).

Britain's coal industry faces jobs crisis

London, Tuesday 13
The Conservative government is bracing for a violent reaction to the Coal Board's decision to close 31 pits and make 30,000 miners redundant. Trade and Industry Minister, Michael Heseltine, said today: "This is the toughest decision I have ever had to take, but that does not make it the wrong decision. I must not allow my heart to rule my head."

The closures will have a devastating effect on the close-knit mining communities. The need to reduce output by 25 million tons a year will mean the end of deep mining in Lancashire, North Staffordshire, North Wales and North Derbyshire. There will be just one pit in South Wales and one in Scotland. An extra £1 billion has been allocated to meet the cost of the redundancies but the money cannot replace a way of life.

Arthur Scargill, president of the National Union of Mineworkers, said the closures are "a deliberate political act of industrial vandalism perpetrated against an already decimated industrial landscape". He called on his men to fight, urging them to take whatever action necessary to save the industry (→ 19).

Golfer Faldo wins Match Play trophy

Virginia Water, Sunday 11
Nick Faldo romped to a six-hole lead in the first 18 holes of the World Match Play golf championship at Wentworth today. He went on to win the prize of $272,000 – the biggest in European golf – at the 29th hole. Faldo's nearest rival, American Jeff Sluman, had knocked out Seve Ballesteros and Ian Woosnam in previous rounds, but could not compete against Faldo's better knowledge of the course. "I kept pushing myself," said the victorious Englishman.

Oct. 15. Russian serial killer Andrei Chikatilo gets death sentence for 52 grisly murders.

European Community leaders seek to salvage Maastricht Treaty

Birmingham, Friday 16
European leaders met here today for a special one-day conference in an attempt to restore the European Community's battered image and salvage the Maastricht Treaty. The "Birmingham Declaration" makes few actual commitments but promises more open decision-making, democratic accountability and respect of national traditions.

Prime Minister John Major, current president of the EC, set the tone for the meeting: "Unless we have the people with us, our enterprise will not succeed." The meeting did not deal with economic stagnation, unemployment or poor economic management (→ Nov 5).

Moves to strengthen Europe's unity face growing opposition in Britain.

Computer industry hit by record losses

New York, Thursday 15
IBM, the computer giant, lost $2.8 billion in the last quarter, with earnings only half what had been expected, and soaring reorganization costs forced "Big Blue" to struggle to keep up with the constantly mutating computer industry.

It is also paying the price of its huge worldwide operations which expose it to fluctuations in the currency markets. Last month's chaos in the European Monetary System meant its European sales froze. Analysts say IBM no longer has a monopoly of new developments and must stop thinking it has.

Katyn massacre secrets revealed

Warsaw, Wednesday 14
Secret KGB documents handed to President Lech Walesa by Russia's chief archivist today reveal the grim secret of how Stalin and his cronies directly ordered the execution of 25,000 Poles at a meeting of the Politburo on March 5, 1940. The documents fit the last pieces into the jigsaw puzzle of the fate of the Polish officers whose bodies were buried in the Katyn Forest. For years Soviets leaders maintained they had been shot by the Germans: Now, at last, the full truth is known.

Guatemalan Indian awarded Peace Prize

Rights activist Rigoberta Menchu.

Guatemala, Friday 16
"Viva Rigoberta!" cried thousands of supporters of the Guatemalan Indian human rights activist Rigoberta Menchu as she drove into the small, rural town of San Marcos, returning from a short trip to the capital after learning that she had won this year's Nobel Peace Prize. She is organizing protests over the 500 years of oppression of native peoples since the arrival of Columbus in the Americas. Menchu began protesting military repression in Guatemala when she was a teenager. In 1980 her father, mother and brother were killed by the Guatemalan Army.

Canadian, Briton share Booker Prize

London, Tuesday 13
The panel found it impossible to agree on who should win Britain's most prestigious literary prize, so, for the first time since 1974, they decided to divide it. This year's £20,000 Booker Prize is to be shared by Michael Ondaatje, whose *The English Patient* tells the story of a bizarre convalescence in post-war Italy, and Barry Unsworth, whose *Sacred Hunger* recounts a mutiny on board an 18th-century slave ship. Ondaatje was the bookies' favorite. Both authors are said to be delighted.

Madison Square Garden rock concert pays tribute to Bob Dylan

His first album was released in 1962.

New York, Friday 16
A young folk singer recorded his first album 30 years ago. He came to be one of the most influential artists in popular music and a symbol of his generation. Tonight a wide range of stars – including Johnny Cash, Stevie Wonder, Tom Petty, George Harrison, the O'Jays and Neil Young – paid tribute to Bob Dylan in a performance at Madison Square Garden. The celebration was marred only when Irish singer Sinead O'Connor fled the stage in tears after being booed by the crowd. A few nights before she had torn up a picture of the pope during an appearance on U.S. television.

Sinead O'Connor is booed off stage.

Oct. 15. Australian top model Elle McPherson launches her own lingerie line in Melbourne.

1992

Su	Mo	Tu	We	Th	Fr	Sa
				1	2	3
4	5	6	7	8	9	10
11	12	13	14	15	16	17
18	19	20	21	22	23	24
25	26	27	28	29	30	31

Colombia, 18
A second earthquake in two days and a volcanic eruption leaves more than 10 people dead and many others injured or missing.

Israel, 18
The West Bank is hit by a resurgence of violence one day after suspected Palestinian guerrillas killed an Israeli woman and wounded nine other Israelis.

London, 19
John Major announces that only 10 coal mines will be closed, not 31 as announced six days ago (→ 21).

Moscow, 19
Russia's Constitutional Court says Gorbachev will be summoned to the court but will not be forced to testify about Communist Party activities.

New York, 20
Despite U.S. opposition, the U.N. and Iraq sign an agreement that will give Iraq greater control over humanitarian assistance.

Beijing, 20
China refuses to define the future democratic status of Hong Kong.

Berlin, 20
Police find the body of Petra Kelly, founder of Germany's Green Party, and say she was killed by her companion, Gert Bastian, a former general.

Egypt, 21
Islamic militants attack British tourists, killing one and leaving two wounded.

Japan, 22
A Japanese scientist claims to have achieved cold nuclear fusion. If true, this could lead to an almost endless supply of safe power.

Moscow, 22
Galeries Lafayette, one of France's major department stores, opens in Red Square.

Johannesburg, 23
Nelson Mandela blames apartheid for the spread of AIDS to black South Africans.

Moscow, 24
The Interior Ministry states that crimes related to alcohol abuse have drastically increased.

Bush fails to score decisive victory in presidential debates

The Clinton camp is buoyed by Democratic candidate's performance.

East Lansing, Monday 19
President Bush performed much more briskly in tonight's final public debate with Governor Bill Clinton and the independent, Ross Perot. He put his message across clearly and did his best to make the voters think about his character rather than their economic woes.

At the end of the debate, however, the consensus was that he had not done enough to cut Clinton's lead. The Democrat came through the debate well, setting off no fireworks but making no errors. Perot lit the fireworks by accusing Bush of using taxpayers' money to help General Noriega and Saddam Hussein gain power (→ Nov 4).

Madonna mania for 'Sex' book launch

London, Wednesday 21
Madonna's greatly-hyped book, *Sex*, a photo-album of sexual exploration, sold 100,000 copies at £25 a time in Britain today within 12 hours of its global launch. Hundreds of people queued in pouring rain to buy the first copies at one minute past midnight. The British launch was, however, more sedate than New York's send-off at which models carried whips and wore dog collars and studded leather jock straps. After a complaint by a member of the public, the book was referred to the Crown Prosecution Service. It took no action.

Oct. 19. **Growing numbers of economic refugees from Africa, seeking Europe's riches, die attempting to cross the Straits of Gibraltar.**

'Sex' sells for $49.95.

Oct. 18. **A tribute to Canadian baseball goes badly wrong when the U.S. Marine color guard mistakenly displays the flag upside down (→ 24).**

Furious miners force Major to back down

An estimated 50,000 people demonstrate in London against pit closures.

London, Wednesday 21

The government was forced to grant more concessions to the miners in order to ensure victory in a rowdy Commons debate on the pit closures tonight. Even so, it scraped home by just 13 votes. The debate took place against a background of a march through London by thousands of protesting miners who are getting much support from the public. Many people see the miners' anger as a way of venting their own frustration over their economic woes.

It fell to Michael Heseltine, minister for trade and industry, to acknowledge the government's retreat by pledging that his enquiry into the closures could save some of the threatened pits and even lead to changes in the structure of the privatized electricity industry (→25).

World Series win ends Blue Jays bad luck

The Canadian players celebrate their 11-inning, 4-3 victory in Atlanta.

Elizabeth II jeered during Dresden visit

Dresden, Thursday 22

The visit by Queen Elizabeth and the Duke of Edinburgh to this city, devastated by British and American bombers in the final months of the war, was marred today by demonstrators who chanted, "Forgiveness Never!" as the royal couple entered the Kreuzkirche for a service of reconciliation.

Most of the anger was directed at the erection of a statue in London of "Bomber" Harris, architect of the RAF's bombing campaign. The majority of the crowd of 3,000 who listened to the service took no part in the protests and the incident was out of keeping with the enthusiastic welcome given to the Queen throughout her five-day visit to Germany.

An egg narrowly misses royal limo.

Atlanta, Saturday 24

Toronto's ball club will no longer be called the "Blow Jays".

Their depressing history of losing when they seemed sure to win almost repeated itself tonight. In the bottom of the ninth inning the Jays were ahead 2-1. They had two outs on the Atlanta Braves and two strikes on the batter. His run-scoring single postponed any victory celebrations. Two innings later 41-year-old Jay Dave Winfield, who had never been on a championship team, sent in two runs off a double to make the score 4-2. But in the bottom of the 11th, the Braves scored again. With the tying run on third, it looked like the game might last all night. The Braves attempted to send their man in on a bunt, but he was thrown out at first. The cycle was broken.

French official convicted in blood scandal

Dr. Garretta gets a four-year term.

Paris, Friday 23

Dr Michel Garretta, former head of the French National Blood Transfusion Center, and other health officials knew in May 1985 that the center was distributing blood contaminated with the AIDS virus. The contaminated blood stocks were not withdrawn until October of that year. As a result, more than 1,250 hemophiliacs have been infected with the AIDS virus and, of those, 273 have died. Garretta and two other health officials were convicted of distributing the tainted blood today. Garretta was sentenced to four years in prison.

Oct. 24. Aussies keep Rugby League World Cup by beating Britain 10-6.

October

1992

Su	Mo	Tu	We	Th	Fr	Sa
				1	2	3
4	5	6	7	8	9	10
11	12	13	14	15	16	17
18	19	20	21	22	23	24
25	26	27	28	29	30	31

London, 25
An estimated 100,000 people demonstrate against the government's planned pit closures.

Lithuania, 25
The former Communist Party wins the first general election since the country broke away from the Soviet Union.

Jerusalem, 25
Prime Minister Yitzhak Rabin reaffirms that Israel does not intend to withdraw from the Golan Heights.

London, 26
The Swedish furniture group IKEA buys 76 Habitat stores in Europe for $125 million.

U.S., 26
Presidential candidate Ross Perot claims that Republicans plotted to wiretap his office and disrupt his daughter's wedding (→ Nov 4).

Ankara, 27
Turkish officials announce that tanks have been dispatched to northern Iraq as a security measure against Kurdish separatist guerrillas.

New York, 29
A jury acquits a young black man implicated in the killing of an Australian Jew in 1991.

New York, 29
Files released by a Russian general indicate that Alger Hiss, convicted and jailed during the "Red Scare", could have been innocent.

London, 31
The 150-mph Rover 200 Coupe is chosen as the best car at the British Motor Show. Rover took ten out of the 33 top design awards.

Florida, 31
British jockey Lester Piggott is injured during the Breeder's Cup Classic at Hallandale. The race was won by A.P. Indy, ridden by Eddie Delahoussaye.

U.K., 31
Business Age magazine reports that Britain has at least 63,000 millionaires and may have as many as 90,000.

DEATH

25. Roger Miller, American country music singer (*1936).

Computer fault causes ambulance horror

Ambulance call-out system is blamed for up to 20 deaths in London.

El Alamein battle recalled in desert

Veterans of Monty's 1942 offensive.

El Alamein, Egypt, Sunday 25
Old foes met today under a scorching sun in the desert to mark the fiftieth anniversary of the Battle of El Alamein, which, with Stalingrad, marked the turn of the tide in World War II. But the old soldiers with their rows of medals had not traveled thousands of miles to talk of victory or defeat but of the comrades who fell.

There are few sights more moving than the Commonwealth cemetery with its crosses marching, row on row, into the desert and there were few dry eyes as Prime Minister John Major read from St John's gospel: "Greater love hath no man than this: that he lay down his life for his friends." A bugler played the Last Post and bagpipes skirled a lament across the desert.

London, Wednesday 28
The failure of a new £1.5-million computerized system for directing emergency ambulance calls is alleged to have contributed to 20 deaths this week. The system was designed to allocate 999 calls more efficiently but for 36 hours on Monday and Tuesday the ambulance service collapsed into chaos and had to revert to manual control.

This is the climax of months of dissatisfaction with the service. Government figures show that only 11% of emergency calls in London are being answered within the required minimum time limit of 17 minutes. John Wilby, chief executive of the London Ambulance Service, said today: "I am deeply conscious of the lack of public confidence ... I have decided that the only honorable course of action is to offer my resignation."

Canada vote boosts Quebec separatists

Toronto, Monday 26
In a national referendum today, Canadians rejected the Charlestown agreement, which would have granted Quebec special constitutional status within the Canadian federation. The agreement was an attempt to meet the province's demands for more autonomy so that it would become a signatory to the Canadian constitution. As of now, Quebec has not done so. Quebec separatists have said that the agreement did not go far enough in granting Quebec autonomy, and critics from the other provinces said it went too far.

The national vote was 52.3% "no". The province with the highest percentage of "no" votes was British Columbia with 67.9%. The result in Quebec was 55.4% "no".

A young Montreal 'no' supporter.

Oct. The first pocket calculator was patented 20 years ago this month.

Angola sinks deeper into war as rebels advance on capital

Fighting between UNITA rebels and the army has left 1,000 dead.

Luanda, Saturday 31
Troops of the guerrilla organization UNITA attacked areas near the Luanda international airport today. The group also shelled the town of Huambo, 250 miles southeast of the capital, and attacked the governor's residence there. Towns in the provinces of Hila and Benguela have been taken by UNITA troops. The attacks seem to signal a renewal of the 16-year civil war that ended last year. President José Eduardo dos Santos and UNITA leader Jonas Savimbi had signed peace accords that made possible this year's elections. The ruling MPLA won the elections, but the outcome was rejected by Savimbi.

The Vatican admits Galileo was right

Vatican City, Saturday 31
The Earth spins on its axis and revolves around the sun. Common knowledge? Perhaps, but heresy to the Vatican, up until today. In 1633 the Roman Inquisition found Galileo Galilei guilty of heresy for espousing this theory. Today a commission of historic, scientific and theological inquiry, appointed by Pope John Paul II, has absolved Galileo of the charges. The commission said the judges who had condemned him were "incapable of dissociating faith from an age-old cosmology." The astronomer, physicist and mathematician spent the last eight years of his life under house arrest for insisting that the Earth was not the center of the universe.

The Earth is indeed round.

Muslim stronghold falls to Serbs

Sarajevo, Thursday 29
The Muslim stronghold of Jajce has fallen to Serbian forces and tonight the town, 100 miles north of Sarajevo, is reported to be burning. The Serbs, gradually tightening their grip, had bombed Jajce in August and September but the defenders, a mixed force of Croats and Muslims, held out until their fragile alliance crumbled because of mutual mistrust. The Muslims accuse the Croats of deserting them while the Croats say the Muslims refuse to face reality. Whatever the cause, the Serbs have emerged victorious and can now cut a path through Bosnia to the Serb-occupied region of Krajina in Croatia.

Car bomb attack in Downing Street

Westminster, Friday 30
IRA terrorists put a gun to the head of a minicab driver today and forced him to drive to Whitehall with a bomb planted in his cab. Obeying orders from the gunmen, he parked outside the Cabinet Office, close to Downing Street. The terrorists ran off and, soon after the driver shouted a warning to policemen, the bomb exploded.

It was a small device and, apart from destroying the car, did little damage and caused no casualties. Nevertheless, the attack, by breaching the tight security in the area, renewed fears about the IRA's ability to strike at the heart of the government.

Liberian rebels kill five American nuns

Monrovia, Saturday 31
Archbishop Michael Francis announced today that five American nuns who have been missing since last week were killed in territory controlled by the National Patriotic Front of Liberia, led by Charles Taylor. Two of the nuns, last seen on October 20, had left their convent in a suburb of Monrovia to attend to a sick or wounded child. They were found shot alongside a road near the convent. The three other nuns, last seen on October 22, had been shot in front of the convent. Searchers had been unable to reach the convent because of the intense fighting between Taylor's troops and the Liberian Army.

October 30. Chancellor Kohl inaugurates the new Bundestag in Bonn.

October 27. Diana and Charles meet Placido Domingo at Covent Garden.

November

1992

Su	Mo	Tu	We	Th	Fr	Sa
1	2	3	4	5	6	7
8	9	10	11	12	13	14
15	16	17	18	19	20	21
22	23	24	25	26	27	28
29	30					

Caucasus, 1
Three thousand Russian troops are dispatched to North Ossetia to help disarm rival factions.

New York, 1
Lisa Ondieki of Australia wins the women's race in the New York City Marathon.

Tehran, 2
Iran increases the reward for killing British author Salman Rushdie.

L.A., 2
Earvin "Magic" Johnson, citing "controversies", quits professional basketball "for good" and plans to focus on fighting AIDS.

Missouri, 2
Jack Smith is appointed president and CEO of General Motors.

Washington, D.C., 3
A presidential commission advises that women be barred from flying combat missions.

Manila, 4
An accord is reached between the Philippine government and Imelda Marcos to transfer her $356 million from Swiss banks back to Manila.

Ireland, 5
Prime Minister Albert Reynolds calls a general election after losing a vote of confidence (→ Nov 25).

Hamburg, 5
A security official says that racist groups have become more organized in their attacks: 1,000 violent incidents were reported in the last two months (→ Nov 8).

Israel, 6
Hitler's book, *Mein Kampf*, is published in Hebrew for students studying German civilization.

Moscow, 7
Twenty thousand Communists march to mark the 75th anniversary of the Bolshevik revolution.

DEATHS

2. Hal Roach, American film producer and director (*1892).

7. Alexander Dubcek, Czechoslovak statesman (*Nov. 27, 1921).

Prime California vineyards ravaged by killer phylloxera bug

Napa Valley, Sunday 1
California vineyards are headed for disaster. The last five, rather dry, years have favored the proliferation of *phylloxera vastatrix*, the demonic bug that ravaged French vines after its introduction into the country from the U.S. in the last century. Grafts of more resistant American vines helped the French vineyards to come back. Now the pest has destroyed nearly 7,500 acres of prime Napa Valley and Sonoma vines, according to provisional estimates. More than 49,000 acres will need to be replanted before the year 2000, at a cost of nearly $2 million. Smaller producers may not be able to afford to repair the damage.

So far, 7,500 acres of prime Napa Valley and Sonoma vines have been hit.

Hal Roach, film great, dies at 100

California, Monday 2
Hal Roach, the producer who made Laurel and Hardy famous, died at his Bel Air home today at the age of 100. Also a writer and director, he played a large part in shaping American film comedy. Among those he helped make stars were Harold Lloyd, Will Rogers and Harry Langdon. In later years his 18-acre "comedy factory" at Culver City became a school for performers such as Janet Gaynor, Jean Harlow and Mickey Rooney, and for directors who included Frank Capra, Leo McCarey and George Stevens. As head of Hal Roach Studios for nearly 40 years, he produced some 1,000 films.

French smoking law sparks controversy

The French, among Europe's heaviest smokers, ponder the new law.

Paris, Sunday 1
The stereotypical image of the French bistro filled with Gauloise fumes (never mind the fact that most cigarettes sold in France are *blondes*, Virginia-style tobacco) may become a thing of the past. An anti-smoking law goes into effect throughout the country today. The French, who in 1989 consumed an average of 2,120 cigarettes per person, may no longer smoke in an enclosed, public space, and restaurants are obliged to provide non-smoking areas. If the police manage to catch a puffer in the act in a non-smoking area, a fine of 600 to 1,300 francs ($115 to $250) may be imposed.

Nov. 1. Willie Mtolo of South Africa struggles to first place in Sunday's New York City Marathon, just ahead of Andres Espinosa of Mexico.

Clinton victory ends 12 years of Republican rule

A defeated Bush comforts Barbara.

Carol Moseley Braun (Ill.) is the first black woman elected to the Senate.

Supporters gather outside the governor's mansion in Little Rock to cheer President-elect Clinton and wife Hillary.

U.S.A., Wednesday 4

The results from yesterday's voting are in. The people of the United States of America have chosen their 42nd president, Governor Bill Clinton of Arkansas. The 46-year-old Democrat will be the first U.S. president of a post-World War II generation.

Clinton received 43% of the popular vote, well ahead of President George Bush, who received 38%. Ross Perot received 19%, the highest showing ever for an independent or third-party candidate. The Democrats also retained their majorities in the House of Representatives and the Senate.

The president-elect began to outline the priorities of his presidency. Creating new jobs, reducing the deficit and reforming the health-care system will be the primary domestic goals. Clinton also revealed the international issues he will address. The new president wants to further global trade talks and peace talks between Israel and its Arab neighbors, complete arms agreements with Russia, aid the famine victims in Somalia and work toward an end to the war in the former republics of Yugoslavia.

At 46, Bill Clinton is the first baby-boomer to reach the White House.

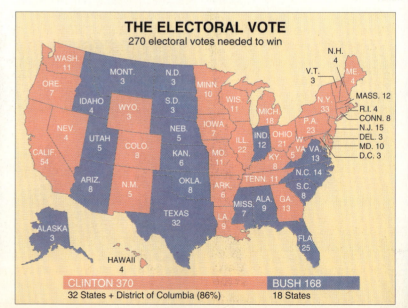

THE ELECTORAL VOTE
270 electoral votes needed to win

WASH. 11
ORE. 7
MONT. 3
N.D. 3
MINN. 10
N.H. 4
V.T. 3
ME. 4
IDAHO 4
WYO. 3
S.D. 3
WIS. 11
MICH. 18
N.Y. 33
MASS. 12
R.I. 4
CONN. 8
NEV. 4
UTAH 5
COLO. 8
NEB. 5
IOWA 7
ILL. 22
IND. 12
OHIO 21
P.A. 23
W VA. 5
VA. 13
N.J. 15
DEL. 3
MD. 10
D.C. 3
CALIF. 54
ARIZ. 8
N.M. 5
KAN. 6
MO. 11
KY. 8
N.C. 14
S.C. 8
OKLA. 8
ARK. 6
TENN. 11
ALASKA 3
TEXAS 32
LA. 9
MISS. 7
ALA. 9
GA. 13
HAWAII 4
FLA. 25

CLINTON 370 — 32 States + District of Columbia (86%)
BUSH 168 — 18 States

Princess Di decries 'hurtful' press rumors

At a recent state banquet in Seoul, tension between the couple is obvious.

U.S. fires first shots in trade war with EC

French white wines are threatened with punitive 200% taxes by U.S.

London, Friday 6

The Princess of Wales, reacting to the critical press coverage of her official visit to Korea with her husband, took the unusual step today of issuing a statement attacking reports of friction between herself and the Queen and the Duke of Edinburgh as "misleading", "untrue and particularly hurtful".

The two main allegations made in the British press were that the Queen had ordered Princess Diana to go to Korea against her will and that there had been an acerbic exchange of letters between her and the Duke of Edinburgh. Cynics say the statement bears the hallmarks of the Palace press office and point out that it does nothing to quell speculation about the state of their marriage (→ 24).

Major delays EC treaty ratification

London, Thursday 5

There was consternation among Britain's EC partners today when it became known that in order to win the House of Commons vote on the Maastricht treaty John Major had promised the Tory "Euro-rebels" that Britain would not ratify the treaty until Denmark has held its second referendum on Maastricht.

This means that ratification will not take place until May at the earliest. The news was badly received in Brussels: "This morning we were celebrating the news of the vote in London", said one official, "but this is not good news."

Prague Spring hero Dubcek dies at 70

Bratislava, Saturday 7

The architect of Czechoslovakia's attempt at "socialism with a human face" died today after being injured in a car accident in September.

Alexander Dubcek was born in Slovakia, but spent much of his childhood in the Soviet Union. He joined the Slovak Communist Party in 1939 and rose through the ranks to become the head of the party in 1968. His democratizing reforms led to the invasion of Czechoslovakia by Warsaw Pact troops. After the overthrow of Communism in 1989, he became chairman of the federal parliament.

Washington, D.C., Thursday 5

The first shots in what could be a damaging trans-Atlantic trade war were fired today when the U.S. trade representative, Carla Hills, slapped tariffs of 200% on $300 million worth of imports from the EC. Worst hit are French white wines, a move which reflects American belief that it is France which is the real stumbling block in the trade negotiations.

EC trade ministers are to meet tomorrow to discuss the American move, but they do so in disarray because Ray MacSharry, EC Agricultural Commissioner and leading negotiator in the trade talks, is withdrawing from the talks. He blames Jacques Delors, President of the EC Commission, for interfering in the stalled discussions (→ 20).

Nov. 4. Elton John signs a £26-million deal with Time Warner.

Bobby Fischer wins chess marathon

Belgrade, Thursday 5

Bobby Fischer has won the 30th and final match of his series against Boris Spassky and will collect the winner's prize of $3.35 million. But Spassky, who won five games to Fischer's ten, will not go away empty-handed. He receives the remainder of the $5-million purse, the largest chess prize ever. Fischer had not played a professional game of chess since he won the world championship by defeating Spassky in Iceland in 1972. The rematch was sponsored by Jezdimir Vasiljevic, a Yugoslav banker (→ Dec 15).

Nov. 7. The Japanese freighter "Akatsuki Maru", carrying 1.7 tons of toxic plutonium, leaves France for Yokohama under naval escort.

November

1992

Su	Mo	Tu	We	Th	Fr	Sa
1	2	3	4	5	6	7
8	9	10	11	12	13	14
15	16	17	18	19	20	21
22	23	24	25	26	27	28
29	30					

Paris, 8
In a surprising comeback, Boris Becker wins the Paris Open after defeating Guy Forget.

Vienna, 8
Russian nuclear officials tell Western experts they will have to keep using Chernobyl-type reactors if the West does not pay for better systems.

California, 9
The U.S. Navy refuses to reinstate Petty Officer Keith Meinhold despite a federal judge overturning his dismissal for being a homosexual (→ 12).

London, 9
The Renoir painting, *A Vase of Flowers*, stolen from a London art gallery five years ago, is recovered. The painting was insured for £450,000.

Sarajevo, 10
The Red Cross begins the evacuation of 6,000 civilians from the battered Bosnian capital.

New York, 11
New York City's chief justice, Sol Wachtler, resigns after being charged with trying to blackmail his former mistress.

Washington, D.C., 11
President Bush fires the State Department official who conducted the search for Bill Clinton's passport and citizenship files.

Peru, 13
A coup attempt to overthrow President Alberto Fujimori fails.

Geneva, 13
The United Nations says that the ozone layer was significantly damaged over the last year due to chemical pollution and gases from volcanic eruptions.

London, 14
The England XV beats South Africa 33-16 at Twickenham in the first game between the two countries since 1984. Sporting relations had been broken over apartheid.

DEATHS

10. Chuck Connors, American television actor (*1921).

14. Maurice Ohana, Spanish composer (*1914).

Over 250,000 Germans join in Berlin march against racism

Berlin, Sunday 8
Leftist anarchist protesters threw rocks, eggs, tomatoes and paint bombs at Chancellor Helmut Kohl and President Richard von Weizsäcker at a march against the increasing anti-foreigner violence in Germany. There have been more than 1,800 violent attacks against foreigners this year. The march was accompanied by security forces, but they had concentrated on keeping the marchers and right-wing protesters apart. The government-organized march included representatives from nearly all of the country's political parties, as well as from industry, organized labor and show business (→ 23).

Chancellor Kohl and President von Weizsäcker lead the demonstration.

Fighting rages at Sarajevo airport

Sarajevo, Sunday 8
Relief flights into this battered, besieged city were again delayed today as fighting raged around the airport, with Serbs and Muslims battling for control of the western suburbs. Mortar shells and small-arms fire exchanged across the runway made it impossible for the aircraft carrying food and medicine to land. Sarajevo has now been without food and water for three days and pressure is building among the people, both Serbs and Muslims, to flee from the shambles (→ 20).

Nov. 10. A highly realistic model of the White House built by John Zweifel is readied for display.

Holocaust survivors to be compensated

Bonn, Sunday 8
The German government will pay millions of dollars in compensation to holocaust survivors who were living in Eastern Europe when a previous compensation program was in effect from 1952 to 1965. The Communist governments in those countries did not allow them to apply for payments. As many as 50,000 European Jews who were forced to live in ghettoes or in hiding for at least 18 months, or who were in concentration camps for six months, will be eligible to file a claim for a monthly payment of 500 German marks ($315).

Iraqgate inquiry ordered by Major

London, Tuesday 10
British Prime Minister John Major announced today that a judicial inquiry will be held into the so-called "Iraqgate" affair, the sale of equipment capable of boosting Iraq's military might. The inquiry, headed by Lord Justice Scott, will have access to all relevant documents and will be able to order ministers to give evidence.

Major made his move to stave off criticism following the collapse of the case against three officials of Matrix Churchill, the lathe manufacturer, on charges of exporting arms-making equipment to Iraq.

Socks, who will officially become First Feline on January 20, is already a favorite for White House press photographers outside Clinton's home.

Clinton may lift Pentagon's ban on gays

A court reinstates Petty Officer Keith Meinhold, a homosexual, in the navy.

Washington, D.C., Thursday 12
Bill Clinton said yesterday that he would end the ban on homosexuals in the armed forces, but that he would consult with the Pentagon on the best way to go about it. General Colin Powell, the chairman of the Joint Chiefs of Staff, said that such a move would be "prejudicial to good order and discipline".

Naval Petty Officer Keith Meinhold, one of more than 17,000 military personnel to be dismissed in enforcement of the ban over the last decade, reported back to duty today. He had been discharged in August, but a federal judge ordered the navy to reinstate him because of the "likelihood" that the ban will be ruled unconstitutional when his case goes to court.

Israel sends troops, tanks into Lebanon

IDF battle tanks take up positions.

Jerusalem, Wednesday 11
Columns of Israeli tanks rumbled into southern Lebanon today following two nights of rocket attacks on northern Israeli towns by Hezbollah, the pro-Iranian guerrilla organization. "We are massing forces as a deterrent measure," said an Israeli spokesman here.

The movement of the tanks into Israel's self-proclaimed "security zone" has been accompanied by air raids on Hezbollah bases. At the Middle East peace talks in Washington, D.C., the Israeli delegate, Uri Lubrani, warned: "If there is no security and quiet on our side of the border, there will be no security and quiet for you either."

Church of England to allow women priests

The historic General Synod vote is greeted with tears and jubilation.

London, Wednesday 11
The Church of England today took a revolutionary step by voting, after 17 years of often bitter debate, to allow women to be ordained as priests. The motion gained the required two-thirds majority in the three houses of the General Synod by a mere five votes.

When the Archbishop of Canterbury, Dr George Carey, announced the result the members remained silent as he had asked, but outside the chamber, men and women wept, hugged and kissed each other in emotional scenes, hardly able to believe that they had won their long fight. It was not all joy, however. Traditionalists, unable to accept women as priests, gave grave warnings that the church was on the brink of a schism.

Nov. 10. During his meeting with Queen Elizabeth at Buckingham Palace, President Boris Yeltsin invites the monarch to visit Russia.

Nov. 13. Riddick Bowe, aged 25, dethrones heavyweight champion Evander Holyfield, 30, in a unanimous 12-round decision at Las Vegas.

Su	Mo	Tu	We	Th	Fr	Sa
1	2	3	4	5	6	7
8	9	10	11	12	13	14
15	16	17	18	19	20	21
22	23	24	25	26	27	28
29	30					

Atlanta, 15
Richard Petty, one of NASCAR's best-known team owners, retires.

U.S., 16
Cambridge becomes the first Massachusetts city to grant legal recognition to homosexual couples.

Germany, 16
The brain-dead woman who was artificially kept alive to allow her fetus to be born, miscarries; the life-support system is switched off.

London, 17
Soccer: Wimbledon player Vinnie Jones is fined £20,000 and suspended for six months for "bringing the game into disrepute"; it is the heaviest fine ever imposed on a footballer in England.

Southern France, 17
Cave paintings discovered at Cosquer are found to be 27,110 years old, making them among the earliest examples of prehistoric art.

Suffolk, 19
Retired gardener Eric Lawes, searching for lost tools, finds a Roman treasure hoard said to be worth £10 million.

U.K., 19
In a landmark decision, a judge gives Tony Bland, a brain-damaged victim of the Hillsborough soccer disaster, permission to die. Life-support systems will be stopped.

Cameroon, 19
Paul Biya is reelected president amid charges that the election was marred by fraud.

Trieste, 20
Twenty watercolors painted by the young Adolf Hitler attract no bids at auction.

Cardiff, 21
Australia, the world champion rugby team, beats Wales 23-6.

France, 21
An avalanche in the Alps kills seven skiers.

DEATHS

18. Dorothy Kirsten, American soprano (*1910).

19. Dorothy Walker Bush, President Bush's mother (*1901).

Thousands of starving refugees flee war-shattered Somalia

A ship packed with 3,000 refugees is escorted to the Yemeni port of Aden.

Somalia, Monday 16
Tonight a French warship is escorting a freighter crowded with 3,000 Somalian refugees to the Yemeni port of Aden. The Somalis are fleeing hunger and inter-clan warfare in their country. Since the toppling of the government and the flight of President Mohammed Siad Barre in January 1991, the north-east African country has been in a state of anarchy. Somalian society is falling apart due to drought, famine and fighting between rival gangs. Veterinarians estimate that more than 30% of the livestock in the country has died in gang raids on herds. The fighting has also hindered relief efforts (→ 26).

Former Communists win Lithuania vote

Vilnius, Monday 16
A party of former Communist reformers has won a majority in Lithuania's parliament. President Vytautas Landsbergis, leader of the anti-Communist party, Sajudis, warned that the vote might lead the country back to one-party rule.

Algirdas Brazauskas, leader of the victorious Democratic Labor Party, said his party favored slower economic reform, but had no intention of returning to the past. Voters also approved direct elections for the presidency. Landsbergis will probably face a challenge from Brazauskas next year.

The former premier and supporters.

Benazir Bhutto held after protest march

Rawalpindi, Wednesday 18
Benazir Bhutto, the former prime minister of Pakistan, was arrested here today after a violent encounter with police who halted a march on government buildings by her supporters. "My arrest won't make any difference. The struggle will continue," she told a crowd of some 30,000 Pakistanis which was eventually broken up by tear gas and baton charges. Bhutto, who wore a bullet-proof vest, was hit several times by batons but appeared unhurt. Government sources said she was driven to a state guest house, where she would stay overnight before being flown to Karachi and placed under house arrest.

Nov. 18. The Man of Steel, a cartoon favorite since 1938, is put to rest.

Nov. 18. Spike Lee cast Denzel Washington as Malcolm X.

Windsor is damaged by seven-hour blaze

The fire broke out at 11:37 a.m. in the Private Chapel in Chester Tower.

A stunned Queen views the disaster.

Windsor, Friday 20
Windsor Castle, home of the Royal Family and the only royal residence in continuous use since the Norman Conquest, was badly damaged by fire today. Flames engulfed the State Apartments in the north-east corner of the Upper Quadrangle, destroying most of the roof and seriously weakening the structure.

It is feared that the priceless collection of art treasures has been badly affected, despite valiant efforts by castle staff, led by Prince Andrew, who formed a human chain to pass paintings to safety. Tonight, while firemen are still damping down the fire, which apparently started in the Private Chapel, questions are being asked about who will provide the millions it will take to restore the castle.

The seven-hour fire left Brunswick Tower and St George's Hall in ruins.

U.S.-EC deal averts trade war at 11th hour

Bush and U.S. Trade Representative Carla Hills announce the accord.

Brussels, Friday 20
The United States and the European Community made a last-ditch deal today to avert a disastrous trans-Atlantic trade war.

Both sides made compromises. The EC agreed to curb farm subsidies and the Americans dropped their demands that European farmers must accept firm limits on the production of oilseeds. The way should now be open for the completion of the Uruguay Round of the GATT talks with immense benefit for the whole world. President Bush and Prime Minister Major have expressed their delight. The agreement is certain to be fiercely opposed by French farmers. Jean-Pierre Soisson, France's minister of agriculture, has already said that he cannot accept it (→ 23).

NATO, Europeans order Adriatic blockade

U.S. Navy warships approach the shores of the former Yugoslavia.

Rome, Friday 20
The North Atlantic Treaty Organization and the Western European Union today ordered their warships in the Adriatic to stop all ships in the territorial waters of Serbia and Montenegro for inspection of their cargo. The blockade, which is similar to action taken against Iraq after its invasion of Kuwait, will implement the U.N. embargo on the former Yugoslavia. It is not certain that the action will help to end the war in Bosnia, because most of the shipments of oil and other supplies are believed to be entering Serbia by road or along the Danube. The warships will be allowed to fire warning shots and inspect ships, but not to destroy any vessels (→ Dec 7).

November

1992

Su	Mo	Tu	We	Th	Fr	Sa
1	2	3	4	5	6	7
8	9	10	11	12	13	14
15	16	17	18	19	20	21
22	23	24	25	26	27	28
29	30					

Madrid, 22
More than 5,000 rightists attend ceremonies marking the 17th anniversary of the death of Generalissimo Francisco Franco.

Brussels, 22
The EC devalues the Spanish peseta and the Portuguese escudo by 6%.

Maryland, 23
General Electric sells its aerospace division to Martin-Marietta for $3 billion.

Australia, 23
The government decides to allow homosexuals to join the military.

China, 24
In one of the worst accidents in Chinese civil aviation history, a Boeing 737 crashes killing all 141 people aboard.

London, 25
Agatha Christie's murder mystery, *The Mousetrap*, celebrates its 40th anniversary in the West End. It has been seen by 9.5 million people.

Moscow, 25
Mikhail Poltoranin, President Boris Yeltsin's deputy prime minister, resigns (→ Dec 14).

U.S., 26
Violent snowstorms cause eight deaths in the Midwest and the Great Plains.

New York, 29
New York Jets defensive lineman Dennis Byrd is paralyzed from the chest down after colliding with a teammate during a football match.

London, 30
Government officials announce that Britain will allow 4,000 Bosnians to seek temporary asylum in the U.K.

Moscow, 30
Russian court upholds ban on the Communist Party.

DEATHS

22. Sterling Holloway, American actor, the voice of Winnie the Pooh and of the snake Kaa in the film *Jungle Book* (*1905).

23. Roy Acuff, American country music singer (*1903).

30. Jorge Donn, Argentine ballet dancer (*1947).

Racist firebombing leaves Turkish woman and two girls dead

Mölln, Monday 23
A Turkish woman and two girls aged 14 and 10 were burnt to death in a racist arson attack in this northern German village early today. The victims, all related, were murdered in their sleep when two fires gutted the multi-family homes occupied by Turkish *gastarbeiters*, German for guest-workers. The 10-year-old was born in Germany.

Anonymous callers to the authorities claimed responsibility, ending with the words, "Heil Hitler". This is the culmination of a weekend of neo-Nazi violence. A demonstration is planned by Turks and Germans in Berlin tonight "to show our fear of the Nazi mob".

Neo-Nazi attack targeted a building housing Turkish residents in Mölln.

Furious French farmers lash out at symbols of American trade

Paris, Monday 23
A Coca-Cola plant, the "symbol of America", was briefly occupied by French farmers today in protest against the trade deal between the European Community and the United States, which the farmers fear will destroy their livelihoods. A spokesman for Coca-Cola said the protest, at Grigny, south of Paris, was carried out "in good humor".

There were other actions in protest at the proposed GATT agreement. At Besançon, a Coke vending machine was burnt. At Valenciennes, farmers smashed Coke bottles, set fire to the British flag and burned 12 piles of hay representing the EC member-states (→ Dec 1).

Coca-Cola, McDonald's and Stars and Stripes burn in anti-U.S. protest.

Nov. 22. Tornadoes rip through Texas, Louisiana, Mississippi, Alabama, Georgia, Kentucky and Tennessee leaving more than 20 people dead.

Birthday boy Boris

Frankfurt, Sunday 22
The fans sang "Happy Birthday to You" as Boris Becker celebrated his 25th birthday today by beating Jim Courier, the world's top seeded player, 6-4, 6-3, 7-5, to win the ATP Tour World Championship and a prize of $1.09 million.

The victory celebrated Becker's return to form after a dismal period when he slumped to number 10 in the world rankings. At one stage he was wondering whether to continue playing, but after today's game he said: "I am playing better than maybe ever." All Courier could say was: "I am a little tired; I got the whole spectrum of tired."

Irish voters call for easier abortion law

A powerful pro-life lobby.

Dublin, Wednesday 25
Staunchly Roman Catholic Irish voters have turned down a government proposal that abortion should be permitted when there is a substantial risk to the mother's life. The defeat of the proposal reflects the fears of the pro-life lobby, who saw it as opening the way to abortion on demand.

At the same time the voters accepted that women should be allowed to travel abroad for abortions and have access to information on abortion services available elsewhere in the EC. This may seem a typically Irish compromise, but it represents a fundamental change in Irish constitutional law.

U.S. offers 30,000 troops for Somalia aid

Relief aid to famine-stricken nation is hampered by heavily-armed gangs.

De Klerk proposes benchmark elections

Johannesburg, Thursday 26
President F.W. de Klerk presented a detailed timetable for the end of South Africa's white-minority rule today. "We cannot turn back, we cannot get bogged down," he said. The president proposed that elections for a non-racial interim government be held by April 1994.

This is the first time that such a positive statement of intent has been made. It did not, however, satisfy the African National Congress, which rejected the timetable as "totally unacceptable" and demanded that an interim government be elected within a year. Despite this rejection, the proposal has broken the stalemate in the negotiations.

White rule could end in 1994.

Czechoslovak split is now official

Prague, Wednesday 25
Czechoslovakia will cease to exist on January 1, 1993. Today 183 of the 300 members of parliament voted in favor of a bill making the split, which has seemed inevitable for some time now, official. Czech and Slovak officials say that the divorce will be an amicable one, without the violence seen in the breakup of Yugoslavia or between some of the former states of the Soviet Union. But there are bound to be at least some disagreements between the Czech and Slovak republics, because the property of the federation must be divided.

Washington, D.C., Thursday 26
The United States has offered to send 30,000 troops to Somalia as part of a United Nations effort to help save the lives of thousands of starving people. So far there are only 500 U.N. soldiers in Somalia, and they can do little against the marauding gangs of heavily-armed robbers who demand tribute from the aid organizations and raid the feeding stations. This surprise offer was approved by President Bush and is being considered by Butros Butros Ghali, the U.N. Secretary General. White House spokesman Marlin Fitzwater said: "We are consulting with the U.N. about the best way to guarantee relief supplies. We want to ensure that assistance reaches these people as soon as possible" (→ Dec 4).

Nov. 22. Designer Andre Van Pier presents a proposed wardrobe for Hillary Clinton, including a $25,000 ensemble for the Inaugural Ball.

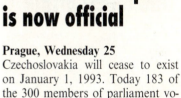

Nov. 26. Briton Nigel Burgess (left) drowns during Vendée Globe round-the-world race; U.S. competitor Mike Plant drowned before the start.

1992 was 'annus horribilis', says Queen Elizabeth

Sad sovereign marks the 40th year of her reign at London's Guildhall.

Four whites die in golf club terror attack

King William's Town, Saturday 28
About 60, mostly white, members of an integrated golf club were eating and drinking in the club's dining room when a group of blacks rolled in hand grenades and then opened fire with automatic rifles on the crowd. Four people, all white, were killed and 17 were injured. This was only one of four deadly attacks in South Africa this weekend. A white family was killed at their farmhouse in what seemed to be a robbery attempt, eight blacks were gunned down at a train station, possibly because of a feud between rival black groups, and six ANC supporters were killed in a grenade attack while at a party.

Black militants leave trail of death.

London, Tuesday 24
The Queen, speaking with evident sadness and in a voice weakened by a cold and the smoke of the Windsor Castle fire, told the guests at a Guildhall banquet in her honor tonight that 1992, planned as a celebration of her 40th anniversary on the throne, has been an "*annus horribilis*".

She did not refer directly to the succession of royal disasters in a year which saw the divorce of the Princess Royal, the separation of the Duke and Duchess of York – along with Fergie's topless photographs – and the marital difficulties of the Prince and Princess of Wales, but admitted wryly that 1992 "is not a year on which I shall look back with undiluted pleasure."

As the year ends, the criticism of the Royal Family grows more insistent. The Queen now faces demands to put some of her fortune toward the cost of the repairs to Windsor Castle and to pay income tax just like her subjects.

Referring to the tabloid newspapers which have hounded her family throughout 1992, she said: "No institution – city, monarchy, whatever – should expect to be free from the scrutiny of those who give it their loyalty and support, not to mention those who don't. But we are all part of the same fabric of our national society, and that scrutiny can be just as effective if it is made, by one party or another, with a touch of gentleness, good humor and understanding" (→ Dec 9).

TV puppets poke fun at Royals.

Venezuela coup bid leaves scores dead

Caracas, Friday 27
Rebel soldiers dropped bombs on the presidential palace this morning and took control of military bases. They then took over the main television station and broadcast a videotaped message by Lieutenant Colonel Hugo Chavez Frias, jailed for leading a coup attempt in February, in which he called for an overthrow of the government. But late today President Carlos Andres Perez appeared on television to announce that the government had regained control of all bases except one, and that the coup, which left scores dead, had been put down.

1992's top names in golf and tennis

U.S., Monday 23
Final standings of the U.S. golf circuit (PGA Tour), in dollar earnings:

1. Fred Couples (USA) 1,344,188
2. Davis Love (USA) 1,191,630
3. John Cook (USA) 1,165,606
4. Nick Price (ZIM) 1,135,773
5. Corey Pavin (USA) 980,934
6. Tom Kite (USA) 957,445
7. Paul Azinger (USA) 929,863
8. Brad Faxon (USA) 812,093
9. Lee Janzen (USA) 795,279
10. Dan Forsman (USA) 763,190
18. Greg Norman (AUS) 676,443
42. Nick Faldo (GBR) 345,168

Paris, Monday 30
Tennis standings (ATP Tour):

1. Jim Courier (USA) 3,599 pts
2. Stefan Edberg (SWE) 3,236
3. Pete Sampras (USA) 3,074
4. Goran Ivanisevic (CRO) 2,718
5. Boris Becker (GER) 2,530
6. Michael Chang (USA) 2,277
7. Petr Korda (CZS) 2,174
8. Ivan Lendl (USA) 1,985
9. Andre Agassi (USA) 1,852
10. Richard Krajicek (NET) 1,816
11. Guy Forget (FRA) 1,717
12. Wayne Ferreira (SAF) 1,679
13. M. Washington (USA) 1,610
14. Carlos Costa (SPA) 1,539

Nov. 27. Fire damages another of Europe's landmarks, Vienna's Hofburg Palace, although the world-famous Lippizaner horses are saved.

December

France, 1
An estimated 50,000 farmers demonstrate in Strasbourg against the GATT agreement.

Washington, D.C., 1
As people around the globe observe the sixth annual World AIDS Day, experts call on the administration to increase funds for AIDS prevention and research.

Moscow, 1
Boris Yeltsin opens a crucial session of the Congress of People's Deputies, dominated by conservatives (→ 14).

Paris, 2
The government says it plans to send 2,000 French Legionnaires to Somalia as part of a U.N-sponsored humanitarian operation (→ 4).

Bonn, 2
The Bundestag ratifies the Maastricht treaty.

Israel, 2
The government asks parliament for the ban on contacts between Israelis and the PLO to be lifted.

Beijing, 2
China threatens to set up its own shadow government in Hong Kong if Governor Patten goes ahead with democratic reforms.

Colombia, 3
In the worst attack in almost two years, a car packed with dynamite explodes, killing 14 people. Authorities believe that the Medellin cocaine ring is responsible.

U.S., 3
The Census Bureau reports that the U.S. population is growing faster than projected, and is expected to reach 275 million by the year 2000.

U.K., 3
Artist Francis Bacon, who died in April, aged 82, leaves his entire £10.9-million estate to a publican who was Bacon's constant friend during the last 18 years.

Paris, 4
At a ceremony making him associate of the French Academy of Political and Moral Sciences, Prince Charles speaks out in defense of French farmers.

Aspen boycott?

Hollywood, Wednesday 2
Christmas without Aspen? That's like a BMW without a carphone. Barbra Streisand angered many of Hollywood's rich and famous by suggesting last month at an AIDS benefit that those who "love the mountains and rivers" of Colorado should be willing to boycott the state in protest at its new statute which voids existing laws, and prohibits new ones, protecting homosexuals against discrimination.

Barbra Streisand causes storm.

Manchester bombs

IRA blasts injure 64 people.

Manchester, Thursday 3
The IRA switched its bombing campaign from London today, setting off two small but powerful bombs which dislocated activity in the business heart of Manchester. People fleeing from the first bomb were caught by the second, and 64, suffering from shock and cut by flying glass, were taken to hospital. The police accused the IRA of giving a confusing warning in order to shift the blame onto the authorities.

Greek tanker causes big oil spill in Spain

The "Aegean Sea", loaded with 80,000 tons of crude, burns off La Coruna.

La Coruna, Spain, Thursday 3
A Greek oil tanker, the *Aegean Sea*, carrying some 550,000 barrels of oil ran aground as it was entering port today, split in two and is spilling huge quantities of crude oil, threatening beaches and marine life in this rich fishing area. The huge tanker is now on fire, and choking black smoke is billowing across the town, while a slick about 20 kilometers (12.4 miles) long is spreading up the rugged coast of Galicia. According to Lloyd's of London, it is a "major disaster". So far there is no explanation of how the tanker ran aground. The crew are safe and are being questioned.

U.S. forces sent on Somalia mercy mission

Washington, Friday 4
"We will not tolerate armed gangs ripping off their own people, condemning them to death by starvation," said President George Bush today, announcing the U.S. military's humanitarian mission to Somalia. The intervention to secure the delivery of food in the famine-stricken country was authorized by a unanimous vote of the United Nations Security Council yesterday. The U.S. will send 28,150 troops, 1,800 of which should arrive on Monday. Bush emphasized that the mission would not last "one day longer than is absolutely necessary" (→ Dec 9).

President Bush's decision is backed by President-elect Bill Clinton.

Su	Mo	Tu	We	Th	Fr	Sa
		1	2	3	4	5
6	7	8	9	10	11	12
13	14	15	16	17	18	19
20	21	22	23	24	25	26
27	28	29	30	31		

Washington, D.C., 6
President-elect Bill Clinton picks Senator Lloyd Bentsen of Texas to be Secretary of the Treasury (→ 11).

U.K., 7
Thom Gunn, a 63-year-old academic living in California, wins the £10,000 Forward Poetry Prize, the most valuable British award for poetry.

Sarajevo, 7
Heavy fighting forces the U.N. to shut down relief operations.

Israel, 7
Three Israeli soldiers are fatally shot by Islamic militants in the Gaza Strip.

Bolivia, 8
Mudslides devastate a gold mining camp north of La Paz, killing at least 80 people.

Milan, 8
Tenor Luciano Pavarotti is booed at La Scala after missing notes in the performance of Verdi's *Don Carlo*.

France, 9
Photographer Daniel Angeli and his agency are ordered to pay $140,000 in damages for taking pictures of a topless Duchess of York embracing her Texan friend, John Bryan.

U.S., 9
The Elvis Presley stamp has postal officials worried that the initial printing of 300 million will not meet demand.

Somalia, 10
The first deaths of Operation Restore Hope occur as French troops fatally shoot two Somalis in Mogadishu.

U.S., 10
Oregon Senator Bob Packwood (Dem.) apologizes for his unwelcome sexual advances to women but does not agree to resign from his position.

Mogadishu, 11
A peace pact is agreed by Somalia's two most powerful warlords (→ 26).

DEATHS

8. William Shawn, American journalist, former editor-in-chief of *The New Yorker* (*Aug. 31, 1907).

9. Vincent Gardenia, American actor (*1921).

Religious rioting sweeps India after Ayodhya mosque is razed

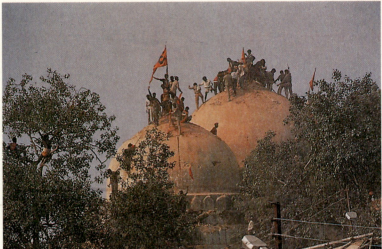

Hindu militants use their bare hands to destroy the 16th-century mosque.

New Delhi, Monday 7
Religious riots are sweeping across India in the wake of the destruction of the ancient Babri Masjid mosque by rampaging Hindu fanatics in the northern Indian town of Ayodhya yesterday. More than 800 people have been killed and hundreds injured as Muslim and Hindu mobs stab, shoot and beat each other.

The violence has thrown the government into chaos and has spilled into the neighboring states of Pakistan and Bangladesh. The army has been called out to restore order in Bombay where street battles have left 41 dead. The stock market has been closed and parliament forced to adjourn in uproar.

Top-secret airplane fascinates experts

U.S., Monday 7
Military aviation buffs are now convinced that the U.S. has developed a secret reconnaissance plane that can reach any point on the globe in three hours. Called *Aurora* by aviation experts, the plane can fly nearly 19 miles high (30 km) at speeds of up to 5,500 mph (8,800 kmh), eight times the speed of sound, or Mach 8. This is more than twice as fast as the previous record. Those who have sighted the plane, which uses liquid methane for fuel, say it is arrow shaped and leaves a trail of smoke resembling "donuts on a rope".

December 6. Designed by Jorma Savolainen of Finland, the sturdy "Urban Bike" weighs less than five pounds and folds away easily.

Swiss voters veto European area plan

Geneva, Sunday 6
Swiss voters today chose to maintain their tradition of isolation and vetoed a government-backed plan to move towards membership of the European Community. The vote specifically barred Switzerland from joining a new European Economic Area comprising the EC and seven of its neighbors, but it was also seen as a rejection of the government's plan to seek full membership of the EC. The vote was close: 50.3% against 49.7%, but 16 cantons voted "No" while only seven voted "Yes".

December 6. By defeating Jakob Hlasek of Switzerland at Fort Worth, Jim Courier guarantees the U.S. team its 30th Davis Cup title.

U.S. Marines hit Somali beaches in relief mission

Mogadishu, Wednesday 9
U.S. Marines and Navy frogmen stormed ashore before dawn today ready to do battle with the Somalian gunmen who have been holding this famine-stricken country to ransom. Much to their embarrassment they found, not bandits, but the massed ranks of the elite press corps who had been tipped off by U.S. officials. No shots were fired as the first troops landed.

The plan is for the 1,800 Marines carried by a three-ship amphibious assault unit to secure the airport and harbor areas before moving out to get food, medicine and other supplies to the Somalis in the hinterland where thousands have died of starvation. The Marines are backed by a naval battle group led by the aircraft carrier *Ranger*.

They are taking no chances, but the followers of the rival warlords,

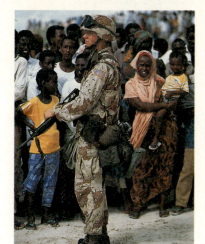
Advance forces secure airport, port.

General Mohammed Farrah Aidid and Mohammed Ali Mahdi, the self-declared interim president, have pulled out of the capital following an agreement between the warlords

The Marines expected trouble, but found instead the world's media.

and a U.S. special envoy.

In New York the U.N. Secretary General, Butros Butros Ghali, said in a statement to the Somali people before the troops landed that the

world had been "deeply moved" by their situation. "The world refuses to accept your suffering and death. An end to hopelessness and despair is possible" (→10).

Europeans opt for downscale fighter

Brussels, Thursday 10
The European Fighter Aircraft, threatened with being scrapped following the end of the Cold War, will go ahead after all – but in a downgraded versionkx costing 30% less. The nations involved, Britain, Germany, Italy and Spain, announced today that the £22-billion program will continue and that the aircraft will be called the Eurofighter 2000. The decision is seen as a victory for Malcolm Rifkind, Britain's defense minister, who prevailed over Volker Ruhe, his German counterpart, who wanted to kill the project.

Charles and Diana: long-expected royal split is now official

No divorce for the royal couple.

London, Wednesday 9
The Prince and Princess of Wales are to separate after 11 years of marriage. The official acknowledgement that the fairy-tale marriage of Prince Charles and Lady Diana is over was made simultaneously by Buckingham Palace and the prime minister in the House of Commons, where some surprise was expressed when Major said that the Princess could still become queen of England in due course.

The news was certainly not unexpected by the readers of Britain's tabloid newspapers, which have been recording every nuance of the troubled marriage. Buckingham Palace said tonight: "We are not

suggesting that the media are to blame, but the cumulative effect of years of intrusive coverage has created an atmosphere that makes life intolerable."

The announcement made it clear that the decision to lead separate lives had been reached amicably, that the Prince and Princess would continue to carry out public duties and that both would take part in bringing up their sons, Prince William, 10, and Prince Harry, 8. There are no plans for divorce. The announcement casts a shadow over the Princess Royal's wedding in three days and completes the miseries of what the Queen has described as her "annus horribilis".

Tokyo is the world's most expensive city

Geneva, Thursday 10
If you're going to Tokyo or Osaka, take plenty of cash. Those places are the world's most expensive in dollar terms, according to a survey of 97 cities published today.

The report uses New York as a base of 100 and takes into account the cost for most products and services except for accommodation. The survey gives Tokyo an index of 183, followed by Osaka at 171. It

shows that West European nations are generally more expensive than the U.S. Oslo tops the European league with 137, followed by Geneva (125), Vienna (121), Paris (119), Dublin (116), Berlin (111), London (110) and Newcastle (94). In the U.S., Washington, D.C., and Chicago have an index of 96, ahead of Los Angeles and Houston (94). The world's cheapest cities are Bombay (70) and Bogotà (67).

Russia's "Thermoplane" can carry loads of 600 tons and cover 4,000 km.

Clinton names three women to top posts

Bill's team: Laura D'Andrea Tyson, Carol Browner, and Donna Shalala.

Little Rock, Friday 11
President-elect Bill Clinton gave three women top jobs in his administration today. Laura D'Andrea Tyson, an economist, will be the first woman to head the Council of Economic Advisers; Donna Shalala, chancellor of Wisconsin University, becomes secretary of Health and Human Services; Carol Browner becomes head of the Environmental Protection Agency.

Clinton said they would bring "energy, dynamism and fresh thinking" to Washington. Others are not so sure. They are seen as politically correct nominees of the "Presidential Partner", Hillary Clinton, and right-wingers have named them "Hillary's harridans" (→17).

Indonesia quake kills 1,500 on Flower Isle

Flores Island, Saturday 12
A violent earthquake measuring 6.8 on the Richter scale, followed by several tidal waves, hit this eastern Indonesia island today, killing at least 1,500 people. Entire fishing communities were wiped out and officials at Maumere, the island's capital, expect the death toll to rise further. An estimated 80% of the coastal town's buildings were destroyed by the offshore quake. The Indonesian government has begun rushing in rescue teams.

Princess Anne weds Royal Navy officer

Commander Tim Laurence is 37.

Balmoral, Saturday 12
The Royal Family, without Diana and without Fergie, turned out today to help the Princess Royal, 42, celebrate her marriage to Commander Tim Laurence, 37. It was a private ceremony in the tiny stone church at Crathie where the loyal Scots still know her as "Wee Annie". On a bitterly cold day the few spectators were outnumbered by 500 reporters and photographers. It was all a far cry from her first marriage to Captain Mark Phillips, a full State Occasion in Westminster Abbey. This time the Princess and her new husband, attended by her children, Peter and Zara, exchanged vows in a simple ritual.

Edinburgh Euro-summit success for Major

Edinburgh, Saturday 12
John Major's turbulent six months as president of the European Community came to a successful conclusion here late tonight with agreement on EC spending levels, and the Maastricht treaty put back on course for ratification. When cases of champagne were delivered early in the evening it seemed that success had been smooth.

The champagne bottles remained unopened, however, while Spain fought a bitter rearguard action to win extra funds for the EC's poorest members. Major gave some ground but eventually Spain surrendered, the deal was agreed and the champagne poured.

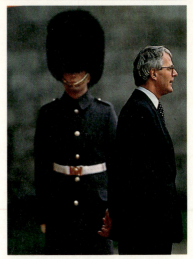

Premier hosts Europe's leaders.

December 12. A ferocious rainstorm with 90-mph winds batters New York City and the surrounding areas leaving at least 15 people dead.

December 12. Miss Russia, 18-year-old Julia Kurotchinka, is crowned Miss World 1992 during a ceremony at Sun City, Bophuthatswana.

December

1992

Su	Mo	Tu	We	Th	Fr	Sa
		1	2	3	4	5
6	7	8	9	10	11	12
13	14	15	16	17	18	19
20	21	22	23	24	25	26
27	28	29	30	31		

Algeria, 14
Muslim extremists ambush and kill five policemen.

London, 14
Damon Hill, son of the late Formula One world champion, Graham Hill, is to succeed Nigel Mansell and partner Alain Prost with the Williams-Renault team.

Israel, 15
Security forces find the stabbed body of an Israeli paramilitary policeman kidnapped two days ago by members of the Muslim fundamentalist group Hamas (→ 18).

London, 15
According to a research paper presented to the British Psychological Society, dieting can seriously damage mental performance.

San Salvador, 15
The 12-year civil war, which left 75,000 dead, officially ends.

Washington, D.C., 15
After winning $3.35 million in a chess match against Boris Spassky in Yugoslavia, Bobby Fischer is indicted on charges that he violated U.S. economic sanctions against Yugoslavia.

U.S., 17
Harvard University scientists announce that an AIDS vaccine has prevented laboratory monkeys from contracting SIV, the AIDS equivalent in monkeys.

Washington, D.C., 17
President-elect Bill Clinton appoints Henry Cisneros, a Hispanic, secretary of Housing and Urban Development; Jesse Brown, a Vietnam veteran, is appointed secretary of Veterans' Affairs (→ 24).

Cambodia, 17
Khmer Rouge guerrillas take 46 U.N. peacekeepers hostage.

New York, 18
American Airlines is rated the top national carrier in the U.S. with Delta Air Lines following closely behind.

DEATH

13. Cornelius Vanderbilt, American entrepreneur, financier, philanthropist, racehorse owner and statesman (*1899).

Hardliners force Gaidar to resign

New Premier Viktor Chernomyrdin.

Moscow, Monday 14
President Boris Yeltsin is fighting for his political life tonight after being forced by hardliners in Russia's parliament to drop his reformist premier, Yegor Gaidar, and replace him with Viktor Chernomyrdin, a former Communist Party functionary and representative of the military-industrial complex. Yeltsin is now under fire not only from the triumphant hardliners, who want to slow down his reforms, but also from disappointed liberals who accuse him of betrayal. Father Gleb Yakunin, a leading radical, says the sacrifice of Gaidar was a catastrophe and that Yeltsin can no longer be trusted (→ 23).

Dec. 13. Over 400,000 people march against neo-Nazi violence in Hamburg and Frankfurt.

Marines reach famine-hit town of Baidoa

Distribution of food, medicine is often hampered by "Mad Max" gunmen.

Baidoa, Wednesday 16
At dawn today U.S.-led forces, in a 70-vehicle convoy, reached Baidoa, 100 miles (160 kilometers) north-west of Mogadishu. A last round of looting and inter-gang fighting preceded the allied forces' arrival, but the gunmen who had been extorting landing fees from aid organizations and the rival gangs withdrew to the north last night. As was the case when the Marines arrived in the country and when they took Bali Dogle, a former Soviet air base, the troops were in full combat readiness, but were able to "walk in peacefully, without a shot being fired in anger", said Colonel Fred Peck, a Marine spokesman (→ 26).

Washington allows Vietnam trade links

Washington, Monday 14
The United States took the first major step today towards ending its 17-year-old trade embargo on Vietnam by announcing that American companies may open offices in Vietnam and sign contracts in preparation for the lifting of the ban. White House spokesman Marlin Fitzwater said the move was in response to Hanoi's cooperation in determining the fate of nearly 2000 Americans still missing from the Vietnam war.

Mystery of Mona Lisa's smile solved?

London, Sunday 13
A British psychiatrist suggests he has solved the mystery of Mona Lisa's smile. "The face looks as though it is the wrong way round," says Dr. Digby Quested. "The key to the mystery is that it is a mirror image." Mona Lisa's smile is more pronounced on the left side, as is common in forced smiles. It is this characteristic, usually a masculine trait, that gives the painting its mystery. Earlier investigations had shown that Mona Lisa's features matched exactly those of a self-portrait of Leonardo da Vinci, and x-rays revealed a beard beneath the surface of the painting. Perhaps it was narcissism that led Leonardo to keep the painting with him in Paris until his death.

Is this Leonardo da Vinci himself?

Expulsion of Arabs sparks Mid-East crisis

Palestinians stuck in the no-man's-land between Israel and Lebanon.

Jerusalem, Friday 18
Israel's expulsion of 418 Palestinians said to be members of the militant groups Hamas and Islamic Jihad has thrown the Middle East into a new crisis. In Washington, Arab delegates to the peace talks boycotted the final session of the eighth round and told President Bush the expulsions could prove a "death blow" to the peace process. Israel, outraged by the killing of a kidnapped policeman by Hamas, refuses to budge. The last chance the deportees have of returning to their homes lies with an appeal to the Supreme Court here. Meanwhile the men, refused admission to Lebanon, are sheltering in a tent camp set up by the Red Cross.

IRA bombs shut down London's West End

London, Wednesday 16
The IRA brought the center of London to a halt today with two small bombs which injured four people, caused chaos among thousands of Christmas shoppers and brought heavy financial losses to the traders of the busy Oxford Street area. Warnings were given, but police accused the bombers of "playing an obscene game" by giving inaccurate warnings. Shoppers were urged to ignore the IRA's attempts to disrupt commercial life (→ 23).

Christmas shoppers are evacuated from Oxford Street by police.

Live Clinton TV teach-in ponders economy

Economists debate at Little Rock.

Little Rock, Tuesday 15
"Bill Clinton is a natural," said Larry King, host of a call-in talk show on CNN, of the president-elect's performance in a two-day televised conference on the economy, which ended tonight. The conference brought together more than 300 business, labor and academic leaders to discuss the U.S.'s economic problems and possible solutions. But the "teach-in" was political, too, with an eye on the opinion polls. Clinton's communications director pointed out that "people just scanning channels will be able to see their president-elect working on the problem they care most about."

U.S. names Balkan war crimes suspects

Eagleburger calls for accounting.

Geneva, Wednesday 16
At a conference on the war in Bosnia-Herzegovina today, U.S. Secretary of State Lawrence Eagleburger listed seven men, five Serbs and two Croats, who should be tried for "crimes against humanity". He also said that those with "political and command responsibility" for war crimes should be tried, citing Slobodan Milosevic, Serbia's president, Radovan Karadzic, Bosnian Serb leader, and General Ratko Mladic, commander of the Bosnian Serb military. Eagleburger said that the international community must consider "more aggressive measures", such as the enforcement of a "no-fly" zone, to end the fighting and the carrying out of "ethnic cleansing".

Australians to drop allegiance to Queen

Sydney, Thursday 17
Paul Keating, the Australian prime minister, well-known for his fervent republican views, announced today that in future new citizens will swear allegiance to Australia and not to Queen Elizabeth.

"There is no oath of allegiance to a foreign queen," was the response of Lloyd Waddy, head of the monarchist movement, to republican critics. "The only oath is to the Queen of Australia, and these lies are harming the country."

De Klerk dismisses 'dirty trick' officers

Cape Town, Saturday 19
In an unprecedented purge of the South African army today, President Frederik de Klerk announced the sacking of 23 officers, including six generals, for engaging in covert intelligence operations, including murder, to undermine his program of political reform. Grim-faced, he said: "I am shocked. I am disappointed. But I am also resolute. If there is a sore, I want to cut it out." He made it clear there are likely to be criminal prosecutions.

December

1992

Su	Mo	Tu	We	Th	Fr	Sa
		1	2	3	4	5
6	7	8	9	10	11	12
13	14	15	16	17	18	19
20	21	22	23	24	25	26
27	28	29	30	31		

Somalia, 20
U.S. Marines reach the southern city of Kismayu (→ 23).

Portugal, 21
A chartered Dutch DC-10 crashes at Faro Airport, killing 54 of the 320 passengers.

London, 21
The High Court rules that the government's planned pit closures are illegal.

London, 22
British Airways drops its $750-million bid for a stake in USAir in face of Bush administration objections.

Libya, 22
A Libyan Arab Airlines Boeing 727 crashes, killing all 158 aboard.

Bosnia, 22
Prime Minister John Major pays a surprise one-day visit to British forces.

Moscow, 22
Pyotr Aven, Russia's foreign trade minister, resigns (→ 23).

Geneva, 23
The World Council of Churches accuses Serbs of using rape as a weapon.

U.K., 23
The Sun newspaper causes a furor by publishing a leaked copy of the Queen's Christmas speech.

Beijing, 23
China orders France to close its consulate in Canton in retaliation for French arms sales to Taiwan.

Somalia, 23
Operation Restore Hope suffers its first U.S. casualty when a U.S. civilian is killed by an anti-tank mine (→ 26).

Ulster, 23
The IRA announces a three-day cease-fire for Christmas.

DEATHS

20. Steven Ross, American businessman, chairman of Time Warner (*1927).

25. Helen Joseph, British-born South African anti-apartheid activist (*1905).

25. Monica Dickens, British author, great-granddaughter of Charles Dickens (*May 10, 1915).

Bush and Major agree on need for no-fly zone over Serbia

The two leaders agree the time has come to end the bloodshed in Bosnia.

Washington, D.C., Sunday 20
In the most serious international escalation of the Yugoslav conflict so far, President George Bush and Prime Minister John Major agreed here today that Serbian aircraft must stay out of the no-fly zone over Bosnia or be shot down. They will ask the U.N. to give the Serbs 15 days to comply.

The agreement is in fact a compromise. The U.S. wanted authority to strike at airfields in Serbia, while the British, fearing retaliation against U.N. soldiers engaged in relief work, argued against the strikes and wanted a 30-day deadline. "If you say we have had enough jaw-jaw and it's time to zap the Serbs, it's going to make it very difficult for the U.N. troops on the ground," said a British official (→ 22).

Cuban flies home to rescue family

Miami, Sunday 20
In a feat worthy of a Hemingway short story, a former Cuban air force major flew a borrowed Cessna 310 across the Straits of Florida from the Florida Keys to Cuba, picked up his waiting wife and two sons and returned to the United States. Orestes Lorenzo Pérez had defected from Cuba in March 1991, flying undetected into U.S. airspace in a MIG-23 to land at Boca Chica Naval Station. After his defection the Cuban authorities had not allowed his family to leave Cuba, despite the fact that they had visas.

Hardliner Milosevic claims poll victory

Belgrade, Monday 21
President Slobodan Milosevic of Serbia claimed a clear victory today over Milan Panic, prime minister of the rump of Yugoslavia, in the election to decide who will control Serbia. Panic is crying "foul", with accusations of fraud at the polls, but early returns suggest that Milosevic did not need to cheat to win.

The hardliner seems certain to win not only a new four-year term of office but also control of the Serbian parliament. This result is a blow to Europe and the U.S. who had hoped Panic would win and fulfill his promise to end the war in Bosnia (→ 29).

Serbia's president denies vote fraud.

U.S. recession over

Washington, D.C., Wednesday 22
The National Bureau of Economic Research determined today that the U.S. recession, which started in July 1990, ended in March 1991. Gross domestic product is the principal indicator for business cycles, and Commerce Department statistics for the third quarter of 1991 showed that GDP was growing at a yearly rate of 3.4%. Even if the news had come before the presidential elections, it probably would not have helped incumbent George Bush. Voters focused more on jobs created than on productivity.

Dec. 20. Folies Bergère, the Paris music-hall which has been a tourist favorite since 1869, loses popularity and is forced to shut down.

Iran-Contra: Bush pardons six officials

Weinberger, former defense head.

Washington, D.C., Thursday 24
President George Bush has pardoned six officials charged with, or convicted of, misleading Congress in the investigation of the Iran-Contra affair. One of those pardoned was former Secretary of Defense Caspar Weinberger, whose trial might have brought to light what Bush, who has repeatedly claimed to have been "out of the loop" on the deal, knew about the operation, and when he knew it. But the investigation may not end here. Lawrence Walsh, the independent counsel in the case, may seek access to notes Bush took during discussions of the operation when he was vice president.

Two Somali warlords sign peace accords

Mohammed Farrah Aidid (left) and Mohammed Ali Mahdi make peace.

Reformers stay on in Yeltsin cabinet

Moscow, Wednesday 23
President Boris Yeltsin, who cut short a visit to China on Saturday fearing that his new prime minister, Viktor Chernomyrdin, would form an anti-reformist cabinet, appears to have won this particular battle with the hardliners. He announced a new cabinet today which not only preserved the liberal core of his old government but added more reformers. Remarkably, because Chernomyrdin is considered a conservative, Yeltsin seems to have gained the support of the prime minister and will be able to continue his economic reforms – but slowly.

Dec. 21. Nathan Milstein, 88, the Russian-born American violin virtuoso, dies (*Dec. 31, 1903).

Clinton's cabinet complete for Christmas

Les Aspin gets Defense.

Warren Christopher gets State.

Washington, D.C., Thursday 24
Bill Clinton today announced his full cabinet (average age 51):
Les Aspin, 54, Defense
Chairman of the House Armed Services Committee since 1985.
Bruce Babbitt, 54, Interior
President of the League of Conservation Voters.
Zoe Baird, 40, Attorney General
Health care specialist and president of an insurance firm.
Lloyd Bentsen, 71, Treasury
Chairs the Senate Finance Committee.
Jesse Brown, 48, Veterans
An executive with Disabled American Veterans.
Ronald Brown, 51, Commerce
Chairman of the Democratic National Committee.

Warren Christopher, 67, State
Negotiated the release of American hostages in Iran.
Henry Cisneros, 45, HUD
The Housing and Urban Development Secretary is a former mayor of San Antonio.
Mike Espy, 39, Agriculture
Opposes farm spending cuts.
Hazel O'Leary, 55, Energy
Nuclear-waste disposal expert.
Federico Pena, Transportation
Aged 45, former Denver mayor.
Robert Reich, 46, Labor
Political economics specialist.
Richard Riley, 59, Education
Former S. Carolina governor.
Donna Shalala, 51, HHS
The Health and Human Services Secretary served in the Carter administration.

Mogadishu, Saturday 26
The two most powerful Somali warlords, Mohammed Farrah Aidid and Mohammed Ali Mahdi, shook hands today and signed a peace agreement brokered by U.S. special envoy, Robert Oakley, who said they had "made a really special effort" to come to terms. A key point in the agreement is the elimination of the so-called "green-line", a free-fire zone between the rival clans.

In fact, the warlords had little option as the U.S. Marines, backed by awesome firepower, tightened their grip on the Somali capital. "From now on", said one U.S. official, "we're going to be doing more enforcement. Heavy weapons will be removed, voluntarily, or, if necessary, by force" (→31).

Dec. 24. Belgian cartoonist Pierre Culliford, creator of the elf-like Smurfs, dies (*1928).

December

1992

Su	Mo	Tu	We	Th	Fr	Sa
		1	2	3	4	5
6	7	8	9	10	11	12
13	14	15	16	17	18	19
20	21	22	23	24	25	26
27	28	29	30	31		

Iraq, 27
A USAF F-16 fighter downs an Iraqi MIG-25 which had flown into the no-fly zone in southern Iraq.

China, 28
In a bid to modernize China's energy industry, 400,000 coal workers are laid off.

Florida, 29
A Cuban pilot uses chloroform on his co-pilot and flies the 53-passenger plane to Miami to seek political asylum.

Washington, D.C., 29
Bill Clinton accepts an honorary degree from his alma mater, Oxford's University College.

Bonn, 29
Author Günter Grass resigns from the Social Democrats to protest the party's stance on limiting the rights of asylum for foreigners.

Nairobi, 29
President Daniel arap Moi wins Kenya's first multiparty elections in 26 years, amid allegations of widespread fraud.

Moscow, 30
President Yeltsin decides that top bureaucrats will no longer be granted state-owned country residences, or dachas.

Ulan Bator, 30
Mongolia announces that all former Soviet troops have left its territory.

Sofia, 30
Bulgaria's parliament elects economist Luben Berov as premier.

Kabul, 30
Islamic scholar Burhanuddin Rabbani is elected president.

Washington, D.C., 30
National Zoo's female giant panda, Ling-Ling, donated by China in 1972, dies.

Czechoslovakia, 31
At midnight, the Czechoslovak Federation ceases to exist and is replaced by the world's two newest nations: the Czech and Slovak republics.

New York, 31
The pound is quoted at $1.514.

DEATH

27. Kay Boyle, American novelist and poet (*1902).

Serbian nationalists oust moderate Panic

The American millionaire has lost both the election and the premiership.

Belgrade, Tuesday 29
Peace hopes in Yugoslavia suffered a decisive setback today. Militant Serbian nationalists and Communist hardliners in Belgrade's parliament combined forces to topple a leading advocate of a negotiated settlement in the war-torn nation. Milan Panic, Yugoslavia's 63-year-old moderate prime minister, was unseated by an overwhelming no-confidence vote. A caretaker premier, Radoje Kontic, has been appointed to replace him.

"We are headed towards disaster," commented Panic, a Serbian-American businessman who left California in July to return to his native land. The clear winner of the trial of strength between moderates and nationalists is President Slobodan Milosevic of Serbia, who routed Panic in fraud-ridden elections a week ago.

Dec. 29. Brazil's Senate forces resignation of President Fernando Collor de Mello.

Bush and Yeltsin to sign missile pact

Washington, D.C., Wednesday 30
George Bush is ending his presidency with a major foreign policy success.

The White House today announced that Bush will by flying from Somalia to Moscow on January 2 to sign a crucial arms accord with President Yeltsin. The pact, known as START-2, was concluded yesterday in Geneva. It pledges to slash U.S. and Russian strategic nuclear missiles by two-thirds over 10 years and eliminate land-based missiles with multiple warheads. Both leaders have hailed the accord: Bush said it was "good for all mankind", while Yeltsin called it "the document of the century".

Europeans set for 1993 Single Market

Brussels, Thursday 31
The European Commission's grand design to create a Europe without frontiers comes into being at midnight tonight. It will consist of a Single Market stretching from the Arctic to the Mediteranean and from the Atlantic to the Oder, encompassing 375 million people gennerating $6.5 trillion.

Difficulties remain. Britain, Ireland, Denmark and Greece will still make travellers show passports in order to "fight terrorism". It has also been found impossible to write a business statute because of disagreements over the appointment of workers to company boards. Businessmen are complaining that the new documents are so complex even the officials who will enforce them are confused.

EC borders will be easier to cross.

Bush flies in for New Year's visit to troops

Mogadishu, Thursday 31
Clad in army fatigues, President Bush stepped out of a USAF C-141 Starlifter under Somalia's broiling midday sun. Security at Mogadishu's war-scarred airport was tight as the president was then flown by helicopter to meet some of the U.S. troops he has come to spend New Year's with. "You all have made the day for this country," he told them at the start of his last scheduled trip abroad before handing over the White House to Bill Clinton. Before leaving he will visit an orphanage and relief centers.

High security for president's arrival.

Some famous names among

Jan. 3, Dame Judith Anderson
The Australian actress, born February 10, 1898, was made a dame commander of the Order of the British Empire in 1960 for her "distinguished contributions to the stage". She is perhaps most famous for her portrayal of the sinister housekeeper, Mrs. Danvers, in Alfred Hitchcock's *Rebecca*.

Jan. 23, Freddie Bartholomew

Bartholomew, born in London in 1924, began his Hollywood career as a child star in *David Copperfield*. Adored by the public, he also appeared in *Little Lord Fauntleroy* and *Captains Courageous* before his "retirement" at the age of 18.

Jan. 26, Jose Ferrer
Born in Puerto Rico, the classical actor and film star began his theatrical career as an assistant stage manager in 1935. He played the title role in *Cyrano* on Broadway in 1946 and won an Oscar for the film version in 1950. He died in Florida at the age of 80.

Jan. 29, Willie Dixon
This American composer of many blues and rock-and-roll hits died at the age of 76 of heart failure. As well as writing songs, he played bass on recordings by Chuck Berry and Bo Diddley for Chess Records in the 1950s and 1960s. Although his own records never sold that well, renditions by white rockers such as the Rolling Stones, Elvis and the Doors made his songs famous.

Feb. 10, Alex Haley
see page 16

Feb. 27, Samuel I. Hayakawa
An American linguist and university professor, Hayakawa began a political career after he served as president of San Francisco State College during student protests in the late 60s. His tough handling of the situation earned him the support of the state's conservatives, and he served as a Republican senator for California from 1977 to 1983. He died at age 85 of a stroke.

March 9, Menachem Begin

Begin, prime minister of Israel from 1977 to 1983, and Anwar Sadat, president of Egypt, signed a historic peace agreement at Camp David in 1978, and jointly won that year's Nobel Peace Prize. Born in Brest-Litovsk on August 16, 1913, Begin had been a part of the guerrilla movement against the British in the 1940s and helped to found the conservative Herut Party after Israel became independent.

March 11, Richard Brooks
Born in Philadelphia on May 18, 1912, Richard Brooks received 11 Oscar nominations for his films. He directed *The Blackboard Jungle*, *Key Largo*, *Cat on a Hot Tin Roof* and *Looking for Mr. Goodbar*, and won an Oscar for his screenplay for *Elmer Gantry*. He died of congestive heart failure.

April 5, Sam Walton
see page 31

April 6, Isaac Asimov
One of the best and most popular science-fiction writers, the Russian-born American was also a biochemist and textbook writer. The work schedule for the prolific author (he wrote more than 500 books) was to rise early and work from 7:30 a.m. to 10 p.m. He died at 72 of heart and kidney failure.

April 17, Maurice Buckmaster
After World War II, Dwight Eisenhower said this Briton's work at the head of allied spies in France helped to shorten the war by six months. He had been a journalist at *Le Matin* before the war, and later worked for the Ford motor company in France. He died at the age of 90 in Forest Row, England.

April 19, Frankie Howerd
The British comedian, master of the innuendo, was essentially a stand-up comic in the old style. He milked audiences, involving them in his act with rambling stories, full of substories and asides. His portrayal of a lecherous Roman slave, Lurcio, in the hit TV series, *Up Pompeii*, was an extension of his stage act with "Mrs. Howerd's little boy" talking to the viewers while the plot swirled around him. He died at 70 after suffering from heart problems.

April 20, Benny Hill
see page 37

April 21, Vladimir Romanov
The pretender to the extinct imperial throne of Russia was born in Finland, then part of the Russian empire, on August 20, 1917, the year his cousin, Czar Nicholas II abdicated. He died during a press conference in Miami.

April 23, Satyajit Ray
Born May 2, 1921, Satyajit Ray was not only a great filmmaker, but a poet, musician, architect and publicist. His work explored with finesse and sensibility the confrontation between the tradition of his country and the modern world. He is best know for his "Apu" trilogy which included *Pather Panchali*, *Aparajito* and *The World of Apu*.

April 28, Francis Bacon
see page 38

April 28, Olivier Messiaen

The French organist and composer, born on December 10, 1908, was inspired by diverse sources which included his Catholic faith, traditional music from all over the world and bird song. He composed organ, choral, chamber and orchestral works and one opera, *Saint Francis of Assisi*.

May 6, Marlene Dietrich
see page 41

May 23, Atahualpa Yupanqui
Born in 1908, the poet and singer celebrated peasants and Indians of his native Argentina. He was imprisoned by Peron, then lived much of his later life in France, where he became a friend of Paul Eluard and Edith Piaf.

May 26, Philip Habib
The American diplomat, born in Brooklyn on February 25, 1920, served as a confidant to every U.S. president from Lyndon Johnson to Ronald Reagan. He had a reputation for speaking his mind, even when, or especially when, his views might be unorthodox or unwelcome to those in power.

May 27, Peter Jenkins
The English journalist specialized in British politics and had worked for most of the major English newspapers. He was the author of two books, *Mrs. Thatcher's Revolution: The Ending of the Socialist Era*, published in 1987, and *The Battle of Downing Street*, published in 1970.

the many who died in 1992

June 3, Robert Morley
see page 47

June 21, Li Xiannian
Born in the province of Hubai in 1909, the veteran of the Long March of 1934-35 was president of China from 1983 to 1988, the first to hold the position since the purging of Liu Shaoqi in 1968. A protégé of Zhou Enlai, he was a critic of Mao's Great Leap Forward and Cultural Revolution.

June 23, John Spencer Churchill
Born May 31, 1909, the nephew of Winston Churchill was a painter and sculptor. The British artist specialized in murals, portraits and frescoes, and his memoirs, *Crowded Canvas*, were published in 1961.

June 29, Mohammed Boudiaf
see page 55

July 5, Astor Piazzolla
Argentina's foremost tango composer, son of Italian immigrants, was born in Mar del Plata on November 3, 1921. He grew up in New York, returning to Buenos Aires in 1937. In the 1950s he developed a new tango style and studied with Nadia Boulanger in Paris. A bandoneon virtuoso, he went on to compose film and theatrical scores, operas and concertos.

July 9, Eric Sevareid
The American journalist was born in North Dakota on November 26, 1912. He was hired by the Paris edition of the New York Herald Tribune in 1938 and was recruited by Edward Murrow to do radio reports for CBS just before World War II. He was later featured on CBS's television news, where he was one of the first prime-time commentators.

July 23, Arletty
Born Léonie Bathiat in Paris, May 15, 1898, Arletty is most famous for her appearance in Marcel Carné's 1938 film, *Hotel du Nord*, where she cried "Atmosphère! Atmosphère!" on a bridge over the Canal Saint-Martin. She was a star of the Paris stage as well, and played Blanche in Jean Cocteau's version of Tennessee Williams' *A Streetcar named Desire.*

Aug. 12, John Cage

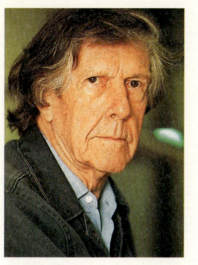

Born September 5, 1912, in Los Angeles, Cage influenced not only musicians, but visual and performance artists. He was as much a *provocateur* as a composer. A 1952 composition, "4'33"," has the performer stand silently for the duration of the piece. Cage did not limit his art to what most would refer to as music, but stated: "If sound is meaningless, I'm all for it."

Aug. 14, John Sirica
John Sirica, born March 19, 1904, achieved fame as the judge who pressed to find the truth about the Watergate affair. He presided over the trial of the Watergate burglars and of President Nixon's top aides, and ordered the president to turn over the infamous Watergate tapes to the House Judiciary Committee.

Aug. 18, John Sturges
Born in 1911, John Sturges was one of America's greatest directors of action films and Westerns. He began his career making documentaries for the Army Air Corps in World War II. His best-known film is perhaps *The Magnificent Seven.*

Sept. 12, Anthony Perkins
American actor Tony Perkins was a star of both the stage and screen, but he is best known for his portrayal of Norman Bates in Hitchcock's *Psycho.* Born April 4, 1932, his first major role was in the Broadway play *Tea and Sympathy* in 1954.

Sept. 28, William Douglas-Home
Born June 3, 1912, the Scottish playwright wrote mostly light comedies with aristocratic characters, such as *The Drawing Room Tragedy* and *Lloyd George Knew My Father.* He was court-martialed and imprisoned for his refusal to follow orders to participate in the attack on the French port of Le Havre in World War II.

Oct. 8, Willy Brandt
Herbert Ernst Karl Frahm, born December 18, 1913, adopted the name Willy Brandt when he joined the underground resistance movement against the Nazis in 1933. Soon after, he fled to Norway. As German chancellor from 1969 to 1974, Brandt worked to improve relations with the Soviet Union, East Germany and Poland, winning the Nobel Peace Prize in 1971.

Oct. 21, Jim Garrison
Jim Garrison was the district attorney of New Orleans who became famous by espousing the theory that the assassination of John Kennedy was a conspiracy by the CIA. He wrote three books on the subject and appeared as Chief Justice Earl Warren in Oliver Stone's film *JFK,* which was based on his theory. He later served as a circuit court judge, retiring last year. He was 71.

Nov. 2, Hal Roach
see page 95

Nov. 7, Alexander Dubcek
see page 97

Dec. 8, William Shawn
Born August 31, 1907 in Chicago, Shawn began working for *The New Yorker* as a reporter in 1933. He succeeded Harold Ross, the founding editor, in 1952 and turned the fashionably witty magazine into a more serious one. He was asked to resign when the ownership changed in 1987. The *New Yorker* has featured writing by the most prominent of American writers.

Dec. 10, Dan Maskell
Tennis was this Briton's life. At 15 he was a full-time ball boy at Queen's Club, at 16 became a junior professional player, and in his 20s was a coach for the British team that won the Davis Cup four times running. He was a squadron leader in a rehabilitation unit in World War II. From 1951 to 1991 he served as a tennis commentator for the BBC and came to be known as "the voice of Wimbledon".

Dec. 21, Nathan Milstein
Born in Odessa on December 31, 1903, Milstein began playing the violin at age four and began to study with Leopold Auer at age 12. He went to Paris in 1926 and was eventually known as one of the world's greatest violinists. He became a U.S. citizen in 1942.

Dec. 21, Stella Adler

The American actress and drama teacher, born February 10, 1901, made her stage debut at four and went on to appear in nearly 200 plays. But her fame came from her students: Robert De Niro, Warren Beatty, Marlon Brando and others studied at the Stella Adler Conservatory of Acting, which she founded in 1949.

Dec. 25, Helen Joseph
Born in England in 1905, Helen Joseph went to South Africa in 1931. She became involved in the anti-apartheid movement in 1953. In 1961 she was charged with treason, and until 1971 was under house arrest, confined to her home from sunset to sunrise. She continued in active opposition to apartheid, and was under government restrictions until 1990.

General Index

Page numbers in roman type refer to articles; those in italic refer to the chronology summaries.

A

Abkhazia (see Georgia)
Abortion
– U.S. Supreme Court to review Pennsylvania abortion law 10
– Irish court orders lifting of travel ban on rape victim 22
– Abortion rights limited in Poland *40*
– U.S. Supreme Court upholds women's abortion rights 55
– German abortion law suspended *66*
– Irish government decides to hold referendum on abortion 85
– Irish voters turn down government abortion proposal 103
Ackers, Thomas 43
Acuff, Roy † *102*
Adidas *88*
Adler, Stella † 115
Adulyadej, Bhumibol 45
Afghanistan
– Muslim rebels force government to surrender *33*
– President Najibullah is ousted 35
– Rebel factions agree to form 51-member interim government *36*
– Combat continues between rebel factions *38*
– Fighting abates as power is assumed by Mojaddidi *38*
– Guerrilla leaders sign agreement *46*
– Women not allowed on television *65*
– Thousands flee fighting *68*
– First public hanging in 20 years *78*
Africa
– Explorers discover first traces of Islam in Black Africa *24*
– Soldiers open fire on ANC marchers in Ciskei, killing 28 78
– Economic refugees die in bid to cross Straits of Gibraltar 91
African National Congress (see South Africa)
Agassi, Andre 58
Ahmed, Mushtaq 68
Aidid, Mohammed Farrah 5, 107, 112
AIDS
– Magic Johnson meets Bush 8
– Heterosexual cases rise by 50% 12
– U.K. government to compensate virus-infected blood receivers *18*
– Pope urges advanced nations to help stop spread of AIDS *20*
– Ex-tennis star Arthur Ashe announces he has AIDS *31*
– Swiss government gives heroin to addicts to reduce virus *42*
– WHO report on AIDS in women *62*
– International conference hears of AIDS-like illnesses 62
– Actor Anthony Perkins dies *78*
– It is revealed that baboon-liver transplant man died of AIDS *78*
– AIDS quilt displayed in Washington 87
– Nelson Mandela blames apartheid for spread of AIDS in Africa *91*
– Dr Michel Garretta convicted in contaminated-blood scandal 92
– American experts push for an increase in AIDS funds *105*
– Colorado boycott proposed 105
Akers, John 9
Akram, Wasim 68
Albania
– Depots raided in food riots 20
– Sari Berisha elected as first non-Communist president *31*
Albertville (see Winter Olympics)
Algeria
– Demonstration against danger of Islamic fundamentalism *4*
– President Chadli Benjedid resigns 7
– General elections cancelled *8*
– Boudiaf appointed president *8*
– Authorities arrest I.S.F. leader Abdelkader Hachani *10*
– Boudiaf is assassinated 55
– Abbasi Madani and Ali Belhadj given 12-year prison sentences *60*
– Terrorist bomb kills nine at Houari Boumedienne Airport 75
– Muslim extremists ambush and kill five policemen *109*
Allen, Woody 72, *82*
Alvarez-Machain, Humberto 50
Amato, Giuliano 81
American Airlines 57, *60*, *109*
Amnesty International 30
Anderson, Judith † 114
Anderson, Terry 40
Andreotti, Giulio 14
Angeli, Daniel *106*
Angola
– First democratic elections *84*
– Truce between government and UNITA rebels set to break down 86
– UNITA guerrillas attack areas surrounding Luanda airport 94
Anh, Le Duc 83
Animal experiments *18*
Anne, Princess Royal 34, 108
Antall, Joszef 23
Antarctica *18*
Apartheid (see South Africa)
Aquino, Cory 51
Arafat, Yasir *14*, 31
Archeology
– A 4,000-year-old lost city is found on Oman-Yemen border 14
– Alpine iceman is 5,300 years old 63
– French cave paintings are 27,100 years old *100*
– Briton Eric Lawes finds Roman treasure worth £10 million *100*
Arens, Moshe *26*
Argentina
– New currency introduced *4*
– Suspends delivery of nuclear material to Iran *12*
– President Menem orders release of Nazi war criminal files *14*
– Suicide bomber destroys Israeli Embassy, killing 10 27
Arletty † 63, † 115
Armenia *12*
Arms and arms control
– U.S. military material bound for Libya is seized in Germany *10*
– Argentina suspends delivery of nuclear material to Iran *12*
– Warships intercept German cargo ship carrying arms to Syria 12
– U.K.-Russia arms control accord 13
– U.S. to close 83 military installations in Europe 13
– Saddam Hussein refuses U.N. missile inspection 21
– Two Russians arrested for trying to sell uranium *22*
– Israel accused of selling U.S. anti-ballistic arms to China 25
– Colt announces bankruptcy *26*
– Bush and Yeltsin sign pact to reduce long-range nuclear arms *50*
– Saddam Hussein continues to defy U.N. on chemical arms issue 59
– U.S. plans to sell planes and armaments to South Korea *65*
– France ratifies nuclear non-proliferation treaty *66*
– Bush backs sale of 150 Fighting Falcon F-16s to Taiwan *77*
– Police seize two kilos of radioactive uranium in Munich *88*
Arnould, Dominique *56*
Arts and entertainment
– Producer Mike Frankovich dies *4*
– Warren Beatty announces plans to wed Annette Bening 5
– American saxophonist Charlie Ventura dies *8*
– American composer William Schuman dies *16*
– American writer Alex Haley dies 16
– Latoya Jackson appears at the Moulin Rouge in Paris 18
– Liz Taylor celebrates birthday 21
– Michael Jackson receives broadcasting industry award 23
– Movie *The Silence of the Lambs* wins Oscars 29
– Jack Palance wins Oscar for role in the film *City Slickers* 29
– Liza Minelli receives award for humanitarian work 31
– Comedian Benny Hill dies 37
– Marlene Dietrich dies in Paris 41
– Bille August receives Palme d'Or for *Best Intentions* 44
– Johnny Carson hosts his last *Tonight Show* 45
– British actor Robert Morley dies 47
– Biography *Diana: Her True Story* causes scandal 48
– Michael Caine appointed CBE 49
– British painter and sculptor John Spencer Churchill dies *52*
– Major agrees to give $7 million for performing arts school *56*
– Composer Astor Piazzolla dies *56*
– Andy Garcia stars in the movie *Jennifer Eight* 57
– Kim Basinger stars in Gabriel Byrne's film *Cool World* 57
– Eddie Murphy stars in the movie *Boomerang* 57
– Kirov Opera performs in the U.S. *58*
– Yancy Butler appears in the film *Mann and Machine* 59
– French film star Arletty dies 63
– Actor Harold Russell sells his 1946 Oscar for $60,000 *66*
– Riots break out after Guns 'N' Roses concert in Montreal *68*
– American singer Tony Williams of the Platters dies *68*
– Mia Farrow accuses Woody Allen of abusing adopted child 72
– Actor Anthony Perkins dies *78*
– Clint Eastwood is guest of honor at Deauville film festival 79
– Sinatra gets Lifetime Achievement honor at US Cinema Awards 81
– French customs officials block entry of Madonna's book *Sex 85*
– Caribbean author Derek Walcott wins Nobel Literature prize 87
– Phillip Glass' opera *The Voyage* opens in New York 88
– Ridley Scott's *1492* released 88
– Booker Prize shared by Michael Ondaatje and Barry Unsworth 90
– Stars pay tribute to Bob Dylan at Madison Square Garden 90
– Madonna's book *Sex* launched 91
– American country music singer Roger Miller dies *93*
– Charles and Diana meet Placido Domingo at Covent Garden 94
– Hitler's *Mein Kampf* to be published in Hebrew *95*
– Film director Hal Roach dies 95
– Stolen Renoir painting *A Vase of Flowers* is found *98*
– Actor Chuck Connors dies *98*
– Composer Maurice Ohana dies *98*
– Soprano Dorothy Kirsten dies *100*
– Denzel Washington stars in Spike Lee's *Malcolm X* 100
– Christie's *The Mousetrap* celebrates 40th anniversary *102*
– Ballet dancer Jorge Donn dies *102*
– Country singer Roy Acuff dies *102*
– Francis Bacon leaves £10.9-million estate to publican *105*
– Barbra Streisand supports Aspen boycott 105
– Opera singer Luciano Pavarotti is booed off stage in Milan *106*
– U.S actor Vincent Gardenia dies *106*
– Australian actress Dame Judith Anderson dies 114
– Actor Freddie Bartholomew dies 114
– Actor Jose Ferrer dies at the age of 80 114
– Blues singer Willie Dixon dies 114
– American film writer and director Richard Brooks dies 114
– Science-fiction writer Isaac Asimov dies 114
– British comedian Frankie Howerd dies 114
– French organist and composer Olivier Messiaen dies 114
– Argentine poet and singer Atahualpa Yupanqui dies 114
– U.S. composer John Cage dies 115
– Film director John Sturges dies 115
– Violinist Nathan Milstein dies 115
– Thom Gunn wins £10,000 Forward Poetry Prize 115
– American actress and drama teacher Stella Adler dies † 115
Arvesen, Jan 56
Ascari, Alberto 44
ASEAN *24*
Ashdown, Paddy 16, 25, *30*, 32
Ashe, Arthur *31*, 32
Asimov, Isaac † *31*, † 114
Aspin, Les 112
Assad, Hafez 79
Astronomy
– Eclipse over southern California 4
– Tenth planet exists *84*
Auctions
– Andy Warhol's 1962 silk screen sold for $2.1 million *40*
– Watercolors by Adolf Hitler attract no bids at Stadion *100*
August, Bille 44
August, Pernilla 44
Australia
– Homosexuals allowed in military *102*
– To drop allegiance to Queen 110
Austria
– Rudolf Streicher leads in presidential race *38*
– Klestil elected president *46*
– Waldheim steps down 59
– Alpine iceman is 5,300 years old 63
– Fire damages Hofburg Palace 104
Automobiles
– U.S. car sales slump by 10% 7
– U.S. car-makers show new models 7
– Number of stolen cars offered for sale to U.K. dealers rises 10
– Ford posts $2.3-billion loss 17
– GM posts biggest loss ever 21
– Lotus stops making the Elan 50
– BMW announces plans to open its first car plant in U.S. *52*
– Jaguar XJ220 car displayed 53
– Rover 200 Coupé chosen best car at British Motor Show *93*
Aviation
– Airbus orders decline *6*
– Richard Branson takes claim against BA to EC Committee 7
– A British Airways Concorde loses parts of its rudder *27*
– Arafat escapes death in crash 31
– F-22 prototype crashes at Edwards Air Force Base in U.S. *36*
– Spitfire explodes at air show *52*
– Cheap air fares threaten U.K. tour operators with bankruptcy 57
– Braniff Airlines ceases operations 57
– BA announces plans to buy major shares in USAir *60*
– U.S. Navy uses QANTAS Boeing 747 as mock target in operation *60*
– BA announces USAir deal 62
– TWA Lockheed L1011 escapes disaster at Kennedy Airport 65
– Four Hercules transport planes begin airlift in Somalia 76
– Yakolev Yak-141 goes on display at Farnborough Air Show 78
– British Aerospace decides to close its Hatfield factory *82*
– U.S. secret spy plane 106
Azerbaijan
– Heavy fighting in Nagorno-Karabakh *12*
– Mutalibov forced out of office 23
– Popular Front takes control of parliament *42*

B

Babbitt, Bruce 112
Babiuc, Victor 83
Bacon, Francis † 38, *105*
Baikal, Lake 69
Baird, Zoe 112
Baker, James 16, 25, *31*, *33*, 69
Baker, Kenneth 34
Ballesteros, Severiano 89
Baltic Council 23
Bank of Credit and Commerce International 11
Barr, William 32, *44*
Barre, Mohammed Siad 100
Bartholomew, Freddie † 114
Baseball
– Nintendo buys first Major League team, the Seattle Mariners 48
– Seaver, Fingers and Newhouser enter Hall of Fame *66*
– Ripken signs biggest contract *75*
– Blue Jays win the America League pennant *88*
– U.S. tribute to Canadian baseball goes wrong 91
– Blue Jays win over Atlanta Braves in World Series 92
Basinger, Kim 27, 57
Basketball
– NCAA Basketball Finals: Duke's men's team beats Michigan *31*
– NCAA Basketball Finals: Stanford women's team beats Kentucky *31*
– Chicago Bulls beat Portland Trail Blazers *50*
– Larry Bird retires *72*
– Magic Johnson returns to Los Angeles Lakers *84*
– Magic Johnson quits professional basketball *95*
Bastian, Gert *91*
Bausch & Lomb 15
Bauwens, Mona 83
Bazin, Marc *47*
BBC *26*
Beatty, Warren 5
Becker, Boris 26, *42*, *98*, 102
Becker, Gary *88*
Begin, Menachem † *24*, † 114
Belgium
– Jean-Luc Dehaene agrees to form 35th post-war government *22*
– Military draft to end in 1994 57
– First trans-Atlantic balloon race is won by Belgian team *82*
Belhadj, Ali *60*
Bening, Annette 5
Benjedid, Chadli 7
Bentsen, Lloyd *106*, 112
Bérégovoy, Pierre 30
Bergen, Candice 44
Berisha, Sari *31*
Berov, Luben *113*
Betancourt, Eduardo *10*
Bhutto, Benazir 100
Biden, Joseph 11
Bird, Larry *72*
Biya, Paul *100*
Blair, Bonnie 20
Bland, Tony *100*
Blundell, Mark 52
BMW *52*, *105*
Boardman, Chris 65
Boat racing
– See also Sailing
– Oxford beats Cambridge in University Boat Race *30*
– Columbus anniversary regatta commences at Liverpool 72
Body Shop *46*
Bogart, Steve 30
Bolivia 100
Bollettieri, Nick 38
Booker Prize (see Arts and entertainment)
Booth, Shirley † *88*
Boothroyd, Betty *38*
Borsellino, Paolo *62*
Bosnia-Herzegovina
– State of emergency declared 32
– Seven men listed for crimes against humanity 110
– Major visits British forces *111*
Botham, Ian 17
Bottomley, Virginia 34
Boudiaf, Mohammed *8*, 55
Bowe, Riddick 99
Bowie, David 21
Boxing
– Evander Holyfield beats Larry Holmes at Caesar's Palace 51
– Riddick Bowe dethrones Evander Holyfield at Las Vegas 99
Boyd-Carpenter, Lord 55
Boyle, Kay *113*
Bradley, Tom 39, 40
Brandenstein, Daniel 43
Brandt, Willy † *85*, 86, † 115
Braniff airlines 57
Branson, Richard 7, 58
Braun, Carol Moseley 96
Brazauskas, Algirdas 100
Brazil
– Earth Summit *47*, *48*, 50
– Chief Paiakan arrested for rape, assault and cannibalism 50
– President Collor de Mello accused of corruption *68*, 84, 113
– Sao Paulo jail riot 85
British Aerospace *82*
British Airways 7, 11, 27, *60*, 62, *111*
British Telecom *22*
Brittan, Leon 47
Brooks, Richard † *24*, † 114
Brown, Jerry 29, *60*
Brown, Jesse 112
Brown, Ronald 112
Brown, Tina 54
Browner, Carol 108
Browning, Kurt 20
Brunei, Sultan of *72*
Bryan, John 73, *106*
Bseiso, Atef *48*
Buchanan, Patrick 11, 19, 24, 73
Buckmaster, Maurice † *36*, † 114
Bugno, Gianni *78*
Bulgaria *8*, *77*
Burgess, Nigel 103
Bush, Barbara 6, 49, 51, 73, 96
Bush, Dorothy Walker † *100*
Bush, George
– Collapses at state dinner in Tokyo 6
– Meets Magic Johnson 8
– Iraqi officials forecast Saddam Hussein will outlast Bush 9
– Buchanan cuts Bush's lead 11
– State of the Union speech 12
– Gives Boris Yeltsin cowboy boots for birthday present 14
– Officially announces his candidacy for a second term 17
– Fails to win landslide victory in New Hampshire primary vote 19
– With six Latin American leaders steps up war on drugs 20
– Wins in eight primaries 24
– Visits Los Angeles after riots 41
– Haitians to be sent back *46*
– Obtains 31% in ABC News/Washington Post polls *47*
– Anti-Bush demonstration in Panama 49
– Arms pact with Yeltsin *50*
– Ecologists hit out at Bush's environmental policies 50
– Objects to new Israeli settlements in Occupied Territories 52
– Promises Tailhook investigation 53
– Administration plans to sell military items to South Korea *65*
– Signs NAFTA agreement 68
– Backs $10-billion loan to Israel 69
– Republican Convention 73
– Gulf War allies establish no-fly zone over southern Iraq 75
– Allocates aid to farmers *77*
– Approves sale of 150 Fighting Falcon F-16s to Taiwan *77*
– Tax bill sent to Bush for approval *85*
– Attends presidential debate at Richmond University 89
– Fails to win decisive victory in debate 91
– Loses presidential vote 96
– Fires official responsible for Clinton file search *98*
– U.S. makes compromises to avert trade war with EC 101
– Sends U.S. forces to Somalia on humanitarian mission 105
– Agrees that Serbian aircraft should stay out of no-fly zone 111
– Pardons Iran-Contra officials 112
– Visits troops in Somalia 113
Business Age (magazine) *93*
Butler, Yancy 59
Byrd, Dennis *102*
Byrne, Gabriel 57

C

Caballe, Montserrat 64
Cage, John † 115
Caine, Michael 49
Calment, Jeanne *18*
Cambodia
– U.N. peacekeeping troops enforce cease-fire *30*
– U.N. chief Butros Ghali pushes for peace 35
– Japan sends its first troops to join U.N. peacekeeping force 82
– U.N. peacekeepers are taken hostage by Khmer Rouge *109*
Cameroon *100*
Canada
– Police to use Cayenne pepper in riot control *26*
– Inuits vote on exchange of territory for political autonomy 40
– Olympia & York files bankruptcy *42*
– Unemployment *47*
– Riots after Guns 'N' Roses concert *68*
– Quebec celebrates its parliament's bicentennial *80*
– Canadians reject Charlestown agreement in referendum 93
Capra, Frank 95
Carey, George, Archbishop of Canterbury 99
Caroline, Princess of Monaco *56*
Carson, Johnny 45
Carter, Jimmy 50
Carville, James 87
Casey, Eamonn 41
Cash, Johnny 90
Cash, Pat *52*
Castellano, Paul 30
Castro, Fidel 5, *10*, *22*, 63, *65*
CBS 15
Chad *4*, *44*
Chaplin, Charlie 37
Charles, Prince of Wales 22, 48, 94, *105*, 107
Cheney, Dick 26, 45, 53
Chernomyrdin, Viktor 109, 112
Cheshire, Lord † *65*
Chess
– Bobby Fischer-Boris Spassky match 77, 97
Chikatilo, Andrei *26*, 89
Chile *16*
Chilton, Edward † *66*
China
– Canadian MPs expelled for placing wreath in Tiananmen Square *6*
– Deng Xiaoping asserts new economic policy *20*
– Prime Minister Li Peng calls for sweeping economic reforms 27
– Military scientists carry out underground nuclear test 45
– Government to suspend export of prison-made items to U.S. *50*
– Diplomatic relations restored with South Korea *75*
– Signs agreement with South Korea to end hostilities *84*
– Threatens to set up shadow government in Hong Kong *105*
– Orders France to close consulate in Canton *111*
Chissano, Joaquim 67
Christie, Agatha *102*
Christie, Linford 67
Chrysler Corporation 7, *26*
Churchill, John Spencer † *52*, † 115
Cipollone, Rose 53
Cisneros, Henry 112
Cleese, John *65*
Clinton, Bill
– Gennifer Flowers accuses Clinton of being a liar 13
– Accused of draft-dodging 17
– Beaten by Tsongas in the New Hampshire primary 19
– Is front-runner in presidential election race 24
– Pulls into clear lead over Paul Tsongas in presidential race 27
– Beaten by Jerry Brown in the Connecticut primary 29
– Visits Los Angeles after riots 41
– Gains 27% in ABC News-Washington Post preference polls *47*
– Criticizes Sister Souljah 49
– Supports right to abortion 55
– Al Gore is running mate 58
– Brown refuses to support ticket *60*
– Has 25-point lead in polls 69
– Attacked by Pat Buchanan 73
– Presidential debates 89, 91
– Wins presidential election 96
– May lift ban on homosexuals in the armed forces 99
– Supports Bush's decision to send troops to Somalia 105
– Chooses Senator Lloyd Bentsen to be treasury secretary *106*
– Puts three women in top governmental posts 108
– Appoints Cisneros and Brown *109*
– Live TV conference 110
– Announces his new cabinet 112
Clinton, Hillary 73, 103, 108
Club Med *16*
CNN 20, 69
Coca-Cola 15, 102
Coleridge, David 52
Colgate-Palmolive Company *16*
Collins, Corinne 63
Collins, Dwight 63
Collor de Mello, Fernando *68*, 84, 113
Colombia
– Medellin drug clan resumes war against rival Cali cartel *6*
– Escobar escapes from prison 63
– Earthquake kills ten *91*
– Medellin clan suspected of car bomb explosion which kills 14 *105*
Colombo, Emilio 67
Colt *26*
Columbus, Christopher 72, 88
Commonwealth of Independent States
– 54 nations attend conference on aid for C.I.S. in Washington *10*
– 25,000 Jews from former Soviet Union apply for immigration *14*
– C.I.S.-NATO conference *20*
– Ex-Soviet army ordered to withdraw from Nagorno-Karabakh *20*
– French mission establishes relief corridor in Azerbaijan *26*
– Western nations agree to give ex-Soviet Union $24 billion 30
– Armenia asks Russia for aid in conflict with Azerbaijan *68*
– *Soyuz* space vehicle lands *68*
Computers
– Michelangelo virus 23
– Industry hit by record losses 90
– Failure in computer system causes ambulance chaos in Britain 93
Confederation of British Industry (see Great Britain, economy and industry)
Conner, Dennis *40*
Connery, Sean 16
Connors, Chuck † *98*
Coren, Alan 29
Cossiga, Francesco 14
Coughlin, Paula 53
Couples, Fred *33*
Courier, Jim *12*, *48*, 102, 106
Courlander, Harold 16
Craxi, Bettino 42
Cresson, Edith 30
Cricket
– England beats New Zealand in First Test *10*
– England beats New Zealand in Second Test *14*
– England and New Zealand draw in Third Test *16*
– England beats New Zealand 17
– Pakistan defeats England by 22 runs in World Cup 29
– England and Pakistan draw in First Test *48*
– Pakistan beats England in the Second Test *52*
– England and Pakistan draw in Third Test *58*
– Test ban lifted on U.K. South African tour rebels 58
– England beats Pakistan in Fourth Test *65*
– Pakistan beats England in Fifth Test, winning Test series 68
– England beats Pakistan to win Texaco Trophy series *75*
– Keith Fletcher becomes England's new team manager *77*
– David Gower left out of tour 78
– Imran Khan retires 84
Crippen, Robert 59
Croatia
– EC recognizes Croatia 8
– First presidential and legislative elections held *66*
Cuba
– Austerity measures introduced 5
– Eduardo Betancourt is executed *10*
– Constitutional changes approved to allow freedom of worship 58
– Castro addresses Ibero-American summit 63
Culliford, Pierre † 112
Curran, James 62

119

Photo Credit

The position of the pictures are indicated by two letters:
b = bottom, t = top, l = left, r = right, m = middle, x = middle left, y = middle right.

Cover
Left to right and top to bottom:
- David Taylor/Sipa Press
- José Nicolas/Sipa Press
- Christopher Brown/Sipa Press
- Sipa Press
- T. Haley/Sipa Press
- Luc Delahaye/Sipa Press
- Greg Smith/Sipa Press
- Lee Celano/Sipa Press
- Copyright Paul Wood
- Sipa Sport
- Carre Christophe/Sipa Press
- Nasa/Sipa Press
- Lionnel Cherruault/Sipa Press

A.A./Sipa Press 84 ml
A. Solomonov/Sipa Press 4 tr
Adenis/Sipa Press 72 tr, 84 mr, 85 bl, 98 tr
AFP 49 tr, 66 bl, 80 m, 83 m, 94 tl
Aimar/Sipa Press 37 bm
Akidiro Mishimura/Sipa Press 6 tl
Alec Russell/Presse-Sports 30 br
Alexandra Boulat/Sipa Press 33 br, mr, tr
Alfred/Sipa Press 107 tl
Allsport 67 mr, 68 bl
Amar ABD RABBA/Sipa Press 31 tr, 35 m
Amis/Sipa Press 21 tr
Angular/Sipa Press 85 mr
Anita Weber/Sipa Press 5 tm, 27 br
Apa/Sipa Press 9 tr
Ariane espace/Sipa Press 21 br
Arkansas Gazette/Sipa Press 31 ml
Art Zamur/Gamma tl
Aslan/Barthélemy/Boccon-Gibod/Sola/Sipa Press 49 br
Associated Press 55 br, 66 br, 110 tl
Baitel/Gamma 99 m
Bajande/REA 42 br
Bardou/Sipa Sport 20 mr, 65 mr
Bardou/Sport +/Sipa Press 64 bl, br
Bardou/Sipa Sport 48 br

Barthélemy/Sipa Press 11 bl, br, bx, by
Barthélemy/Sipa Sport 20 ml
Battisni/Sipa Press 30 m
Baumann/Sipa Press 114 tr
Benani/Média/Sipa Press 52 tm, 60 tm
Benaroch/Sipa Press 79 mr
Ben Radford/Allsport 78 bl
Bill Gentile/Sipa Press 73 tr
Blacke Sell/Sipa Press 79 bl, 99 tl
Bob Black/Chicago Sun-Times/Sipa Press 96 ml
Bob Kusel/Sipa Press 24 tl
Bob Strong/Sipa Press 27 bm, 37 tr, 91 bl, 100 bl, 110 tr
Boccon-Gibod/Sipa Press 53 ml, 114 m
Boiffin/Gamma 91 mr
Bongarts/Presse sport 95 bl
Bravo el Tiempo/Sipa Press 63 bl, tl
Bret Cygne/Sipa Press 108 tl
Cavalli/Sipa Press 83 br
Ceghilani/Sipa Press 55 tm
Cerrari/Sipa Press 21 tl
Cham/Nicolas/Sipa Press 36 br
Cham/Sipa Press 50 tr, 90 tm
Charlier/Sipa Press 74 tr
Cherruault/Sipa Press 92 m, 93 tl
Chesnot/Sipa Press 59 tm, 76 bl, br, 108 tr
Chine Nouvelle/Sipa Press 35 br
Christopher Brown/Sipa Press 18 br, 32 tr, 38 bl, 74 b, ml, mr, tl, tr
Cipelli/Sipa Press 54 tm
Colorsport/Sipa Sport 58 ml, mr
Courtesy of Bandai France 48 m
Courtesy of Donnay 55 bl
Courtesy of Jaguar 55 bl
Courtesy of Kodak 80 tl
Courtesy of US Air 62 ml
Courtesy of Zippo 27 ml
Dagoy/Sipa Press 58 br
Dalmais/Sipa Press 31 bl, 86 bl
Dan Helms/Sipa Press 83 tr
David Hartley/Rex Features 101 ml
David Sams/Sipa Press 61 bl, ml, 85 tr
David Taylor/Sipa Press 44 tr, 72 tr
David Taylor/Sipa Sport 52 br
Devries/Sipa Press 72 mr
Dhomme/Sipa Press 37 br
Dijkstra/Sunshine/Sipa Press 86 tl

DR 63 br, 87 bm
Duclos/Van Der Stockt/Sipa Press 112 hd
E. Dirk/Sipa Press 25 bm
East News/Sipa Press 6 mr, 9 bl, 15 bl, 23 mr, 25 ml, 28 mr, 51 tr, 109 tl
Ed Truzik/Sipa Press 40 bl
EFE/Sipa Press 63 m, 105 tr
Facelly/Sipa Press 46 br, 53 br
Florence Durand/Sipa Press 53 tm, 62 br
FNS/Sipa Press 63 bm
Foulon/Sipa Press 41 br
Frank Zullo/Sipa Press 4 br
Frederico Mendés/Sipa Press 22 m, mr, 84 pm
Frilet/Sipa Press 19 tr, 84 bl, 88 br
Futy/Sipa Press 8 mr, 22 tr, 77 tm
G. Piko/Sipa Press 77 bm
Gamma 107 bl
Gary Horlor/Sipa Press 104 ml
Giannini/Sipa Press 95 tr
Gilles Klein/Sipa Press 103 bd, bm
Gilles Klein/Sipa Sport 43 br, tr
Greg Newton/Sipa Press 113 bl
Gromik/Sipa Sport 68 t
Guibbaud/Sport +/Sipa Sport 67 bl, br
Gustavo Ferrari/Sipa Press 66 tm
H.H.A./Sipa Press 58 tm
Handani-Liaison/Gamma 100 m
Haskell/Sipa Press 37 ml
Herzau/Signum/Sipa Press 102 tr
Hochart/Sipa Press 60 b
Hornbak Christensen/Sipa Press 47 tr
Houston-Post/Sipa Press 102 bl
Hussein/Sipa Press 107 ml
Ilhami/Sipa Press 49 tl
Imax/Sipa Press 89 tl, 93 ml, 100 tl, 103 tr
Iso Press/Sipa Press 112 bd
ITN/Sipa Press 69 tr
J. Moatti/Sipa Press 24 br, 53 br
Jean-Pierre Berthomé 114 tl
Jim Tiller/Sipa Press 8 bl
Job/Sipa Press 22 tl, 95 mr
John Mantel/Sipa Press 17 bm, 30 bl, 31 br, 40 br, 54 br, 55 bl, 61 br, mr, tr, 81 mr, 83 bl, 97 bl, 103 bl
Jordon/Sipa Press 79 br
Juhan Kuus/Sipa Press 7 tm, tr, 34 bl, 51 tl, 78 ml, 108 br

Karim Daher/Gamma 76 tl
Kessler/Sipa Press 42 m, 94 bl
Kevin Frayer/Sipa Press 56 tl, 69 br
Kipa-Interpress 115 md
Kokilopoulos/Sipa Image 89 m
Kurt Viavant/Sipa Press 112 mg
L.R.C./Sipa Press 94 mr, 97 tl
Laffont/Sipa Press 94 mr
Lagarde/REA 9 ml
Lari/Sipa Press 41 br
Laski/Sipa Press 16 tl, 89 br
Lazic/Sipa Press 26 br
Lee Celano/Sipa Press 4 bl, 39 br
Le Secretain/Sipa Press 111 bg
Live Action/Sipa Press 90 br
Lotus France 50 br
Luc Delahaye/Sipa Press 32 ml, 35 tr, 48 tr, 56 mr, tr
Magellan 57 tm, 73 br, 75 t, 96 br
Malanca/Sipa Press 76 ml, 92 tl, 107 tr, 109 tr, 113 bd
Malcolm Croft/Press Association 72 bl
Maous/Sipa Press 112 bg
Marc Peters/Sipa Press 27 tm
Marc Viellard/Sipa Press 14 tl
Markel/Liaison/Gamma 112 md
Matt Mendenson/Sipa Press 41 tl
Max/Sport +/Sipa Press 15 tr
Max Louis/Sipa Press 12 mr
Maxwell Pica/Sipa Press 41 mr
Michel Isaac/Air et Cosmos 78 tl
Mike Melson/AFP 98 br
Mike Pearson/Sipa Press 60 mr
Mirkovich/Sipa Press 54 ml
Moatti/Niekiefenm/Sipa Press 115 tl
Motta/Dossier/Sipa Press 45 tm
Nahassia/Al Jawad/Sipa Press 81 bl
NASA/Sipa Press 37 m, 43 tl, 79 ml, 88 ml
National pictures/Sipa Press 48 bl
Neal Lauron/Sipa Press 99 br
News/Gamma 112 hg
Newsport/Sipa Sport 51 br
Nicolas/Chamussy/Sipa Press 36 mr, tr
Nightingale-Spooner/Gamma 110 bl
Nikolai Jakobsen/Courtesy of Herald Tribune 45 bl
Nina Berman/Sipa Press 13 ml, 28 br, 29 ml, 30 tr, 32 bl, 37 ml, 108 mr
NTB/Sipa Press 19 br

Nuri Vallbona-Houston post/Sipa Press 96 tl
OCR/Paul Rodrigues/Sipa Press 39 mr
OCR/Sipa Press 39 tr
Orton/Sipa Press 18 tr
Pasaila/Sport +/Sipa Press 64 ml
Patrick Piel/Gamma 109 bl
Paul Wood 32 bm
Peter Northall/Sipa Press 6 bl
Peterson/Gamma 86 m
Pitchal/Sipa Press 97 br
Prashant Panjiar/India Today/Sipa Press 106 tl
Press Association 75 mr, 79 bm
Presse-sport 106 br
Presse sport 67 tr, 80 bl, 91 br, 92 br, tr
Quill/Sipa Press 96 tr
R.M.N. 109 tr
R. Robert/Gamma 25 mr
Rajak/Sipa Press 56 bl
Raphael Gaillarde/Gamma md
Rex Features 34 br, mr, 38 br, 77 bl
Rex Features/Sipa Press 5 br, 6 br, 8 br, 9 br, 13 tm, 15 br, 16 bl, mr, 22 bl, 25 tr, 26 m, 32 br, tm, 34 tl, 42 bl, 45 tl, 46 bl, 47 tl, 52 ml, 56 br, 57 bl, bm, br, 60 ml, 63 tr, 65 ml, 81 br, 82 br, 83 tl, 86 br, 90 bl, bm, 99 tl, tr, 103 m, 104 tl, tr, 105 ml, 106 mr, 108 bl
Richard Gardner/Sipa Press 16 br
Richard Sobol/Sipa Press 11 tm, 92 bl, 96 bl, 98 bl
Rick Talco/Sipa Press 4 br
Robert Maass/Sipa Press 73 mr, tl, 97 tr
Roberts/Sipa Press 38 tl
Roger Wilson/Sipa Press 40 mr, tr, 41 ml
Rooke/Sipa Press 25 mr
S. Henry/SABA/REA 17 tl, tr
S. Sarkis/Sipa Press 90 ml
Sam Mircovitch/Sipa Press 17 br, 81 br
Sanhani/Sipa Press 24 bm
Schreiber/US Press/Sipa Press 59 ml
Schwarz/Sipa Press 24 mr, 101 tr
Scott Andrews/Sipa Press 59 mr
Scott Wallace/Sipa Press 50 mr
Seitman/Sipa Press 51 bl

Sichov/Sipa Press 26 tm, tr, 64 m, mr, 77 br
Simmons Ben/Sipa Image 29 tm
Simmons Ben/Sipa Press 7 br
Simon Danger 93 br
Sintesi Gentile/Sipa Press 62 tr
Sipa Press 10 mr, 13 br, 41 bl, 44 br, 59 bl, 64 br, 65 br, 73 bl, 81 tr, 82 tl, tr, 87 tr, 88 bl, 100 br, 103 tl
Sola/Sipa Press 44 ml
Soren/Rasmussen/Sipa Press 88 tr
Star Tribune/Sipa Press 13 bl
Stephano Micozzi/Gamma 87 tl
Stumpf/Sipa Press 28 t
Sunday Times/Rex Features 101 bl
Swanson/Sipa Press 19 ml, 23 tm, 42 bm, 69 tl
Tabacca/Sipa Press 42 br
Talfoto/Sipa Press 72 mr
Tavernier/Sipa Sport 20 tl, tr, 82 bl
Thierry Potier/Sipa Press 23 ml
Today/Rex Features London 101 tl
Tom Haley/Sipa Press 4 tl, 46 tm, 102 mr, 111 md
Tony Savino/Sipa Press 4 m, 10 tl, 12 bl, 19 bm
Topham 59 br
Toussaint/Sipa Press 49 bl
Tracy Baker/Sipa Press 7 bl, m, 91 tl
Tringale/LGI/Kipa-Interpress 10 bl
Trippett/Sipa Press 8 tl, 12 tl, 17 ml, 23 bl, 29 tr, 55 ml, 69 m, 87 br, 89 tr, 105 br, 110 mr, 111 hg
Turiak/Gamma 105 tl
U.S. Features/Sipa Press 104 br
US postal service/Sipa Press 47 br
Valdez/Sipa Press 14 bl
Villard/Sipa Press 18 ml, 50 bl
Voja Miladinovic/Sipa Press 45 br
Wallis/Sipa Press 90 tr
Wessley Bocxe/Sipa Press 14 mr, 34 tr, 79 m
Witness/Sipa Press 76 mr
Y. Breton/Sipa Press 13 br
Yan Philiptchenko/Mégapress/REA 93 mr
Yates/SABA/REA 21 bl
Zeng/Chine nouvelle/Sipa Press 35 tl
Zizola/Dossier/Sipa Press 101 br, 101 br

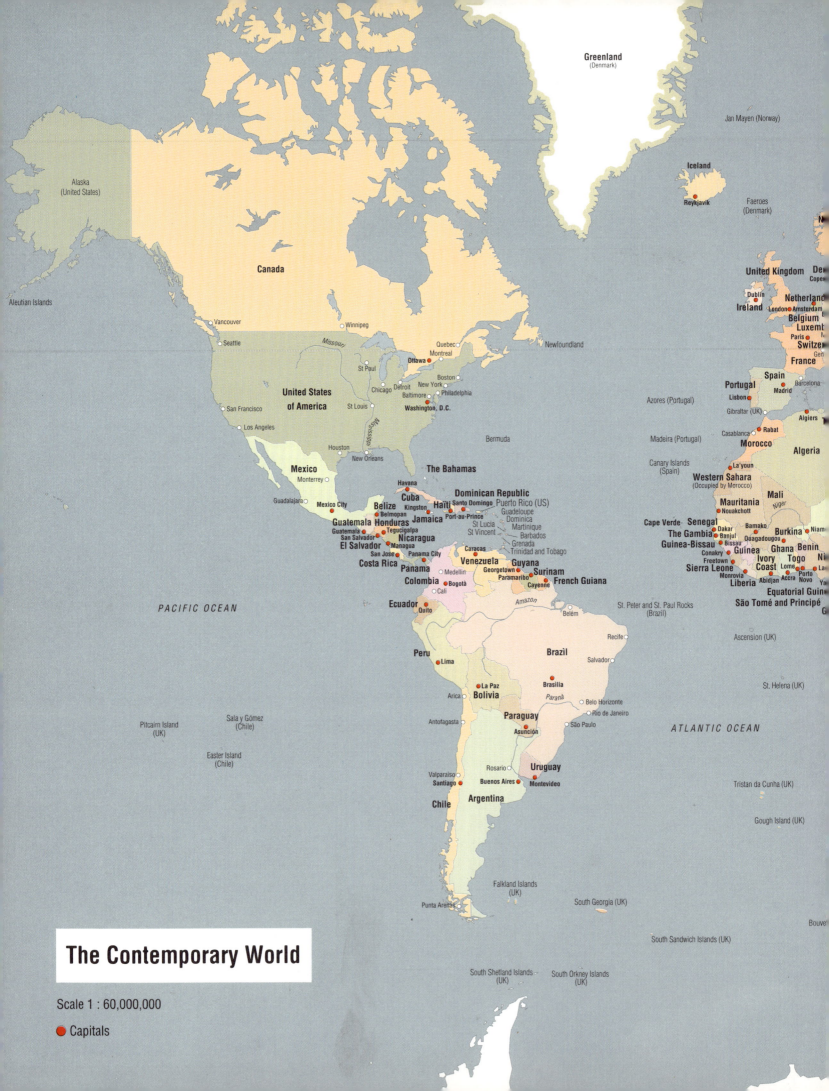

The Contemporary World

Scale 1 : 60,000,000

● Capitals